# GOD, MAN, AND MORTALITY

# GOD, MAN, AND MORTALITY

## The Perspective of Bediüzzaman Said Nursi

Hasan Hörküç

TUGHRA
BOOKS
New Jersey

*Published by* Tughra Books
345 Clifton Ave., Clifton,
NJ, 07011, USA


www.tughrabooks.com

Series Description: Perspective of the Risale-i Nur in Islamic Studies
Series Editor: Colin Turner

Library of Congress Cataloging-in-Publication Data
God, man, and mortality : the perspective of Bediuzzaman Said Nursi / [edited by] Hasan Horkuc.
pages cm. -- (Perspective of the Risale-i nur in Islamic studies)
Includes index.
ISBN 978-1-59784-329-4 (alk. paper)
1. Nursi, Said, 1873-1960. 2. Nurculuk. I. Horkuc, Hasan.
BP252.G63 2014
297.2'043--dc23
2014032403


ISBN: 978-1-59784-329-4


*Printed by*
Imak Ofset, Istanbul - Turkey

# Contents

# Acknowledgements

T he book has come together of some chapters written by distinguished scholars and experts of their particular area of studies. I, therefore, am grateful to all of the contributors.

I am particularly grateful to my colleague, my teacher and my friend (if I may), Dr C P Turner of Durham University. I am also grateful to Yusuf Alan and Fikret Yaşar for their support. They have recognized the importance of this project to come out. Also, there are many others who involved throughout that I cannot name and I am grateful, among them just one or two to mention are Süleyman Tiftik, Adnan Azak and Ali Çiftçi. I also would like to dedicate this book to Mr Abdullah Aymaz, the author, scholar, columnist, for his moral and spiritual support throughout my academic life.

I am also grateful to my wife and daughters for their understanding for the time that I have spent for this project. For your love and support, I am always grateful. Thank you, Halide, Esma and Zehra.

# Series Aims and Scope

This new series will offer insight and make an important contribution to contemporary Islamic studies from Nursian perspective, and will appeal to a wide range of readers who seek to understand the important contributions made by Nursi.

Each book in the series will provide an introduction to a different topic of Nursian discourse. It will inform and show how Nursi's discourse developed, what particular subjects he specialized and the impact he left on society.

The key themes will be covered in the series throughout are: relation between man, universe and God, the Qur'an and its Miraculousness, Modernity, Civilization and Man, plurality, harmony and dialogue, spirituality, jihad and politics in Nursi's discourse.

# Foreword

One of the many paradoxes which have been thrown up by the so-called 'Islamic revival' of the past hundred and fifty years is the fact that the majority of revivalist thinkers in question have been lay intellectuals. Jamal al-Din al-Afghani, Hasan al-Banna, Sayyid Qutb, Shariati, Mawdudi, Ghannoushi, to mention but a few, are examples of revivalist leaders who had little or no background in the traditional *madrasa* disciplines of legal theory (*fiqh*) and Prophetic Tradition (*hadith*). Many of them were, of course, exposed to the traditional 'Islamic sciences' in one way or another, but none of them—with the exception of Ayatullah Khomeini—could claim expertise as a jurist.

Yet it is painfully obvious that the Islam which today enjoys such a high global profile is overwhelmingly legalist in nature and subsequently '*sharia*-obsessed'. At the heart of current Islamic revivalism there appears to be one recurrent theme: the call for a return not only to 'Islamic values', but also to Islamic government and the rule of Islamic law. Calls for the establishment of Islamic regimes and republics, and the actual formation of such entities, as in the case of Iran and Sudan, have been paramount, and the question of governance and the rule of Islamic law underpins the ideologies of all of those groups commonly known as 'Islamist' or, in other words, advocates of a highly politicized form of Islam which places the notion of caliphate or *sharia* rule at center stage.

While on the societal level, Muslim revivalists proffer the notion that the ills of the Muslim world can be ameliorated only by the establishment of Islamically-driven political structures, on the level of day-to-day life there seems also to be the perception that Islam is basically reducible to the *sharia.* What this means in practical terms is that the beauty, virtues and meaning of Islam has become obscured by a veil of medieval Islamic legalist discourse—the discourse of *fiqh*—which lacks the intellectual depth of Muslim philosophy and theology and which is devoid of the spirituality of Sufism and other Muslim mystical traditions. We live in an era of *sharia*-compliant banking and *halal* hamburgers; we ponder over the legality of replacement heart valves derived from pigs and we agonize over the propriety of women shaking hands with men; and we spend untold mental and intellectual energy debating the minutiae of legal rulings on the correct position in which to place our hands during the canonical prayer. Paradoxically, however, all serious legal matters—state-military relations, for example, or international financial transaction—have little or no input from Islam or Muslim jurists, since the so-called 'Muslim world' is content to follow the conventions laid down by international law. Islamic legalism, therefore, is confined primarily to the private and personal domain of worship.

There is one thinker, however, who appears to buck the trend. Unlike so many of his revivalist contemporaries, Said Nursi made the revival of belief and the reform of the individual his primary and overriding concerns. In this respect he is one of only a handful of Muslim thinkers in the twentieth century who have little if anything to say about the socio-economic or political externalia of Muslim life. Over the past thirty years, 'Islam is a complete way of life' has been the mantra of choice for the vast majority of Muslim movements. Consequently, emphasis has been largely on the implementation of Islam at the socio-political level, with debate and discussion focusing mainly on issues such as Islamic law, Islamic education and the concept of the Islamic state. As such, most Muslim movements can be said to adopt an "externalist" approach to the Islamic revelation, seeing in the strict adherence of Muslims to the *sharia*—and, where necessary, the imposition of such adherence through legislative means—the key to the formation of the ideal Muslim society. For the "externalists", reform has come to mean chiefly the reform of society, the underlying aspiration of which must be to return to the "golden age" of Islam typified—for the externalists at least—by the community-state of Medina during the lifetime of the Prophet.

These "dreams of Medina", and the concomitant desire to share—or, even, impose—those dreams on others, are responsible in part for the current Western perception of Islam as more political ideology than Divinely-revealed religion. For a religion that has at the very heart of its message the concept of Divine unity, it is ironic that the profile it currently enjoys on the world stage is as a discourse of power and control that concerns itself more with the implementation of God's laws than with the notion of God itself. While to a certain degree this monochrome image of Islam is a result of certain anti-Islamic trends in politics and the media, to a greater extent it is a domestic issue, and concerns the overwhelming preponderance in the world of Muslim learning of the scriptural sciences such as *fiqh* and *hadith* over the rational sciences such as philosophy and theology. That Muslim scholarship is weighted inordinately towards the 'transmitted sciences' (*'ulum-i naqli*) should not, of course, come as that much of a surprise. Nor is it a recent phenomenon: al-Ghazali himself, eight centuries ago, bemoaned the fact that Muslim scholarship was being reduced to nothing more than expertise in canon law.

Yet the impact of this phenomenon is felt today more acutely than ever before, even if its dangers are not articulated as ardently as they were by al-Ghazali. In Christianity, for example, while theology may no longer wear the mantle of 'queen of sciences' that was conferred upon it in the late medieval period, it still enjoys the kind of attention that Muslim theology could only dream of. Karl Barth, Rudolf Bultmann, Hans Kung, Reinhold Niebuhr—it is not difficult to name any number of modern Christian theologians of international renown. When it comes to counting contemporary Muslim theologians, however, the fingers of one hand would probably not be exceeded in doing so.

Which is why a work such as *God, Man and Mortality* is such a breath of fresh air. For although Said Nursi does not yield easily to compartmentalization, he is arguably a theologian at heart, albeit with a mystic's spirit. Some students once complained to him that their high school teachers 'never talk about God'. One may be forgiven for thinking that Nursi's *Risale-i Nur*, his magisterial, 6000-page work of Qur'anic exegesis, was written partly with the grievances of such students in mind. The Risale was for all intents and purposes a missive written to a Muslim world which was under attack not from the sword or the bomb but from the immaterial enemies of ignorance, poverty and conflict. In it, Nursi attempted to reconnect the Muslim masses with the ideals and realities of belief, which he believed was the bedrock of personal and societal salvation. Nursi believed in the need for change, but knew that to be lasting, it had to be evolutionary. If he was in support of a revolution, it was a revolution of belief, and not one that was fuelled by political aspirations. If he believed in a state, it was not an Islamic state but an Islamic state of mind. This alone sets him apart from his coevals, lending him the kind of authenticity that many of his followers believe other revivalists lack, and which connects him directly to the great theologians and mystics of the medieval era.

*God, Man and Mortality* is a collection of essays written both by seasoned and by up and coming scholars working in the field now known as Nursi studies. The aim of these essays is to hold a mirror up to Nursi's teachings on a number of theologically important issues, just as Nursi held a mirror up to the teachings of the Qur'an. The scope is broad, covering subjects such as Divine immanence and transcendence, human spirituality and man's role as Divine vicegerent, Divine determining and free-will, and human conscience as evidence of the existence of God. The topics presented by our authors are unashamedly theocentric in nature; discussions on politics and legal theory are conspicuous by their absence. We benefit from the depth of awareness that the contributors clearly have of Nursi's teachings and his place in the Muslim academe, as well as from their lucid expository styles and strong authorial voices. The field of Nursi studies is no more than twenty years old, but already it can claim a number of distinctive works on Nursi and his teachings that are exemplary in their scholarship. *God, Man and Mortality* is, I believe, another.

Colin Turner
Durham, November 2013

# Chapter 1

## The Human Conscience as a Proof for the Existence of God: Nursi's Perspective

*Bilal Kuşpınar*

Since time immemorial, the existence of God has been a pivotal subject of inquiry in the history of philosophy. Proofs and arguments that have been proposed for this crucial question appear to have been classified in philosophical dictionaries into three broad categories: (i) cosmological, (ii) ontological, and (iii) teleological.[1] Cosmological arguments, generally speaking, begin with the observable objects and facts and proceed further with an analysis of such things as motion, contingency, cause, and order in the universe, and finally arrive at the conclusion that God exists as their primal origin or prime mover or uncaused Cause or the Necessary Being. In contrast to this first group of arguments are placed the ontological arguments, which proceed from the acceptance of an abstract definition of God's Essence in mind and reach God's Existence.[2] The exponents of this group of arguments, like Anselm (c.1033–1099), who was in fact regarded as the first to propound it, thought and argued that in our mind and understanding nothing greater than God can be conceived. This also means for them that God is "that than which noth-

---

[1]  See, for a study of some of these arguments in the context of Islamic and Jewish philosophy, Herbert A. Davidson, *Proofs for Eternity, Creation and the Existence of God in Medieval Islamic and Jewish Philosophy* (New York: Oxford University Press, 1987).

[2]  For a good analysis of cosmological arguments see W. L. Craig, *The Cosmological Argument from Plato to Leibniz* (London: Macmillan, 1980) and *The Kalam Cosmological Argument* (London: Macmillan, 1979).

ing greater can be conceived."[3] Later, in the seventeenth century, Descartes developed his own version of ontological arguments through self-contemplation of God as the completely perfect Being.[4] Both Anselm's and Descartes' finite thinking appear to posit a self-awareness on the part of the infinite and greatest and most perfect Being, that is, God. As for the third and last group of arguments, the teleological ones, also known as arguments from design, which share some commonalities with the cosmological arguments, proceed from an analysis of order and purpose in the universe and arrive at the conclusion that order as such cannot exist without an orderer and that God exists as the origin and source of that order.

Depending on their respective schools and orientations, Muslim philosophers and theologians from the classical period to modern times have been using these three groups of arguments in their philosophical writings, even sometimes with their own further additions, modifications and sophistications. But there are several other thinkers who stand outside this conventional philosophical circle and adopt, in their attempts at the demonstration of God's existence, a different path and method, though they still incorporate some of the aforementioned philosophical arguments in their discourses. Nursi, whose intellectual formation draws mainly on the traditional Islamic scholarship via a self-taught style of learning, is in fact one of these trans-philosophical and unconventional figures of the contemporary Muslim world. His mind-set, as he himself declares explicitly in his *Risale*, is Qur'anic *par excellence*, which can be understood as meaning that his reasoning and thinking runs in accordance with the *mind* of the Qur'an, and that his arguments are molded according to the *logic* of the Qur'an.[5] It is in this particular sense, therefore, that his intellectual personality cannot be characterized by any of the traditionally accepted

---

[3]  N. Malcolm, 'Anselm's Ontological Arguments,' *Philosophical Review* (1960), 69: 41–62.

[4]  René Descartes, *Discours de la method* (Paris: Larousse, 1969); *Discourse on Method and the Meditations*, trans. and introd. F. Sutcliffe (Harmondsworth: Penguin, 1968).

[5]  Even Nursi attributes the composition of his *Risale* to the perfection of the Qur'an, which he regards as his "master, teacher, leader, and guide for every conduct in his life" (*Risale-i Nur Kulliyatı, Mektubat*, 28, vol. 1, 522). "I must openly confess that the treatises [*risaleler*] do not belong to me; they are the property of the Qur'an and they spring forth from the Qur'an and hence bring to light its virtues ..." (ibid., 523).

appellations of erudition such as philosopher, theologian, or even mystic or Sufi.

The subject of God's existence and unity, to begin with, occupies a central place in the writings of Nursi. The way he treats this subject, however, and the style he uses for its exposition are different from any typical literary form of argumentation and standard presentation. For the sake of convenience we may call it 'the Nursian style of writing' and 'the Nursian mode of argumentation.' He himself confesses his distinct style on several occasions throughout his works, especially in one particular place in his *Al-Mathnawi 'Arabi al-Nuri* where he responds to those who complain about the lack of clarity of his words as follows:

> [Some] people complain that my words cannot be understood clearly. Yes, I accept that. For I feel sometimes as if I am speaking from the top of a minaret and sometimes crying out from the bottom of a well. What can I do? This is the way it is. [I must warn that] the speaker in this book is my feeble heart and the addressee is my rebellious soul. The real listener, however, is one who searches for the truth. So, anyone who desires to read this book should heed this [admonition].[6]

It is not coincidental, we presume, that Nursi professes these words just before he commences to set down his proofs for the existence of God. He probably seeks to say, or at least he seems to imply, that the arguments and proofs he will put forward in the lines following the above-quoted admonition may not necessarily run and develop within the widely accepted philosophical or theological discourse and that they should therefore not be viewed and judged according to the principles of the conventional logic.

Like any other religious thinker, Nursi believes that there are innumerable proofs for the existence of God. He often recalls and stresses the celebrated maxim of his predecessors that "the paths leading to God are

---

[6]   *Al-Mathnawi 'Arabi al-Nuri*, Noqta, manuscript copy, transcribed by Ceylan Çalışkan (İstanbul: Sözler, 2003); cf. printed copy, ed. İhsan Kasım, Vol. 6, 420; Turkish trans. Abdulmecid Nursi (İstanbul: Sözler, 2006), 316. All references refer to the original manuscript copy of the *Al-Mathnawi 'Arabi*, unless otherwise indicated.

as numerous as the breaths of the creatures."[7] In his Turkish writings such as *Sözler, Mektubat, Şualar,* and *Lem'alar,* he uses various kinds of proofs and arguments, including the aforementioned cosmological, onto-logical and teleological ones, though without naming them as such. It is in his Arabic masterpiece *Al-Mathnawi,* however, that he singles out only four proofs as leading directly to God. The first is the Prophet Muham-mad, peace and blessings be upon him, himself, the second the universe, the grand cosmos (or macrocosm) (*al-kawn*), also called the macro-hu-man (*al-insan al-akbar*), the third the miraculous sacred book the Qur'an, and the fourth the conscience (*wijdan*), the human conscience (*al-wijdan al-bashari*).[8] Not only in the *Mathnawi* but also in his other works does Nursi delineate the first three of them, the Prophetic, the Cosmic and Qur'anic proofs, with ample illustrations and elaborate explanations. But the last proof, which can briefly be called the conscience proof, he expos-es mainly in his former work, though he appears to make mention of it in his other works rather in passing. At any rate, each of these proofs deserves to be studied first in its own individual context and then collec-tively in terms of its relations with the others. Although in this essay we shall focus mainly on the conscience proof, we will nonetheless offer a short synopsis of the other three proofs in order to give a general idea about them to the reader and also to better situate the conscience proof in the context of the others.

The Prophetic proof, also designated by Nursi as the Muhammadan truth, that consists essentially in the excellent character of the Prophet Muhammad, peace and blessings be upon him, stands as the greatest tes-timony to the consensus of all the Prophets on the Divine Revelations, as well as the most definite confirmation of the veracity of their prophecy. Muhammad's Messengership, that is to say, is an indisputable proof, accord-ing to Nursi, not only for the existence and oneness of God but also for the unity and truthfulness of all the Prophets, just as Islam is a self-evi-dent truth for the affirmation of their Divinely revealed scriptures. This Prophetic proof therefore can be considered as historical, ethical and epis-

---

[7]  See e.g., for this statement, in his *Al-Mathnawi 'Arabi,* Noqta, 5; İhsan Kasım's edn, 423.

[8]  *Al-Mathnawi 'Arabi,* Noqta, 5; İhsan Kasım's edn, 423; *Risale-i Nur Külliyatı, Mesnevi-i Nuriye,* 1568.

temological proof, in that it testifies *historically* to the continuity of all Prophets, *ethically* to the uniformity of their individual characters, and *epistemologically* to the overall consistency and essential unity of their respective messages, all of which consequently and apparently demonstrate the unity of their original source.

The Cosmic proof, on the other hand, bears the characteristics of the aforementioned cosmological and teleological arguments. By this proof Nursi urges us to ponder on the Great Cosmos and read everything there, both individually and collectively, as the letters and points of the Book of Creation, and try to hear how each of them proclaims, in their respective tongue, the existence and unity of their all-Great Creator, as if they are gently chanting 'Glory be to Him and Praise be to Him.' All particles in the Universe, declares Nursi, with their very existence bear witness to the existence of the Necessary Being, and with their well-designed and balanced constitutions and particular attributes, they all testify truthfully to the perfect harmony implanted by their Creator in them individually and in the Universe as a whole.[9] Moreover, each being, he further states, is like a micro-organism and a prototype of creation, and as such it exhibits in itself a meticulous orderliness, a wonderful system and a subtle mechanism, all of which again point to the existence of the All-Wise Creator.[10]

As for the Qur'anic proof, it is, as Nursi characterizes it, a conclusive proof (*burhan an-natiq*) articulating the existence and unity of God specifically to those who wholeheartedly place their ears to its chest and hear thereof the most pleasant and coherent heavenly melody, 'There is no deity but God.' This is, for him, a luminous proof composed of six transparent sides: on the top, it bears the stamp of its inimitability; inside it holds the light of guidance; at the bottom it supplies logic and evidence; on the right it has the assent of reason; on the left it has the *testimony of conscience*; at the front it has goodness; and it aims as its goal at the happiness of the two worlds. As such, it is the foundation of revelation.[11] In saying so, Nursi forcefully asserts that the Qur'an comprises most cogent arguments and most compelling evidences for the existence and unity of God. In the *Mathnawi*, he summarizes the Qur'anic proofs under two head-

---

[9]  *Al-Mathnawi 'Arabi*, Noqta, 4–5; İhsan Kasım's edn, 422.

[10]  Ibid., 5; İhsan Kasım's edn, 423.

[11]  *Risale-i Nur Külliyatı, Hutbe-i Şamiye*, vol. 2, 1980; *Al-Mathnawi 'Arabi*, Noqta, 14.

ings, one the proof of purpose and final goal (*ghayat*), the other the proof of origination and creation (*ikhtira'*).[12]

A close examination of these two proofs reveals to us that they reflect more or less certain dominant characteristics of both the cosmological and teleological arguments of the philosophers and theologians. The most striking difference that distinguishes Nursi from the others is that he holds the Qur'an up as a window to the universe and observes the latter through the glasses of the former, rather than looking directly at the universe with a naked eye. One of the most important reasons for him to do so is probably his self-conviction that the *raison d'être* of the cosmos and of all that exists therein, as well as its wisdom, can be meaningfully acknowledged and adequately comprehended by the logic of the Qur'an. He expressly and repeatedly states that anyone who has a stainless heart, a sound intellect and an untroubled conscience can easily notice the miraculous style and the extraordinary eloquence of the Qur'an. "Such a person can also detect in the Qur'an the existence of a special eye that sees the entire universe like an open page and clearly views and reads all of its outward and inward dimensions."[13] Such a person, again, whom we may conveniently call the Qur'anic man, is capable of decoding, deciphering and interpreting the signs and symbols of the Book of the Creation. This being the case, the proofs and truths of the Qur'an, according to Nursi, can be better discerned and appreciated by a man who possesses an upright mind, a pure heart, and a sound conscience.[14]

Now let us return to our main subject, namely the fourth proof, the human conscience. It must be noted at the outset that Nursi offers no clear-cut definition for the term 'conscience' (*wijdan*). Instead he provides a substantive yet interesting description for it as follows:

> It [the conscience] is the self-conscious primordial disposition (*fitrat dhi shu'ur*) that divides and connects as an interval (*barzakh*) between the physical world and the world of the Unseen. Indeed, the primordial disposition (*fitrat*) and the conscience (*wijdan*) are [like] a

---

[12]  *Al-Mathnawi 'Arabi*, Noqta, 15–18.
[13]  *Risale-i Nur Külliyatı, Sözler,* 25, vol. 1, 187.
[14]  Ibid.

window [opening] to the intellect, as they diffuse the rays of *Tawhid* (belief in God's Unity).[15]

Apparently, Nursi's above-quoted account bears several significant components of the traditional definition of the conscience as recorded in the classical dictionaries of Islam. At the same time, it comprises several other components, as will be displayed soon, which seem to be lacking in the traditional definitions.

The well-known technical dictionary of at-Tahanawi furnishes two definitions for the conscience: the first according to the Sufis, and the second according to others, namely philosophers and theologians. The former defines it as an instant (rapturous) encounter with God, as it is derived essentially from the Sufis' ecstatic state (*wajd*). This mystical definition, quite specific in its use, has very little to do with the other technical notion of conscience, for which at-Tahanawi suggests two definitions, one well-known and the other less known. According to the well-known definition, the conscience stands for the soul (*al-nafs*) and all its internal faculties (*al-quwwa al-batinah*). In this sense, it refers to that through which everyone finds him- or herself by pure intellection by oneself by or perceiving through the internal faculties. According to the less-known definition, it simply refers to that which is perceived by the internal faculties.[16] All that we come to discover within ourselves through our conscience, as Tahanawi further expounds, can be termed *al-wijdaniyat*, an example of which is that we are aware of the existence of ourselves.[17]

What appears to be commonly shared and almost equally emphasized in the well-known traditional definition of conscience and that of Nursi's is that the conscience is a kind of metaphysical entity or spiritual faculty inherent in every human being and that it is at the same time conscious of itself. It can be viewed as man's inward realization. While Nursi calls it '*fitra*', the primordial disposition or pristine-original state of every human being, the traditional definition characterizes it as '*nafs*,' the soul or the self. Although both of these terms may in the final analy-

---

[15] *Al-Mathnawi 'Arabi*, Noqta, 3; İhsan Kasım's edn, 421.

[16] Al-Tahanawi, *Kashshaf Istilahat al-Funun*, Beirut: Dar al-Kutub al-Ilmiyya, 1418/1998, vol. 4, 293.

[17] Ibid.

sis denote the same substance, the former, that is also used both in the Qur'an and the Hadith, essentially for the inborn-natural creation of man, bears theological implications, while the latter contains more psychological and philosophical connotations.[18]

Be that as it may, this human conscience, as has been noted, is invested, in Nursi's articulation, with an extraordinary function of *dividing and connecting* the two worlds, this physical world and the immaterial world. This seems quite innovative and peculiar to Nursi's genius, since, so far as our research goes, no Muslim thinker before Nursi has ever assigned to the conscience such an unusual function. Though it is difficult for us to verify whether or not the human conscience performs such a function, we can see, if we analyze it further, how well it makes sense within the system of Nursi's religious thought. By equipping the conscience with such a functional power, Nursi intends to show that man, by virtue of his conscience, can establish communion with the world of the Unseen, provided that the conscience remains unadulterated and uninfluenced. In other words, the pristine nature of man (i.e. the *wijdan*), so conscious of itself and so close to the realm of spirituality, is capable of finding its Creator, God, as it serves as a window, so to speak, to the intellect through which the latter sees the Truth. That is why Nursi vigorously states that the conscience receives the illumination of the *Tawhid* from the world of the Unseen and transmits it to the intellect.

On the other hand, Nursi remains virtually silent on the nature (*mahiyya*) of the conscience, and even he does not bother to discuss what it is and how it is, and whether it is a faculty or something else. Rather, he tends to admit that the nature of the conscience may not necessarily be known; its existence nevertheless is known. For there are many things, he argues, whose existence (*wujud*) is known, though their essence (*mahiyya*) cannot be known. For instance, everyone is definitely cognizant of a will or a choice in himself through his conscience; yet he does not necessarily know the true nature of this will. Besides, to know the nature of beings is one thing, Nursi remarks; to know that they exist is

---

[18]   See e.g. Fazlur Rahman, *Avicenna's Psychology: An English Translation of Kitab an-Najat, Book II, Chapter VI, with Historico-philosophical Notes and Textual Improvements on the Cairo Edition* (London: Oxford University Press, 1952).

something else.[19] Likewise, although everyone is aware of the existence of his conscience, not everyone is cognizant of what it is.

Because of the mysterious nature of the conscience, Nursi instead draws our attention to its power and function and cares to distinguish it from the other well-known internal faculties. In one particular instance, for instance, he speaks about the four elements of the conscience, will (*irada*), mind (*zihn*), emotion (*hiss*), and the Divinely subtle faculty (*al-latifa ar-Rabbaniya*), all of which are at the same time, as he maintains, the four faculties (*hawas*) of the spirit (*ruh*). If we examine these 'faculties' more closely in their present context, we may conceive them to be the necessary immaterial constituents of the conscience. Each of these faculties, Nursi goes on to proclaim, has an ultimate goal. The goal of the will is worship of God, that of the mind is the knowledge of God, that of the emotion is the love of God, and that of the Divinely subtle faculty is the witnessing of God. The perfect form of worship, known as *taqwa*, essentially includes all of them.[20] All of these faculties, moreover, can be better cultivated, Nursi further stresses, and refined by the Divine Law and rightfully directed toward their respective goals.[21]

As has been noted, the conscience, in Nursi's view, has an intimate and intricate relation with the other internal faculties. Like all others, the conscience, too, ought to be well preserved without being impaired by any hindrances and without being obstructed by the plague of worldly indulgences.[22] As a matter of fact, Nursi issues a stern warning about the protection of the conscience, indicating that if a human being who faces numerous challenges and misfortunes during his short life in this world does not place his trust in God, his conscience will be troubled and afflicted with pain. Consequently, all the torments and pains may either suffocate him or turn him into a beast. Hence, man's sound conscience must be well sustained by his reliance on God.[23]

It is the conscience that lets man realize through his cognitive intuition (*hads*) that a fundamental aspect of his constitution, namely his spir-

---

[19]  *Risale-i Nur Külliyatı, Sözler*, 26, 205.
[20]  *Risale-i Nur Külliyatı, Hutbe-i Şamiyye*, vol. 2, 1980.
[21]  Ibid.
[22]  *Risale-i Nur Külliyatı, Şualar*, 11, 976.
[23]  *Risale-i Nur Külliyatı, Sözler*, 6, vol. 1, 10.

it, continues to live after his death.[24] Nursi further expounds this point as follows:

> Man's conscience, which is his conscious primordial nature, looks to and points to the eternal happiness. Yes, whosoever listens to his own vigilant conscience will certainly hear the sound crying, "Eternity! Eternity!" Even if the whole universe is given to that conscience, it cannot meet and satisfy its needs for eternity. In this case, the conscience has been created for such eternity. Furthermore, the conscience is attracted by and drawn to a true goal (*gaye-i haki-ki*) and a captivating truth (*hakikat-i cazibedar*)."[25]

As is clearly seen, Nursi goes deeper into the human conscience and draws as it were an anatomy of it from his own perspective and specifies for it, among others, two essential qualities. One is that, apart from being self-conscious, it has almost infinite needs and as such it cannot be satisfied with the things of this temporal world; nor can it be ever happy in this world. The other quality of the conscience is that it has a longing and yearning for the truth and God to whom it is naturally and inevitably attracted.[26] In other words, man, owing to his weakness, poverty, and defects, as Nursi remarks, is always in search of what he calls a "point of support" (*nokta-i istinad*) and a "point of assistance" (*nokta-i istimdad*).[27] It is indeed this particular quality of the conscience that compels and prompts man to discover within himself the Infinite, the Absolute, the Most Perfect, the most Ultimate Truth, the Most Compassionate, etc., in whom alone he can trust and on whom alone he can rely, through whom he can keep his nobility and dignity, and to whom he can confess his helplessness and weakness.

The two points we have just mentioned, namely the point of support and that of assistance, are like two small windows in the conscience, as Nursi depicts them, opening to the court of the All-Merciful and All-Compassionate One, who in turn uses them to diffuse the light of His knowl-

---

24   *Risale-i Nur Külliyatı, Sözler*, 29, 231.

25   *Risale-i Nur Külliyatı, Sözler*, 29, 234.

26   *Risale-i Nur Külliyatı, Sözler, Lemaat*, 321.

27   *Risale-i Nur Külliyatı, Sözler*, 33, 316; *Al-Mathnawi 'Arabi*, Noqta, 20; İhsan Kasım's edn, 430.

edge (*ma'rifa*) into that conscience.[28] Thanks to these windows, further-more, and through their opening, the conscience constantly looks to that Merciful One and also leans on His court.[29] To look at them from a differ-ent angle, these two points are two necessary realities of the human con-science and hence virtually every man feels them within himself. Since man is the noblest of all creations, Nursi asserts, and since his spirit is the most sublime of all, he cannot be devoid of these two points. Other-wise, in the case of their absence in him he would be reduced to the low-est of all creatures.[30] The spirit, furthermore, receives pleasure from the conscience, and so does the body from the spirit.[31]

To revert, again, to Nursi's conception of the human conscience (*wij-dan bashari*), as cited earlier, it signifies the primordial disposition or original nature of every human being. Being a self-conscious faculty, far different from all other external and internal senses, it is by itself capa-ble of finding and recognizing God. It even, as Nursi firmly asserts, "testi-fies decisively to the existence of a Necessarily Existent Being, Who is the possessor of Glory and Beauty."[32] For this faculty, like many other unknown internal faculties, serves for man as a kind of window that opens to the world of the unseen.[33] Furthermore, this conscience faculty, like the sixth sense of urge (*sawq*) and the seventh sense of craving (*shawq*), neither lies nor misleads. On the contrary, its testimony is always true and "whatev-er it says is the truth."[34] This is, in the eyes of Nursi, an undeniable fact, which can easily be discerned from a close observation of the original state of any being. This point he takes up again in the *Mathnawi* and he substantiates it with a few examples, as follows:

> The primordial disposition does not lie. For instance, a seed has a [natural] inclination to grow, which says, "I shall sprout and yield fruit." It says the truth (namely, what it says is proved true). Or, for example, an egg has a [natural] inclination towards life, which says,

---

[28]   *Al-Mathnawi 'Arabi*, Noqta, 21.

[29]   *Risale-i Nur Külliyatı, Sözler,* 33, 316.

[30]   *Al-Mathnawi 'Arabi*, Noqta, 20; İhsan Kasım's edn, 430.

[31]   *Risale-i Nur Külliyatı, Sözler* (Lemaat), 342.

[32]   Ibid., 321.

[33]   *Al-Mathnawi 'Arabi*, Noqta, 19; İhsan Kasım's edn, 430.

[34]   *Risale-i Nur Külliyatı, Sözler* (Lemaat), 321.

"I shall become a chick." And it becomes so by God's leave. It says the truth. Or, for instance, if a handful of water has a [natural] inclination to freeze and expand, it says, "I shall cover more space." Strong iron cannot prove it wrong, as the water's [natural] truthfulness [and honesty] cracks the iron. All these [natural] inclinations are the manifestations of the creative commands decreed by the Divine Will.[35]

The natural inclination (*mayalan*) can be understood, in the terms of the philosophers, as an internal faculty (*al-quwwa al-batinah*) that exists in the vegetable soul, the animal soul, and the human soul. As is well-known, the souls of plants and animals, according to the philosophers, have in common the faculty of growth (*al-quwwa al-numuwwa*), which Nursi designates here as the natural inclination to grow (*mayalan-i numuwwa*). But interestingly, Nursi, the philosophers of the past attributed no faculty to so-called inanimate things, such as water. In any case, every being manifests in itself, through its own peculiar inclination or desire as Nursi terms it, or a particular faculty as the philosophers specify it, the creative command (*amr takwini*) of God that corresponds to His cosmic-dominical command (*amr Rabbani*). Exactly in the same way, man in turn manifests in himself, through his own conscience, the same creative command of God, which, however, appears in the form of what Nursi names "ecstasy" (*jadhba*) and "attraction" (*injidhab*),[36] which can be interpreted as man's natural inclination toward God.

In other words, so long as the human conscience remains in its original purity and unaffected by any negative external or internal factors, it naturally moves and is constantly drawn toward what Nursi has previously termed "a captivating truth," that is, God, who is the source and force of attraction. To express it more precisely in the nomenclature of the philosophers, the conscience's natural inclination turns from the state of *potency* into that of *actuality*, through its ecstasy and attraction, both of which are the manifestations of God's creative command.

Moreover, since the conscience is originally pure and naturally invested with self-awareness, it, together with the heart, as Nursi states, is the

---

[35] *Al-Mathnawi 'Arabi*, Noqta, 19; İhsan Kasım's edn, 430. See, for a similar passage, *Risale-i Nur Külliyatı, Sözler* (Lemaat), 321.

[36] *Risale-i Nur Külliyatı, Sözler* (Lemaat), 321.

locus (*mahal*) of belief. And both intuition (*hads*) and inspiration (*ilham*) are the evidence of belief, whereas thought and mind are the safeguards of belief.[37] Of course, each of these cognitive and intuitive faculties, which are interrelated and indispensable for man's overall sound function, performs a task pertaining to its respective position and condition. Nevertheless, it is the human conscience that is distinguished from the rest and even from the intellect on account of what is notably its most distinct power, as articulated by Nursi in the *Mathnawi*:

> Even if the intellect ceases to function properly and fails to reason, the human conscience [still continues to function and] does not forget the Creator. Even if it denies its own self, it still sees Him, contemplates Him, and turns [or maintains its inclination] toward Him. Intuition (*hads*), which is like lightning, an instantly occurring wit, constantly stirs it up, while its manifold form, inspiration, illuminates it. Moreover, the inclination's manifold form, 'desire,' and its manifold form 'yearning' (*ishtiyaq*), and its manifold form 'Divine Love' (*ashq ilahi*) persistently urge and direct it [i.e. the conscience] to [become acquainted with] the knowledge of the All-Glorious Almighty. The attraction and ecstasy inherent in this conscience are due to the [existence of] a Captivating Truth who attracts it.[38]

Immediately following these remarks, Nursi concludes by saying:

> Once you have become familiar with these points, you should look into this self-evident proof, namely the conscience, and see [how strong a proof it is]! Just as the heart ensures life [by pumping blood] throughout the body, the knowledge of the Creator as the pivotal source of the heart's [spiritual] life gives life and activates all the ambitions and inclinations of man commensurate with his unlimited potentials and aptitudes. It also casts into them pleasure, increases their value, develops and expands them.[39]

All in all, in order for the conscience to execute its naturally invested task, Nursi insistently warns, its pristine sound state (*fitrat-ı selime*) ought to be maintained. Once this original state has been secured, the

---

[37] Ibid., 336.

[38] *Al-Mathnawi 'Arabi*, Noqta, 20; İhsan Kasım's edn, 431.

[39] Ibid.

eyes of the conscience always remain open, even if the eyes of the intellect may be blind.[40] Moreover, such a well-preserved and uncorrupted conscience, he firmly stresses, not only recognizes God but confirms the veracity of the message of the Qur'an as well. At the same time, the satisfaction of the conscience, as well as the tranquility of the heart, comes about through the enlightenment of the Qur'an.[41] Finally, truth can only be addressed to and appreciated by a man who has a sound conscience and who respects, and acts with, the principle of freedom of conscience. On the other hand, speaking of truth and reality to a person whose conscience has fallen to the lowest level of baseness would be not only a waste of time but also, to use the famous proverbial (Biblical) maxim, would be "casting pearls before swine,"[42]—so admonishes Nursi in conclusion.

---

[40]  Ibid., 21.

[41]  *Risale-i Nur Külliyatı, Mektubat*, 19, 444.

[42]  Matthew 7: 6; *Risale-i Nur Külliyatı, Mektubat*, 28.

# Chapter 2

## What Is Man?: Bediüzzaman Said Nursi on Man as God's Representative on Earth: A Christian Reading Report

*Revd Marten de Vries*

"What is man that You take thought of him, and the son of man that You care for him?" A quotation from Psalm 8. David is awed by the greatness of the universe. When he observes the moon and the stars he feels lost, and he asks himself in wonder how it is possible that God should concern Himself with insignificant man. He then proceeds to sing man's praises, crying out: "Yet You have made him a little lower than God, and You crown him with glory and majesty!"[43]

God has given man an elevated position. He has entrusted man with control over the earth. "You make him to rule over the works of Your hands", is what it says in the Psalm. At the same time it remains clear at the beginning and at the end of this same passage of Biblical poetry that man's authority is second-hand. "A little lower" is what we hear, which means: directly under God. Man is God's 'vice-regent' or vicegerent. But God is and remains the great King. The Psalm ends as it began: "O Lord, our Lord, how majestic is your name in all the earth!"[44]

---

[43] In the Septuagint, the Greek translation of the Old Testament that was current at the beginning of our Christian year-notation, "little lower than a God," is translated as "little lower than the angels": "βραχυ τι παρ αγγελους." This recurs in the quotation in Hebrews 2; see below.

[44] Psalm 8,1.8 (New International Version).

This text contains at least three elements which Bediüzzaman Said Nursi also emphasizes continually. The Great Creator surpasses everything and everyone. Man has received a special position within God's creation. But this also entails responsibilities. Responsibilities towards God and towards creation.

Let us now focus on man's position. What is man, in the light of God's revelation?

## Caliph on Earth

On the very first page of the Old Testament it is mentioned that God created man "in His own image," "according to His likeness."[45] This by no means implies that God created something godly next to Himself, a clone of Himself. What it does mean is explained directly: "rule over all the earth" and "subdue the earth," rule over other creatures in God's Name, as His representative on earth. The earth should be "cultivated" and "kept" by man.[46] It should be brought to development by man as steward and servant of the Highest Majesty.[47]

Where Christians reflect the Bible by speaking of man as the "image of God,"[48] Islamic theology uses the term "caliph." In Surah al-Baqarah

---

[45] Genesis 1: 26–28. In the Hebrew expression 'וְנִתְמֹדְךָ וְנִמְלָצָב' both words can be seen as synonyms. In the New Testament the expression recurs in I Corinthians 11: 7, where the man is called "εικων και δοξα θεου."

[46] Genesis 2: 15.

[47] The Hebrew gives 'עבד' = 'عبد' for 'cultivate.'

[48] When Jesus is called "image of God" in the New Testament, it is emphasizes that God Himself was present in this man. 2 Corinthians 4: 4: "η δοξα του χριστου ος εστιν εικων του θεου"; Colossians 1: 15: "ος εστιν εικων του θεου του αορατου." The similarity is that both Adam and Jesus ("the last Adam", 1 Corinthians 15: 45) represented God. When it states in Romans 8: 29 that God "predestined" man "to become conformed to the image of His Son" ("προωρισεν συμμορφους της εικονος του υιου αυτου"), this must mean that men may share in the glory that Jesus, by becoming one of them, gained for them. And that is: restoration of the honorary position that God had intended for man in his Creation. It is interesting that in J. van Genderen and W. H. Velema, *Beknopte Gereformeerde Dogmatiek*, 2nd edn, Kampen 1992, different accents are placed by both authors. Where Velema, in the chapter *De mens het beeld van God*, relates being "the image of God" in Colossians 1: 15 to Christ's human nature (305), Van Genderen in *Christus, de Middelaar* connects this to his godly nature (416). This difference in interpreta-

the first man, Adam, is titled "caliph." Before calling man to life, God imparts His intentions to the angels. He announces that He will appoint a "caliph" as a crown on His creation, a being that can represent Him on earth.

God's willing servants have their doubts as to whether this is a good idea. They already envision it. While they are in heaven praising and glorifying God, this creature is capable of working against God. The man that God has in mind will spill blood and bring decay upon the earth. But God knows what He is doing. He does not take unwarranted risks. "I know what you know not", He answers the angels.[49] The evil of men will not surprise Him, it will be overruled by man's goodness.[50]

In the last verse of Surah al-An'am people as such are also called "caliph." Thus we are reminded of our high calling.[51] The caliphate is not just a task for one specific person, Adam or a successor of Muhammad, placed above other people as *primus inter pares*.[52] It is a task entrusted[53]

---

tion of one text cannot be explained by the difference of subjects: 'dyophysite' cannot lead to a double exegesis.

[49] Surah al-Baqarah, 30.

[50] In his exegesis, Nursi paraphrases the words of God: "There is much good and many advantages in mankind, and there is sinfulness but this is minor. It would be opposed to wisdom to abandon the former due to the latter. Humanity also holds a mystery, and this qualifies man for the vicegerency," Bediüzzaman Said Nursi, *Signs of Miraculousness*, The Inimitability of the Qur'an's Conciseness: 270. From the *Risale i-Nur* Collection. Translation by Şükran Vahide (İstanbul: Sözler), 2004.

[51] Surah al-An'am, 165. In verse 133 the verb 'اِسْتَخْلَفَ' is used, but there it concerns disobedient people who are replaced by others.

[52] In Surah Sad, 26 the word is specifically applied to David. Nursi gives the title of 'vicegerent' also especially to the Mahdi at the end of times and to other reformers, given by God to keep the sharia and Muhammad's religion, Bediüzzaman Said Nursi, *Letters*, Twenty-Ninth Letter, Seventh Section: *The Seven Signs*, Fifth Sign: 514. From the *Risale i-Nur* Collection 2. Translated from the Turkish *Mektubat* by Şükran Vahide (İstanbul: Sözler), 2001 edn.

[53] Nursi often uses the concepts 'Vicegerent' and 'Supreme Trust' together: The *Risale i-Nur* Collection, *passim*, such as: *The Words*, Twentieth Word, First Station: 254; *idem*, Second Station, *On the Miracles of the Prophets*: 268; *idem*, Twenty-Third Word, Second Chapter, First Remark: 329. Further: *The Flashes*, Seventeenth Flash, Fifteenth Note: 188. From the *Risale i-Nur* Collection 3. Translated from the Turkish *Lem'alar* by Şükran Vahide (İstanbul: Sözler), 2000 edn. *The Rays*, Eleventh Ray, *The Fruits of Belief*, Seventh Topic: 233.238. From the *Risale i-Nur* Collection 4.

to the whole of mankind:[54] not to each individual *per se*, but to the human race.[55]

We consequently read in Surah al-Baqarah of how God prepared man to fulfill his task. "He taught Adam all the names".[56] In the Bible Adam gives names to all the living creatures under his command, thereby proving that he is equipped for the task.[57] Just so the equivalent verse in the Qur'an encompasses the fact that God first granted man the ability to express himself and to name his fellow creatures. In this way he was able to rule in His Creator's name.[58]

God gave man knowledge of affairs, situations and events,[59] and in doing so, He placed man above the animals, but above the angels too.[60] Man, unlike the angels, was able to choose between good and evil. Yet he was created or born with the capacity to fulfill his calling without fault, of his own free will, to comply with his destiny of being God's caliph on earth.[61]

---

[  ] Translated from the Turkish *Şualar* by Şükran Vahide (İstanbul: Sözler), 2002 edn. See the use of 'الأمانة' in Surah al-Ahzab, 72 for the Qur'anic of 'trusteeship'.

[54] Nursi, *The Words*, On the Nature and Purposes of Man, Life and All Things, Twentieth Word, Second Station, *On the Miracles of the Prophets*, 265. From the *Risale-i Nur* Collection 1. Translated from the Turkish *Sözler* by Şükran Vahide (İstanbul: Sözler), 2002 edn.

[55] Nursi, *The Words*, Twentieth Word, Second Station, *On the Miracles of the Prophets*: 265.

[56] Surah al-Baqarah, 31.

[57] Genesis 2: 19–20.

[58] Most probably this is a parallel to Surah ar-Rahman, 4: "علمه البيان"

[59] Nursi, *The Words*, Twentieth Word, Second Station, *On the Miracles of the Prophets*: 265.

[60] They had to bow before man because of his knowledge. Iblis, the devil, a jinn and as such also a being with a free will, refused to do this. He felt exalted above man because he had been created from fire and not from clay, Surah al-A'raf, 11–12. Here Nursi points out a pattern, a 'universal principle,' see: Nursi, *The Words*, First Station: 254.

[61] In Christian doctrine, the God-given capacity is distilled from the New Testament, where it says about man: "in the likeness of God has been created in righteousness and holiness of the truth.": Efeziërs 4,24. In Colossians 3: 10 it speaks of: "the new self who is being renewed to a true knowledge according to the image of the One who created him."

# God Is the Great King

Nursi does not tire of emphasizing that God did not let go of His control over the earth when He made man. He is called "the Monarch of Pre-Eternity and Post-Eternity,"[62] and also, "Sustainer of All the Worlds."[63] Earlier, Nursi already spoke of God's "glorious dominicality to all beings."[64] God uses His caliph, but keeps a tight hold on the reins.[65] God remains sovereign.[66] Man may be called the "throne verse,"[67] but what the 'Throne verse' in the Qur'an says remains standing: in the end heaven and earth are preserved by God alone.[68]

Man, in himself, created out of clay,[69] is weak, weaker and more vulnerable than other beings.[70] His superiority does not lie in his quantity, in his numeric majority: there are many more animals.[71] Nevertheless he has received a high position from God. Nursi sings man's praise: "For man is a well-composed ode of wisdom."[72] In the Name of the One who rules,[73] he received a high station.[74] In spite of his potential rebellion and unbelief[75] he is "the final fruit on the tree of the universe."[76] He is the

---

[62] Nursi, *The Rays*, Eleventh Ray, *The Fruits of Belief*, Seventh Topic: 238.
[63] Nursi, *The Words*, Eleventh Word: 138.
[64] Nursi, *The Words*, Tenth Word, *On Resurrection and the Hereafter*, Eleventh Truth: 100.
[65] Nursi, *The Words*, Twentieth Word, Second Station, *On the Miracles of the Prophets*: 268.
[66] Nursi, *The Words,* Thirty-Third Word, *Thirty-Three Windows making know the Creator*, Twenty-First Window: 704.
[67] Nursi, *The Rays*, Eleventh Ray, *The fruits of belief*, Seventh Topic: 238.
[68] Surah al-Baqarah, 255.
[69] Surah al-A'raf, 12.
[70] Nursi, *The Words,* Tenth Word, *On Resurrection and the Hereafter*, Eleventh Truth: 100.
[71] Nursi, *The Flashes*, Seventeenth Flash, Sixth Note: 166.
[72] Nursi, *The Words*, Twenty-Third Word, Second Chapter, First Remark: 329.
[73] Nursi, *The Words,* Twentieth Word, Second Station, *On the Miracles of the Prophets*: 268.
[74] Nursi, *The Words*, Twelfth Word, Fourth Principle: 146.
[75] Nursi, *The Words*, Tenth Word, *On Resurrection and the Hereafter*, First Addendum, First Part, Second Point, 115. *Idem, The Rays*, Ninth Ray, Second Point: 209. (Repetition.)
[76] Nursi, *The Rays*, Eleventh Ray, *The Fruits of Belief*, Seventh Topic: 238.

"micro-cosmos."[77] Within creation he is the most complete mirror of God's Names,[78] called to life to proclaim the manifestation of God's holy and beautiful Names in creation.[79]

In His wisdom, God gave man understanding.[80] Man is equipped to perform the thousands of tasks that God laid aside for him.[81] Man is the spiritual and material leader on earth,[82] monarch of the animals,[83] called upon to proclaim God's glorious dominion with words and deeds.[84]

Man in himself is small and weak.[85] He can fall into sin. But God equips him to function as His representative. Therefore God addresses man. He speaks to all creatures, especially to His caliph. He does that through scriptures, books, and regulations.[86] With the light spread by Muhammad, man can conquer animals that are stronger than himself.[87] If man wishes to be a worthy representative of God, he must believe in the One God. In this way he is fully man, "worthy of bearing the Trust."[88]

All and everyone, and especially God's representative on earth, is dependent on the Creator and His decisions.[89] So man must always continue to admit his dependence.[90] His humbleness should be evident in

---

[77] Nursi, *The Rays*, Fifteenth Ray, *The Shining Proof*, Second Station, Seventh Step: 631.

[78] Nursi, *The Letters*, Twenty-Eighth Letter, Fifth Matter, *On Thanks*: 431.

[79] Nursi, *The Words*, Twenty-Third Word, Second Chapter, First Remark: 329.

[80] Nursi, *The Words*, Twentieth Word, Second Station, *On the Miracles of the Prophets*: 265.

[81] Nursi, *The Flashes*, Twenty-Second Flash, Second Indication: 226.

[82] Nursi, *The Words*, Twentieth Word, Second Station, *On the Miracles of the Prophets*: 264.

[83] Nursi, *The Flashes*, Twenty-Second Flash, Second Indication: 226.

[84] Nursi, *The Words*, Thirty-Third Word, *Thirty-Three Windows making know the Creator*, Twenty-First Window: 704.

[85] Nursi, *The Words*, Nineteenth Word, *On the Messengership of Muhammad*, peace be upon him, Fifth Droplet: 245. Nursi, *The Letters*, Nineteenth Letter, *The Miracles of Muhammad*, peace be upon him, First Addendum, Fifth Droplet: 238. (Doublure.)

[86] Nursi, *The Rays*, Eleventh Ray, *The Fruits of Belief*, Ninth Topic, First Point: 258.

[87] Nursi, *The Words*, Nineteenth Word, *On the Messengership of Muhammad*, peace be upon him, Fifth Droplet: 245.

[88] Nursi, *The Words*, Twenty-Third Word, Second Chapter, Fifth Remark: 339.

[89] Nursi, *The Letters*, Twenty-Eighth Letter, Fifth Matter, *On Thanks*: 431.

[90] Nursi, *The Words*, Twenty-Fourth Word, Fifth Branch, Second Fruit: 371. Nursi there refers to Surah al-Fatiha, 5 (4 in his manner of counting).

his humble worship of God.[91] He must express his thanks.[92] His ritual prayers, especially, he must not forsake. Through Friday prayer in particular, the hearts of men are united in a mysterious way, so that "a miniscule creature in the universe" becomes the vicegerent of the Creator of the heaven and the earth.[93] Particularly because he has received this station from God, God will certainly accept his prayers.[94]

## God's Unity

The unity of God belongs, just as does the necessary existence of the Creator, to the indubitable Islamic belief, to which God's vicegerent should strictly adhere.[95] When he fails to do that, he goes against the godly, human, and cosmic perfection.[96] Denial of God's unity runs counter to the universe, that glorifies its Creator in union.[97] It is an insult to the universe and the wonderful Names of God. They are then derogated.

In this manner creation becomes aimless, dependent on chance. Man becomes a sign without any meaning. He lowers himself to a level lower than a perishable beast,[98] which is in itself stronger than a man.[99] He is transformed into a diabolical animal, just like some Europeans and those that imitate them. Finally God will consign those animals to "the hell they deserve"![100] Yet, when man successfully endures life's temptations and remains true to Islam, he will be rewarded with eternal joy, the dwell-

---

[91] Nursi, *The Words*, Eleventh Word, First Group: 138; Twentieth Word, Second Station, *On the Miracles of the Prophets*: 265; Twenty-Third Word, Second Chapter, Fifth Remark: 339.

[92] Nursi, *The Letters,* Twenty-Eighth Letter, Fifth Matter: *On Thanks*: 431.

[93] Nursi, *The Flashes*, Seventeenth Flash, Ninth Note: 174. With a reference to Surah al-Baqarah, 43: "واقيموا الصلوة".

[94] Nursi, *The Rays*, Eleventh Ray, *The Fruits of Belief*, Eight Topic, Fourth Benefit: 248.

[95] Nursi, *The Rays*, Fifteenth Ray, *The Shining Proof*, First Station, *A Brief Summary of Surah al-Fatiha*, Seventh Phrase, 'The path of those whom You have blessed': 588.

[96] Nursi, *The Rays*, Seventh Ray, Second Chapter, *Concerning Proofs of the Divine Unity*, Third Truth, *Perfections*: 174.

[97] Nursi, *The Words*, Twenty-Fifth Word, *On the Miraculousness of the Qur'an*, Second Light, Second Beam, *Ten Points of Eloquence*: 442.

[98] Nursi, *The Words*, Twenty-Third Word, Second Chapter, First Remark: 329.

[99] Nursi, *The Words,* Nineteenth Word, *On the Messengership of Muhammad*, peace be upon him, Fifth Droplet: 245.

[100] Nursi, *The Flashes*, Seventeenth Flash, Sixth Note: 166.

ing-place of peace that surpasses all expectation.[101] In any case, physical pleasures await him in the eternal kingdom that he desires by nature.[102] Eternal joy and immortality await him in the afterlife, where the reality of God's Names comes gloriously to light.[103] This passage in the Belgic Confession of Faith could have been a quote from Nursi's *Risale i-Nur*:[104]

> The creation, preservation, and government of the universe, which is before our eyes as a most beautiful book, wherein all creatures, great and small, are as so many letters leading us to perceive clearly the invisible things of God, namely, His eternal power and deity.[105]

All that is, and all that takes place, reflects the Names which God revealed of Himself.[106]

All is created by God and determined in a perfect order. As if He were wielding a pen, He described beginning and end, origin and destination of the seed and the fruit of each ordinary plant and every tree.[107] Each state and phase of every living creature is depicted, including the life-history of man. God, with His power, laid down all the patterns.[108] And His caliph, man, has the task of putting into words God's greatness upon the earth,[109] in this way respecting the order and balance which God placed in creation.[110]

## Creation Is for the Benefit of Man

Man is the center of the universe. Without man as monarch, the firmaments would not have been created.[111] God brought the universe under

---

[101] Nursi, *The Words*, Eleventh Word: 138. The words Nursi uses remind us of 1 Corinthians 2: 9. He himself refers to Bukhari and Muslim.
[102] Nursi, *The Rays*, Eleventh Ray, *The Fruits of Belief*, Eight Topic, Fourth Benefit: 248.
[103] Nursi, *The Rays,* Eleventh Ray, *The Fruits of Belief*, Seventh Topic: 233.
[104] Nursi, *The Words,* Nineteenth Word, *On the Messengership of Muhammad*, peace be upon him, Fifth Droplet: 245.
[105] Belgic Confession of Faith, Article 2.
[106] Nursi, *The Words*, Twenty-Third Word, Second Chapter, First Remark: 329.
[107] Nursi, *The Rays*, Second Ray, Conclusion, Fourth Matter: 47.
[108] Nursi, *The Words*, Twenty-Sixth Word, *On Divine Determining*, Third Topic: 486.
[109] Nursi, *The Words*, Twenty-Third Word, Second Chapter, First Remark: 329.
[110] Nursi, *The Words*, Twenty-Sixth Word, *On Divine Determining*, Third Topic: 486.
[111] Nursi, *The Words*, Nineteenth Word, *On the Messengership of Muhammad*, peace be upon him, Fifth Droplet: 245.

the yoke of mankind and decorated it and fitted it as a dwelling.[112] Directly after describing man's function and task as God's image, the story of creation in the book of Genesis in the Bible also tells us about God giving man the use of the fruits of the earth: food for him.[113]

The ruling over fauna[114] and flora[115] is depicted by Nursi in terms of the metaphor of an officer with his soldiers.[116] God taught Solomon the language of the birds.[117] Nursi connects this with the human capacity for making use of animals, like using bees to make honey. He can make doves deliver letters and make parrots talk. More usefully, he can use sparrows to fight a locust plague. But the great animals, too, God placed under man's control.[118]

Man is a privileged being. As the highest creature he is vicegerent on earth. He gained knowledge of God's Attributes and Qualities.[119] But these privileges bring obligations. He must use both his mouth and his hands[120] to glorify God.

It is up to man to exploit and develop the earth.[121] The naming-knowledge that he gained from God stands for a general principle.[122] Man must

---

[112] Nursi, *The Rays*, Eleventh Ray, *The Fruits of Belief*, Seventh Topic: 233. See also Surah al-Baqarah, 29 and Nursi's exegesis of it in *Signs of Miraculousness*, in particular 257.

[113] Genesis 1: 29.

[114] Genesis 1: 28.

[115] Nursi, *The Rays*, Eleventh Ray, The Fruits of Belief, Seventh Topic: 238.

[116] Nursi, *The Words*, Twenty-Fourth Word, Fifth Branch, Second Fruit: 371.

[117] Surah an-Naml, 16.

[118] Nursi, *The Words*, Twentieth Word, Second Station, *On the Miracles of the Prophets*, 267–268.

[119] Nursi, *The Words*, First Station: 254.

[120] Nursi, *The Words*, Twentieth Word, Second Station, *On the Miracles of the Prophets*: 264.

[121] Nursi, *The Words*, Twentieth Word, Second Station, *On the Miracles of the Prophets*: 265. Nursi says: "Strive to transform the face of the earth into a garden every part." The picture the Bible paints is that God first makes a garden and that man then cultivates it, Genesis 2: 8–15. While the naming of animals is not part of God's preparatory work but of man's performing of his task; see above. Nursi here reminds us of Surah al-Mulk, 15. God placed the earth at man's disposal and man may profit from it. But he must also get to work in it!

[122] Nursi, *The Words*, First Station: 254.

practice science and arts,[123] dig for ore and work metals,[124] bring to development craft and industry. Man's task is to bring development and prosperity.[125]

Nursi was aware of man's weakness. He states that when men do not believe in God, death will take away the meaning of their existence.[126] Their life becomes meaningless and leads nowhere.[127] This does not refer only to the afterlife. Man must produce something of worth in God's eyes right here and now. But—is man really capable of creating a paradise here on earth? And if not, is the cause to be found in faulty political systems like socialism and bolshevism, that defy the laws of nature?[128]

We are living half a century after Nursi. Science and technique have developed even more explosively after his death. Through computer technology man can perform and control the unthinkable. Yet men have not grown more optimistic. The earth is becoming exhausted. The whole world runs on oil, but provisions are not endless. Animals become extinct and are mistreated in bio-industry. Some nations are capable of, and their political leaders not averse to, spreading destruction on a large scale. Already millions of people have been killed by ethnic and religious violence. What kind of a being is man that he does this to himself?[129]

Faith seems to make no difference. Muslims, Christians, Hindus or atheists can blame each other, but everyone is part of world events, gets dragged into them and takes an active part himself in one way or another. Were the angels right in saying that man is only capable of *fasad* (corruption) and *safk* (bloodshed)? Is this inherent in being human? Or did the angels know this because they had insight into the "Well-preserved Tablet," one of the possibilities assumed by Nursi in his explanation of

---

[123] Nursi, *The Words*, Tenth Word, *On Resurrection and the Hereafter*, First Addendum, First Part, Second Point, 115.

[124] Nursi, *The Words*, Twentieth Word, Second Station, *On the Miracles of the Prophets*: 264.

[125] Nursi, Nursi, *The Flashes*, Seventeenth Flash, Sixth Note: 166.

[126] Nursi, *The Words*, Twenty-Third Word, Second Chapter, First Remark: 329.

[127] Compare the biblical book of Ecclesiastes (or Preacher).

[128] Nursi, *The Flashes*, Twenty-Second Flash, Second Indication: 225–226.

[129] Compare Surah al-Maedah 5, 32.

Surah al-Baqarah, 30?[130] Was Nursi, as a man of his times, not too optimistic about man and his possibilities?

## Above the Angels

Christian theology orients itself by Jesus Christ, in Whom (the one and only) God descended to earth. In the New Testament, Psalm 8 recurs in Hebrews 2. That which David said of man is applied to Jesus on the basis of the Septuagint. In His godly nature Jesus is certainly stationed higher than the angels. By His incarnation as fallen (into sin) man (yet Himself without sin!),[131] and by His death on the cross, He was for a short time[132] placed below the angels. Yet it is exactly because He defeated death that He received glory and was able to repair man's honorary position: above the angels, who were created to serve man.[133]

What is man that this should happen to him? Christians do not become lacking in motivation because of this. It brings relief in a devastated world. They believe that creation, dragged down with man at the Fall into sin,[134] will, together with man, be set free from slavery to corruption on the day that Jesus returns.[135]

What is man? What is man capable of? Is he equipped for his high station? Or no longer equipped? Must he then limit his ambitions to planting pointers to paradise, while awaiting the world to come? Should we be waiting for the Mahdi? A *sayyid* from the descendants of the Prophet of the Muslims?[136] In what manner can you address people? Should you tell them that they should live in harmony with the "laws

---

[130] Nursi, *Signs of Miraculousness*: 268.

[131] Hebrews 7, 26.

[132] When 'מיהלא' is expressed as "αγγελους" in Psalm 8,6, 'βραχυ'starts to take on a different meaning: 'short time' instead of 'just under.' In Hebrews 2: 7–9 Psalm 8 is quoted from the Septuagint, and that is why the application is different from what the Psalm originally wants to say. Not "almost godly," but "for a short time even lower than the angels." See note 1.

[133] Hebrews 1:2.

[134] Genesis 3:17.

[135] Romans 8: 19–21.

[136] Nursi, *The Letters*, Twenty-Ninth Letter, Seventh Section: The Seven Signs, Fifth Sign: 514, 515.

of nature"?[137] Even when they do not share your faith? But what if the natural balance is broken?

The discussion of theological anthropology should be continued. As a right-minded Muslim, Said Nursi had a positive view of mankind. Man is created in God's image and is still ever able to realize a good world as long as he lets himself be led by the laws of the Creator. Christians, on the other hand, consider man to be born a sinner and their positive view is derived from their belief in Jesus Christ, who will deliver the earth, together with man, from sin and all its consequences. For the time being, man can do no more than establish signs of hope. Moreover, that is his duty according to his high station, of which he is reminded by God's Word and, in particular, through the Gospel of Christ.

---

[137] Nursi, *The Flashes*, Twenty-Second Flash, Second Indication: 225.

# Chapter 3

## Transcendence–Immanence of God: How Humans Relate to God in the Theological Discourse of Bediüzzaman Said Nursi

*Mehmet Özalp*

W hile almost all faith traditions more or less agree on the existence of God and in the unity of God or Godhead, the main theological differences between faiths stem from each one's distinctive response to the fundamental question of how humans should relate to God. This response is invariably associated with the transcendence–immanence problem in theology. If one claims that God is transcendent, above and beyond space and time, then God is rendered unreachable and hence relating to God becomes exceedingly difficult. In such faith systems Divine intermediaries inevitably follow to close the gap between the transcendent and the mortal human. Conversely, if one argues that God is immanent in order to make God more accessible, this approach invariably leads to tendencies to anthropomorphize God into worldly images, or to imagine that God is part of the universe. Said Nursi addresses this fundamental theological problem by arguing that the Qur'anic presentation of God as *transcendent and immanent at the same time* gives immediate access to God without violating God's divinity. God is transcendent in His Self, but immanent in the way God reflects His Qualities and Attributes on the cosmos in general and on the earth in particular. God's *al-Asma al-Husna* (the Most Beautiful Names)—and the Attributes of God which are manifest and apparent in the universe through these Names—are the signposts that have been encrypted throughout the book of the universe. This approach accentuates the immanence of God, hence rendering God approachable and personal. At the same time, it preserves the transcendence of God and preserves *tawhid*—the absolute, unshared unity of God.

There is a natural tendency in human nature to believe in and develop an intimate relationship with the Person (*Dhat*) behind the transcendental Will and Power actively governing the universe. There are three important concepts and aims with respect to how Muslims relate to God in the Islamic spiritual framework that we need to bear in mind: *Iman billah*—belief in the existence of God; *ma'rifatullah*—knowledge of God; and *muhabbatullah*—love of God. Our relationship with God starts with the discovery of His signatures in nature and a firm belief in His existence. A natural curiosity, coupled with an innate yearning to get to know God, leads one to the knowledge of God. *Ma'rifatullah* is attained by identifying and accessing the Names, Attributes and Qualities of God as they reflect in the human heart, the universe and the Holy Qur'an. Love of God naturally emerges out of knowledge of God, for one cannot love the unknown. Since this is a vast field, discussion in this essay relates to the *ma'rifatullah* aspect of the way Islam facilitates the human need to relate to God.

## Ways of Relating to God

Excluding the insane among us who claim to speak to God,[138] we currently have no direct channel or human agency via which to communicate with God other than our personal prayers.[139] How, then, does one have access to and relate to an unseen, transcendent God,[140] who is above and beyond space and time? "Eyes comprehend Him not, but He comprehends all eyes. He is the All-Subtle, the All-Aware," declares the Qur'an.[141] Our inability to openly see God or enter into a direct line of communication

---

[138] The concept of Messengership in Islam is that God appoints a rather reluctant human being to convey revealed words of God to people.

[139] Muslims believe that the Qur'an is literally the word of God. Therefore, reading the Qur'an equates with speaking with God. Reading the Qur'an with this belief does give the experience of speaking with God.

[140] Qur'an, Al-Baqarah, 2:3.

[141] Qur'an, Al-An'am, 6:103. Qur'an translations are from Ali Ünal's *The Quran with Annotated Interpretation in Modern English* (New Jersey: Light Publishing, 2006).

with Him renders God distant to us. Yet, believers have a need to develop a close relationship with God and feel God's immanent presence in their daily lives. In many faith traditions and spiritualities, human beings had to find ways of gaining a satisfactory level of intimacy with God. In Islam, while God's transcendence is clearly asserted,[142] we are also given the news that God is not so distant after all. He is more immanent and closer than we may actually realize.

A number of Qur'anic verses give the impression that God is absolutely close to His creation. "So, All-Glorified is He in Whose Hand is the dominion of all things,"[143] "No living creature is there but He holds it by its forelock and keeps it under His complete control,"[144] "We are nearer to him than his jugular vein,"[145] remarks the Qur'an. However, at the same time there are verses that give the impression of distance. Verses such as "and to Him you are being brought back,"[146] and "The angels and the Spirit ascend to Him, in a day the measure of which is fifty thousand years [of earthly years],"[147] infer a distant and transcendent God.

How can God be infinitely transcendent, hence distant, and absolutely immanent, hence close, at the same time? Said Nursi begins by saying that this is not a contradiction but an expression of the difference between the way God relates to His creation and how we relate to God. He addresses this fundamental theological question by distinguishing three ways in which humans relate to God.[148] In order to bring such an abstract matter of theology closer to our understanding he utilizes an analogy which we will call the *sun analogy*. He employs variants of this analogy in addressing a number of theological questions throughout his works.

---

[142] Qur'an, Ikhlas, 112:4. This verse clearly states that God is unlike any of His creation.

[143] Qur'an, Ya Sin, 36:83. This verse and the five verses that follow are cited by Said Nursi himself.

[144] Qur'an, Hud, 11:56.

[145] Qur'an, Qaf, 50:16.

[146] Qur'an, Ya Sin, 36:83. Taken literally, if we will be brought back to God then we must be now distant from God.

[147] Qur'an, Al-Ma'arij, 70:4.

[148] Bediüzzaman Said Nursi, *Sözler* (Words) (İstanbul: Soz Basim Yayin Nursi, 2003), 276. I have used primary sources in referring to Said Nursi's works.

There are three ways in which one can relate to the sun. In the first way, the sun is close to us with its unrestricted light and intangible reflection. In spite of our being separated from it by a great distance, its light reaches our eyes and penetrates the iris. The image of the sun appears in our perception and feels intimately close to us. On the other hand, since we are restricted in space and time and have a physical and solid body, we are immensely distant to the sun. The only reasonable way we can relate to the sun is through its reflection and manifestation. However, if one wishes to meet directly with the sun itself, one must overcome many restrictions and travel long, hazardous distances to reach the sun.[149] This is the second way.

The third way to relate to the sun is to assume that the sun literally comes to us itself and we do not need to travel to it. The sun incarnates in a single object, or an actual spark of the sun is embedded within everything. However, although this option is conceivable, incarnation of the sun is quite impossible as no entity has the capacity to behold the actual greatness of the sun.[150]

In a similar way, different faith traditions have developed one of the following three ways of relating to God. First, assuming that God is transcendent and inherently distant from humans in His Person (*Dhat*), people may try to reach God through a spiritual journey. In this way, the travelling is from the human to the Divine, involving a spiritual struggle to reach perfection and achieve an actual communion with God. Success in this approach depends on one's ability to ascend spiritually through multiple layers of existence and may take many years of special focus and struggle.[151] Although it is possible to complete the journey in one lifetime, very few people can actually complete the journey. Hence relating to God is not open to everyone. Then there is the problem of whether it is possible to have true communion with God. Consequently, multiple lifetime and reincarnation doctrines developed in certain faith traditions such as Hinduism.

---

[149]  Ibid., 277.

[150]  Nursi, *Lemalar* (Flashes) (İstanbul: Söz Basım Yayın, Nursi, 2003), 299.

[151]  Nursi, *Sözler*, 278–279.

The second way is to assume that God would come down to the human level by incarnating in earthly forms or in a human being (as with Jesus in Christianity). This is another way in which people conceive means whereby they can directly relate to God. According to this notion, one can relate to God directly through the incarnate person without having to go through a long and arduous spiritual journey themselves. However, such a belief also assumes that earthly objects, or human beings, have the capacity to comprise the essence of a transcendent God. According to the Qur'an such beliefs invariably lead to *shirk* (associating partnership with God) as they violate God's unity (*tawhid*).[152]

The third way to relate to God is to focus on God's personal Names, Attributes and Qualities as reflected in the universe and the human heart. One needs to realize that while we are distant from God, God is already close to us just as the sun is intimately close with its light, heat, and reflection in spite of its distance. By focusing on God's ever-present immanent closeness through Attributes, one can relate to God far more deeply and safely without having to go through a long, arduous spiritual journey and without having to violate God's unity.[153]

The Qur'an, and hence Islam, focuses on the third way of relating to God. It is for this reason that the Names of God are so often emphasized in the Qur'an,[154] and therefore there is a famous list of the 99 Names of God in the Islamic tradition.[155] But how does one get access to God's Names or Attributes? It is in God's Light, Nursi argues, that God's Names and Attributes are conveyed to the empirical and visible world around us.

## Accessing God's Light

The Qur'an declares, in the chapter An-Nur (The Light) and verse 24:35, that "God is the Light of the heavens and the earth." The verse goes on to furnish a metaphor[156] of God's Light as a never-ending unknown source and finishes with the expression "Light upon light":

---

[152] Qur'an, An-Nisa 4:36, 4:48; Al-An'am 6:22, 6:71–94.

[153] Nursi, *Sözler*, 278.

[154] Qur'an, Al-Hashr, 59:22–24. In just three verses, 19 Names of God are mentioned.

[155] Canan, İbrahim, *Kutub-u Sitte* (İstanbul, 1996), Vol. 17, 507.

[156] Qur'an 3:7 acknowledges that there are metaphorical (*mutashabih*) verses in the Qur'an. Such verses are usually about how God governs the universe and inter-

God is the Light of the heavens and the earth. The example of His Light is like a niche wherein is a lamp; the lamp is in a crystal; and the crystal, shining as if a pearl-like star, lit from the oil of a blessed olive tree that is neither of the east nor of the west. The oil would almost give light of itself though no fire touches it. Light upon light! God guides to His Light whom He wills. God strikes parables for people. God has full knowledge of all things.[157]

One possible meaning of this verse, for Nursi, is that belief in God illuminates our world view and such a belief enables a believer to see things as they really are. More specifically, the universe is created with multiple realms circling around one another like a rose with many petals. Each Divine Name becomes the source of light that illuminates these realms.[158] Therefore, God's Light carries with it knowledge about God in terms of God's Names and Attributes, which becomes apparent as God's Light reflects over the mirror of the universe and the human heart.[159] If God's Light is available to our human perception and the universe acts as a mirror to God's Light, how does one gain access to this light?

It is at this point that many religions and philosophical ideas about God differ greatly. How is it possible for religions to have major differences if each claims to hold the *truth about God*? How is it that monotheistic religions, which are so closely related, have fundamental differences about God? Even highly spiritual and mystical people from the same faith tradition sometimes contradict one another, while at the same time successive philosophers race to refute each other's rational arguments about truth. Furthermore, why is it that in some religions God is absent[160] and in some others the afterlife has very little focus[161] while God, the afterlife, and, for that matter, all key aspects of belief have a strong emphasis

---

acts with His creation, or when abstract concepts and relative realities are expressed. We are warned that, when these verses are interpreted, one must use extreme caution since unqualified interpretations may easily lead to theological deviation.

[157] Qur'an 25:31.

[158] Nursi, *Sözler*, 582–585.

[159] Ünal, Ali, *The Qur'an*, 736–737.

[160] Some forms of Buddhism, for instance, do not talk about God.

[161] In Judaism, the afterlife does not have the prominence given to it by Islam and Christianity.

in Islam?[162] Ultimately, what is the root cause of differences about *God* and the *truth of God* within a faith tradition and between faith traditions if there is only one God? Said Nursi gives the following introductory explanation in his long answer to this important question:

> The wisdom of this mystery is this: certainly, the human being is capable of mirroring all the Divine Names and has the capacity for all possible human perfections. However, having a limited power, a minor will, varying abilities and a diversity of desires, he searches for truth through thousands of veils and obstacles. For this reason, in his discovering of reality and witnessing of the truth, multiple barriers intervene. Some people cannot overcome such barriers. In most cases, human spiritual capacities are very varied. The capacity of some is not capable of unfolding some of the truths of belief. Moreover, the colors of the reflections of Divine Names vary according to the mirror over which they manifest. People, who receive such reflections, sometimes cannot be the means to a complete manifestation of a Divine Name. Furthermore, manifestations of the Divine Names take on different forms with respect to universality and particularity, shadow and actual. Some human capacities are not able to transcend the particularity and some get stuck in the shadow. For some others, in proportion to their spiritual capacity, a Divine Name dominates their nature. That Divine Name exercises command over their complete spiritual capacity at the expense of other capacities.[163]

In expanding his answer, Nursi further develops his *sun analogy*, this time focusing on the way we may feel, perceive and have access to its light. There are three different ways in which the sun's light reaches us.

The first relates to how the sun's light reaches us through *reflection on objects*. The sun's light reflects on all flowers, for example, on earth. Light has a particular reflection over a whole flower species, and sometimes uniquely over a single flower. When the pure light from the sun hits the flower it dissipates, and some colors are absorbed and some are reflect-

---

[162] Nursi, *Sözler*, 449–450. I have looked at Şükran Vahide's translation as a first template and then rendered it into a new translation based on the original text to improve its readability and in my view present a meaning closer to that of the original.

[163] Ibid., 450–451.

ed. The reflected light reaches our eye, giving the flower its unique color and beauty. However, in the process pure light is altered by the limited reflecting capacity of the flower.[164] The second way for the sun's light to reach us is via *reflection from the moon and planets*. The moon, for example, receives a tiny fraction of the reflection of the sun's light. Although the moon is exposed to the full grandeur of the sun, only a shadow of the light is forwarded to the seas,[165] the earth, the air, and other objects in proportion to the capacity of the moon.[166] Since the moon's capacity is limited we do not see things as they really are if we purely depend on the moon's light. *Direct reflection* of the sun over every transparent object is the third way the sun's light reaches us. Because there is no intermediary, the light received is pure, universal, and actual as every transparent object, glass, window and bubble receive the full attributes of the sun in this direct light.[167]

In a similar manner, God's Light can also be received in three ways. In the first, the human nature is like the flower in the analogy. Although each and every one of us is capable of receiving God's Light, the pure light is inevitably dissipated in the limited capacity of our human nature, especially if it has not fully flourished.[168] Even if someone were to unfold his innate potential through mysticism, he develops and beautifies himself. God's Light beautifies him in the same way as the sun exhibits the beauty of a flower. Nevertheless, human nature is an opaque mirror, so it invariably dissipates and refracts God's Light. It becomes impossible to get the full truth of God in this way just as it is impossible to see the full reflection of the sun through a flower. A person may attain a certain level of human perfection but he cannot comprehend the full reality of God by relying purely on personal experience. His *subjective reality* colors the way he comprehends God's reality.[169] While such a subjective reality may not be completely false, it falls far short of being complete and pure.

---

[164]  Ibid., 451.
[165]  Francis Bacon proved that the light reflected from the moon does not have heat.
[166]  Nursi, *Sözler*, 452.
[167]  Ibid., 452.
[168]  Ibid., 453.
[169]  Ibid., 454.

Accessing the sun's light through the moon represents truth as perceived and expressed by the philosopher and his reason. Although a philosopher's access to the truth of God is of a higher order than that of ordinary human experience, it is nevertheless only a shadow of the pure light of God, just as the light received from the moon is only a shadowy fraction of the sun's light.[170] Even if the philosopher is elevated all the way to the moon by the stairs of reason, he will find the moon to be a dark and desolate place without a real light of its own. For as long as he trusts the ability of reason alone to reach the truth, he will not be able to access it in its totality. The philosopher may only find the truth of God by a rational inference behind multiple layers of intellectual veils.[171] Hence, the philosopher has an *incomplete reality.*

The third case represents the light received by revelation conveyed through a true Prophet of God. Prophethood and its inspiration directly open a window on God in every object. An ordinary believer in this path does not depend on himself to decipher the truth of God, nor does he rely on an intermediary like the moon. He gets direct access to God's Light.[172] Such a believer leaves his self behind, vaporizes into the atmosphere and burns with love in the full grandeur and intensity of God's Light. Because he understands that a universal and transcendent God is the source of all truth, opaque objects and puzzling mirrors do not baffle him. He knows that what is seen on these mirrors are only colorful reflections, not the sun itself. Every object in the universe, and the universe as a whole, become a mirror to God's Names and Attributes.[173] Such a believer can confirm his personal but subjective reality with the *objective reality* of God's Light as reflected in the universe and understood by the guidance of revelation.

Therefore, people will get partial or complete access to truth depending on which way they try to access the truth of God. While all avenues provide some access to God's Light, going through philosophy, and a pure reliance on one's spiritual experience or reason, invariably fall short of giving a full, universal, and pure understanding of God. Since human experience depends on an individual's wide-ranging capacities and level of

---

[170] Ibid., 453.
[171] Ibid., 455.
[172] Ibid., 453.
[173] Ibid., 455.

spiritual and intellectual development, we end up having a diversity of claims to truth. Only guidance received from an unadulterated revelation teaches us how to gain access to full grandeur of God's Light and hence understand God by directly opening, in everything, a window on God. This approach enables one to understand God in a universal way with His full Names and Attributes without ignoring other truths of faith that naturally emanate from a complete understanding of God.[174]

If God's Light reflects over the mirror of the universe, then it should be possible to discover its content through events and objects around us. Every observable and measurable event and entity in the universe acts like a prism, leading the discerning eye of the observer to empirical clues that point to the existence, unity, and Attributes of God. It is possible to draw *patterns of action* from observable events on earth and in the universe. Using these patterns, we can then identify certain *titles* or *names*, and as a consequence would be able to deduce (with the guidance of the Qur'an) God's Divine *Attributes*. Before this is explored further, we need to make a distinction between a *name* and an *attribute*.

## Identifying the Names and Attributes of God through the Book of the Universe

When we use the word *name* in a theological context, we do not mean the personal name or the identifier of a person. In our context, a *name* (*ism*) refers to a *title* given to a person because of a particular *skill*. When we say Adam is a carpenter, we mean he has the skill of carpentry. When we say, Adam is an architect, we know that he has the *skill* to design and plan buildings. For this reason, when we see a building, we say that it can only be the creative work of an architect.

An *attribute* (*sifat*), on the other hand, refers to a capability or *complete competence* that has become the second nature of a person. When we say Adam has the attribute of communication, we mean that he is a master in the art of communication. That is, he is competent in different forms of communication such as listening, writing, speaking, presenting, etc. If one of these key skills is missing, we can say he is skilled in some aspects of communication, but we cannot say he is a competent commu-

---
[174] Ibid., 455–456.

nicator. Therefore, a competence is a complete complementary set of skills combined in the same person.

Similarly, a Divine *Attribute* is a combination of a set of Divine Names in God's Self. For example, one of the Attributes of God, the Attribute of *Takwin* (Creation, Production), includes the Names of God *Al-Bari* (The Provider of Appropriate Features), *Al-Muhyi* (The Giver of Life), *As-Sani* (The Artistic Creator), *Al-Musawwir* (The Shaper), *Ar-Razzaq* (The Sustainer), and so on. Hence, each Attribute of God is a combination of Names, the important point being that a given name may be associated with more than one attribute. A note of warning: one should not imagine God as divided into Names and Attributes; rather, all of these Names and Attributes collectively make up the Qualities or the 'character' of God.

|  | *God Almighty* | *Car Manufacturer* |
|---|---|---|
| *Observable patterns of action (Divine Acts)* | • Act of cleansing (e.g. decomposition of corpses, plants cleaning the air by converting CO2 to O2). <br> • Act of balancing and ordering (e.g. the distance of the Earth from the Sun; the limbs of the body in proportion). <br> • Act of purposeful design (e.g. the organs); every being has a place in the ecology. | • Car is running smoothly owing to aerodynamic design. <br> • Electrical systems are working for all needs and environments. <br> • Every feature of the car has purpose and is fitted with the driver and passengers in mind. |
| *Names* | • *Al-Quddus* (Most Holy) <br> • *Al-Adl* (All-Just) <br> • *Al-Hakeem* (All-Wise) | • Aerodynamic engineer <br> • Electrical engineer <br> • Ergonomic designer: knows customers' (driver's and passengers') needs). |
| *Attributes* | • All-knowing <br> • All-encompassing will <br> • All-powerful (etc.) | • Has knowledge covering many areas of discipline <br> • Has technological competency. <br> • Has production competency. |

The table above outlines how we can reach God and get to know God by observing *Divine acts* in nature and the universe. The example of a car manufacturer is also given in the table as an analogy to aid understanding, not as a direct comparison.

In the case of the car manufacturer, let us assume that everything about the car is made by a single person. Even though we don't see the car manufacturer, we see the many cars that he produces because they are everywhere, with the same design and trademark. When we examine a single car more carefully, we notice that the car runs smoothly because of its aerodynamic design. Electrical systems are there and working, as are lights, indicators, etc. Every feature of the car has a purpose and is fitted with the driver and passengers in mind. For example, the steering wheel is right in front of the seat at a certain height, the gear stick is at arm's length and so on. All these observations lead us to conclude that the car manufacturer has the titles (names) of aerodynamic engineer, electrical engineer and ergonomic designer. From these titles we can conclude that the car manufacturer has certain general capabilities or competencies (attributes). He is all-knowing about car manufacturing. He has technology and production capabilities. From this, in turn, we gain an appreciation of the strong personal qualities of the car manufacturer.

This enables us to logically go from *observable works* (acts) to *names*; from names to *attributes*; and, then from attributes to personal *qualities*. It is possible to apply this method to the way in which we decipher Divine Names and attributed from the natural world, as illustrated in the figure below.

The Qur'an points our critical attention to the natural world around us: "can you see any rifts?"[175] Everything around us is designed with perfect features to survive in the natural world and function in a harmonious ecosystem. When we closely examine natural events and the features of living beings, we realize that there are discernable acts of universal proportions and scale. For example, we see an *act of cleansing* in the way corpses are removed and the air is cleaned by plants.[176] We also see an *act of balancing* in the way the earth is placed in its orbit and the proportion

---

[175] Qur'an, 67:3.
[176] Nursi, *Lemalar*, 555–557.

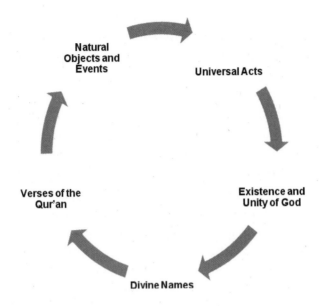

in limbs of the body.[177] We might also see an *act of frugality* in the way our bodily organs carryout multiple functions and nothing is wasted in the natural world.[178] The sheer scale, complexity and faultless execution of these observable acts show us that there is a God who is *Most Holy, All Just and All Wise.* These titles or names, in turn, inform us of the perfection of God's Attributes of *Knowledge, Will,* and *Power.* Our appreciation of these Attributes tells us the perfection of God's Personal Qualities. At this point, Said Nursi directs our attention to the Qur'anic ethical teachings not to be wasteful,[179] to be just[180] and to be clean[181] as evidence that the Qur'an's teachings perfectly align with what we observe in the natural world.

## Conclusion

The theological writings of Said Nursi elaborate on one of the most fundamental question of theology—how do believers relate to a distant and transcendent God? In human history, this need has led to interpretations

---

[177] Ibid., 561–65.

[178] Ibid., 566–574.

[179] Qur'an, 7:31.

[180] Qur'an, 55:7–9.

[181] Qur'an, 2:222.

and theologies such as belief in a hierarchy of gods who function as intermediaries between God and humans; elaborate spiritual progressions and journeys designed to take one towards a final communion with God; and acceptance of a spark of divinity in every object, or God incarnating in a human being. Ultimately all such doctrines violate the monotheistic element in just about all religions. According to Said Nursi, this problem lies at the heart of why religions differ from their very inception or through their changing interpretations over time.

Islam, according to Said Nursi, addresses the transcendence–immanence problem by tapping into God's immanent closeness to humans through God's ever-present Light. When we merely raise our awareness to comprehend this fact we become able to detect God's Light as it reflects in the universe and the natural world. In this scheme, there is no need to journey spiritually towards God, or imagine lesser Divine intermediaries as populating the immense gap between God and humans; or assume that God incarnates in earthly forms and images. Once one has detected God's Light guided by the objective reality made available by revelation (the Qur'an), it becomes possible to decipher God's Names and Attributes by identifying empirical patterns of actions and works detectable in the natural world and across the universe. We are then able to identify each of God's innumerable Names and witness how it operates giving us an objective and complete understanding of God's character. When we get to know God, we could then cultivate an intimate love and closeness with God. While the Qur'an acts as an instruction manual teaching us this invaluable methodology of reading the book of universe, the universe becomes an objective source of knowledge to test the veracity of the Qur'an's theological and ethical teachings.

# Chapter 4

---

# Man as Vicegerent of the Earth: How New Is Said Nursi's Interpretation?

*Şükran Vahide*

Said Nursi's main purpose in composing the collection of writings known as the *Risale-i Nur* was to offer convincing proofs and explanations of the essentials of faith as taught by the Qur'an that would answer the needs of ordinary believers, whose faith, he felt, was being challenged by the scientism and currents of materialist thought that gained strength in late Ottoman and early Republican Turkey. His aim was to demonstrate the validity and truth of the Qur'anic vision of existence and its continued relevance for human life. Arguably, one of the most noteworthy features of the *Risale-i Nur* is its treatment of man, descriptions of whose nature and functions are woven into its numerous proofs and arguments. Nursi most probably focused on the human being in this way not only in order to explicate the high position accorded him by the Qur'an, but also to reply to those European philosophies that had reduced him to the status of a rational animal. Where the Enlightenment had in effect demoted man, Nursi sought to reinstate him at the center of the cosmos, and to redefine his functions that relate both to the Maker and to other beings. In undertaking these tasks, Nursi drew on many traditions within Islamic thought and learning, which he sought to coalesce within a method he claimed was derived from the Qur'an.

This chapter, by examining Nursi's interpretation of man as vicegerent of the earth, and comparing it with views of the vicegerency in Islamic thought of various types and periods, aims both to set out Nursi's views and to discover in what respects, if any, his interpretation is original, and so to throw light on the composition of his thought, the influences upon it, and aspects of his method. The chapter consists of three main sections. The first offers a summary discussion of the term 'vicegerent', as found in exegetical material, its adoption by Sufi writers, and its usage by modernist writers of the nineteenth and early twentieth centuries. The second section investigates Nursi's interpretation of man as vicegerent and his two main approaches to the subject. The final section points out, in three subsections corresponding to the previous discussions, some parallels for and possible sources of Nursi's ideas in Islamic thought. The conclusion attempts to evaluate the findings and to determine in what ways Nursi's interpretation is original.

## The Term 'Vicegerent' (*Khalifa*)

'Vicegerent' is a term that occurs nine times in the Qur'an in various contexts in reference to human beings, twice in the singular and seven times in either of two plural forms,[182] with its first mention, in 2:30, being the source of the notion of man's vicegerency of the earth. This verse–

> Remember (when) your Lord said to the angels: 'I am setting on the earth a vicegerent.' The angels asked: 'Will You set therein one who will cause disorder and corruption on it and shed blood, while we glorify You with Your praise ...?'

–and the following one, which begins "And He taught Adam the names of all things," were from earliest times the cause of speculation, the term *khalifa* being met with uncertainty by commentators and thus giving rise to different interpretations.[183] Besides the angels' querying the corruption that would be caused by the *khalifa*, the main questions revolved around whom the title referred to and its precise meaning. Was the *khalifa* Adam, or his righteous descendants, or all his progeny, that is, humankind, in addition to himself? And if the term was understood in the sense

---

[182] The singular, *khalifa*, 2:30, 38:26; and plural forms, *khala'if*, 6:165, 10:14, 10:73, 35:39; and *khulafa'*, 7:69, 7:74, 27:62.

[183] See, Wadad al-Qadi, 'The Term "Khalifa" in Early Exegetical Literature,' *Die Welt des Islams* 28 (1988), 397–404.

of the basic meanings of the root *kh-l-f*, to succeed or come after, or replace, whom did the *khalifa* succeed on the earth? Various explanations were given in the light of narrations from the Prophet and his companions. All or some of these interpretations were included in the commentaries of the major exegetes.

It was not till later Sufism that the idea of man's vicegerency gained importance, emerging with the development of the notions of the Perfect Man and the Spiritual Pole; the earliest Sufis had not dwelt on the concept. The first scholar to give it Sufistic significance was al-Ghazali (d. 505/1111), who stated that it was only by virtue of the hidden relationship formed when God breathed into man of His spirit, as described in 15:29, that Adam became God's *khalifa*.[184] According to this, *khalifa* clearly signifies all the children of Adam; however, the relationship is realized only through the continuous performance of supererogatory worship in addition to obligatory worship.[185] Later, Muhyiddin 'Arabi (d. 638/1240) accorded the vicegerency a high place, making it fundamental to his system of thought. His conception is based on the notion of the Perfect Man, who with his comprehensive nature as the microcosm reflects all the Divine Names manifested in the macrocosm. The Perfect Man is God's vicegerent on earth, as are the Prophets and saints.[186] A key factor in the vicegerency is knowledge, the capacity to acquire which was bestowed on Adam with 'the teaching of the names,' described in 2:31. It is by virtue of knowledge that the vicegerent, manifesting God's Names and rulership in the cosmos, deputizes for God.[187] A noteworthy point concerning the vicegerency in the writings both of Ibn 'Arabi and of subsequent writers influenced by him is its being confined to the elect, although potentially all human beings have the ability to achieve its high station.[188]

---

[184] 'Halife,' *TDVİA*, 15 (1997), 299–300 by Süleyman Uludağ.

[185] İmam Gazali, *İhyau 'Ulumi'd-Din*. Turk. tr. Ahmed Serdaroğlu (İstanbul: Bedir, n.d), iv, 554.

[186] See Süleyman Uludağ, 300; William C. Chittick, *The Self-Disclosure of God: Principles of Ibn al-'Arabi's Cosmology* (Albany: SUNY Press, 1998), xxi, 77.

[187] Ibid., 213.

[188] See e.g. William C. Chittick, *Faith and Practice in Islam: Three Thirteenth Century Sufi Texts* (Albany: SUNY Press, 1992), 35, 92, 105.

Another school of Sufism, that of the Naqshbandi reformist (*Mujaddid*) Shaikh Ahmad Sirhindi (d. 1034/1624), advanced a quite different interpretation of the vicegerency. Its followers saw the need to purify Sufism and bring it closer to the Sharia, and they differentiated between the ways of Prophethood and sainthood. In the Prophetic way, God bestows on the lover of faith "real conviction (*iman-i haqiqi*) and elevates him to the position of His own deputy (*khalifat Allah*) ... and helps him to establish His Sharia."[189] This linking of the vicegerency and faith are also to be observed in Nursi; indeed, numerous aspects of Sirhindi's thought were, by his own admission, influential on Nursi.

Moving on to the so-called Islamic Modernists of the nineteenth and early twentieth centuries, notably Muhammad 'Abduh and his school, a new emphasis is to be observed in treatment of the concept, and an expansion of its meaning, arising from the Modernists' espousal of the ideas of self-strengthening and material progress. 'Abduh notes that the Qur'an directs man's attention toward the universe so that he should ponder over it and investigate it, and suggests that it urges him to study the creation and its secrets so that he may derive the sciences for human progress.[190] 'Abduh's stress on human reason and knowledge is reflected in his interpretation of the vicegerency. He cites some previous interpretations but concludes that the meaning of the vicegerency is general, referring to Adam and all his descendants, and is in respect of everything by which God has favored man over other creatures. The chief of these faculties, by which man rules over the universe and subjugates it as he wishes, is reason (*'aql*). Despite being created weak and ignorant, by virtue of the power of reason man has unlimited potential, knowledge, and actions, the purpose of which is to disclose the secrets of creation. It was owing to these characteristics that God made him vicegerent of the earth. He was the most appropriate creature for the vicegerency.[191]

---

[189] Muhammad 'Abduh Haq Ansari, *Sufism and Shari'ah: A Study of Shaykh Ahmad Sirhindi's Effort to Reform Sufism* (Leicester: The Islamic Foundation, 1406/1986), 70.

[190] See e.g. Muhammad 'Abduh, *Tafsir al-Qur'an al-Hakim* (Cairo: Dar al-Manar, 1366/1947), i, 249, 250.

[191] Ibid., 258–260.

## Nursi's Interpretation of the Vicegerency

To come to Said Nursi's interpretation of the vicegerency: he makes reference to it in two main contexts: the first is in explanations of the miracles of the Prophets, as mentioned in various verses of the Qur'an, and chiefly 'the teaching of the names.' This latter Nursi describes as a "miracle of Adam ... indeed of mankind, related to the question of the vicegerency."[192] Although he included an expanded version of the discussion in the *Risale-i Nur* as the Second Station of the Twentieth Word (written ca. 1927), originally it was part of his expositions of verses 30–33 of Surah al-Baqarah in his commentary *Isharat al-I'jaz*, which was composed in 1913 and 1914 in the early period of his life. These pieces emphasize the development of science, human progress, and material aspects of the vicegerency, and almost certainly owe something to the ideas of the Islamic Modernists.

The second main context in which Nursi makes reference to the vicegerency is his proofs of the truths of belief, in some of which he includes descriptions of the nature and position of man. These proofs form an integral part of the *Risale-i Nur* and analysis of them will aim to throw light on both Nursi's method of Qur'anic interpretation and the composition of his thought and the extent of its originality. Discussion of this latter will follow discussion of the former, along with a brief look at some related key concepts.

## The Vicegerency and Human Progress

Nursi's main purpose in expounding the miracles of the Prophets, in connection with which he mentions the vicegerency, is to illustrate aspects of the Qur'an's miraculousness (*i'jaz*), namely: universal principles and the tips of general laws being concealed in minor incidents the Qur'an mentions; and secondly—by way of explanation of the verse "neither is there a grain in the dark layers of earth, nor anything green or dry, but is (recorded) in a Manifest Book" (6: 59)—everything being found in the Qur'an. The idea, that is to say, is that on some level the Qur'an makes allusion to all events and all things—in this case, that it alludes to the wonders of

---

[192] Bediüzzaman Said Nursi, *Signs of Miraculousness. The Inimitability of the Qur'an's Conciseness*. Eng. tr. Şükran Vahide (İstanbul: Sözler, 2004), 271–272.

modern science and technology through the miracles of the Prophets. Nursi's thesis is that by mentioning the miracles, the Qur'an is pointing to the final goals of human scientific and technological progress and is urging men to work to achieve them.[193]

In his commentary *Isharat al-I'jaz*, while expounding the verses describing the creation of Adam and the teaching of the names (2:30–33), Nursi explains that it was because of his comprehensive disposition and the diversity of [his] abilities that he was taught the names of all things and so was made vicegerent of the earth in preference to the angels. Adam's superiority lay in his ability to acquire complete knowledge of the names. Knowledge is thus "the pivot of the vicegerency," for the execution of God's ordinances and the application of His laws, which constitute the vicegerent's function on the earth, is dependent on full knowledge.[194]

In his commentary, Nursi cites two interpretations of the names: they are "the attributes and appellations that signify things, or the myriad languages ... that the sons of Adam use," and he adds that the syntax "suggests that the names are identical to what they signify."[195] In the *Risale-i Nur*, however, he states that the names comprise three sorts of knowledge, that is, "countless sciences, and numerous all-embracing branches of knowledge about the universe, and extensive learning about the Creator's Attributes and acts."[196] As has been mentioned, this knowledge is contingent on the innate human capacity to receive it.[197] It thus comprises knowledge of man, of the cosmos, and of God. The remaining discussions in this chapter should assist in illuminating Nursi's conception of these branches of knowledge.

In interpreting what the Qur'an is alluding to with this verse, Nursi posits that since men are the progeny of Adam and the inheritors of his abilities, it is incumbent on them to learn the names, that is, to explore the cosmos and through their combined efforts develop the sciences that reveal its functioning. As holders of the Supreme Trust, they have also to

---

[193] Nursi, *Signs of Miraculousness*, 272; Nursi, *The Words*. Eng. tr. (İstanbul: Sözler, 2002), 262.

[194] Nursi, *Signs of Miraculousness*, 274, 276.

[195] Ibid., 276.

[196] Nursi, *Words*, 254.

[197] Nursi, *Signs of Miraculousness*, 275.

"demonstrate their worthiness" before other creatures. Nursi seems to be suggesting that since it is through human development and scientific and technological progress that man gains mastery over the universe and "vast creatures like the earth are subjugated to [him]," it is only by such progress that man actually rises to "the exalted rank" of the vicegerency. Fulfillment of this duty is, moreover, tied to acquiring knowledge of the third type mentioned above, knowledge of the Divine Names and Attributes. While investigating and advancing the sciences, men should study the Divine Names, on which the physical sciences and all branches of knowledge are ultimately based, so that progress in science becomes an ascent to knowledge of God. For Nursi understands from the allusions of the verse that the sciences, arts, and all human attainments "have an elevated reality which is based on a Divine Name," and by being based on the name find their perfection and "become reality."[198]

Although in his expositions of the miracles of the Prophets, in which he propounds these views of the vicegerency, Nursi's emphasis is on the development of science, material progress, and civilizational advances, as is seen above the vicegerency in fact has various sides to it, and is a moral and spiritual (*manevi*) position rather than a material one.[199] A brief look at two related concepts, Divine dominicality (*rububiyet*) and universal worship (*ubudiyet-i külliye*), may assist in clarifying this.

In Nursi's writings, by dominicality is meant the regulation, administration, and ordering according to laws of the universe with all its interdependent parts and beings.[200] These laws are in force in all beings and encompass the universe, from particles to the planets.[201] As an essential part of his position of vicegerent, man's "acts and deeds closely pertain to God's universal dominicality," and in his dominance over the earth he can intervene in its workings.[202] He is, indeed, "the chief pivot of the works of [Divine] dominicality,"[203] and, in so far as he preserves the balance of

---

[198] Nursi, *Words*, 270.
[199] Nursi actually states this. See *Words*, 254.
[200] See Nursi, *The Rays*. Eng. tr. (İstanbul: Sözler, 2002), 131, 168.
[201] Nursi, *Letters 1928–1932*. Eng. tr. (İstanbul: Sözler, 2001), 344–345.
[202] Ibid., 89, 90.
[203] Nursi, *Rays*, 78.

the Earth's "vast administration," he may serve the smooth application of its laws.[204]

What is required of man in the face of God's universal dominicality is "universal worship (*ubudiyet-i külliye*)," which is one of the purposes of the universe's creation. Hence, in conclusion to the above discussion Nursi says:

> In the face of the manifestations of dominicality, the elevated pur-
> pose of the universe is man's universal worship and submission to
> God, while man's furthest aim is to attain to that worship by means
> of ... sciences and perfections.[205]

That is to say, in so far as man recognizes God's direct governance of the universe, and by penetrating to the Divine Names on which the sciences he develops are based makes those sciences a means of approaching God, his striving to advance and to fulfill the obligations of the vicegerency is deemed a part of his universal worship. Universal worship thus embraces the vicegerency, and like the vicegerency has various aspects, material and spiritual. The latter will be discussed in the next section.

## The Vicegerency as a Proof of the Tenets of Faith

It will be useful, in examining Nursi's interpretation of the vicegerency in the context of his proofs of what he calls "the truths of belief," the second area in which he makes reference to it, to situate the notion within his conception of the cosmos in general and of the human being in particular. For in the *Risale-i Nur* he does not treat the vicegerency as a separate topic, but cites it together with various human attributes as a component of his proofs, to underline the loftiness of man's rank in the scheme of things and demonstrate the importance of the functions attendant on his position. In doing this he often mentions the related concept of the Trust (*emanet*), mentioned in Qur'an 33:72, which is touched on below.

As with his overall method, Nursi's conception of existence is derived from the Qur'an and is based on the view that all events and

---

[204] Nursi, *The Flashes*. Eng. tr. (İstanbul: Sözler, 2000), 414.
[205] Nursi, *Words*, 272.

phenomena in the world are signs (*ayat*)[206] and bear a symbolic meaning. One of his objectives in writing the *Risale-i Nur* was to both to convey and instil this idea, and to offer a practical way of deciphering the signs of beings and of 'reading' them for their meanings. To this end he developed a method based on reasoning reflective thought (*tefekkür*) on the natural world which, in making the beings and processes of the natural world evidences, seeks to offer logical proofs for the truths the Qur'an teaches, such as Divine unity and the resurrection of the dead. Following the Qur'an, which very often links descriptions of Divine acts in the universe to Divine Names and Attributes,[207] Nursi made the Names central to his system of thought and based many of his proofs on them. The natural world is thus seen to comprise multiple evidences for the truths of belief, which, being one within the other, prove and corroborate each other.

Nursi's conception of the world emerges from the above view; the fact that all beings are signs and evidences of their Maker suggests that they perform a function or functions; according to one of the many metaphors he uses, they are "officials" with "duties." The performance of these duties is their worship, which varies according to their ontological realities; that is, their innate dispositions and the Divine Names they manifest.[208] Nursi thus conceives of existence in terms of Divine dominicality on the one hand and universal worship on the other.[209] Although his conception is hierarchical and he categorizes beings according to their innate capacities and resultant duties of worship, his stress is not on hierarchy but on the performance of the duties and the manner of the various beings' glorifications and praise of God, the degree of perfection of which may be higher with inanimate creatures than with those possessing will.[210]

---

[206] See e.g. Qur'an, 41:53, 45:3.

[207] See e.g. Qur'an, 7:54, 10:31–32, 23:12–14, 24:43–45, 30:50, 36:38, 87:1–4.

[208] Nursi, *Words*, 361.

[209] See ibid., 273, where Nursi states that it is "the Qur'an's basic duty is to teach the perfections and acts (*ṣuunat*) in the sphere of dominicality, and the duties and circumstances of the sphere of worship." See also ibid., 242.

[210] See e.g. ibid., 361–367.

## Aspects of Man's Ontological Reality

Similarly to other beings, man is thus an official with duties; it is only by virtue of the wealth of his faculties and the comprehensiveness of his disposition that he has been made vicegerent of the earth, and the obligations and functions that it entails have been made incumbent on him. Whenever Nursi mentions the vicegerency in proving the truths of belief, he almost invariably lists with it a number of basic facts about man's ontological reality, thus elucidating the numerous sides and elements of his universal worship, which all his functions as vicegerent comprise.

In the *Risale-i Nur*, Nursi allots much space to expositions of man and his many faculties and their purposes. Our discussion will be limited to those attributes and their purposes that he mentions in connection with the vicegerency. It should be pointed out at the outset, however, that while continually stressing the loftiness of man's innate disposition (*fitrat, istidad*) and his elevated rank, Nursi draws attention to his boundless need and innate powerlessness and weakness, recognition of which hinges on a correct understanding of the human 'I' or ego *vis-à-vis* the Maker. This question is touched on below.

As with many of his discussions, with this subject Nursi makes wide use of metaphors and comparisons rather than offering learned or detailed expositions of the concepts involved. Those descriptive of man's being may be subsumed under three headings: man the microcosm, man's comprehensive disposition, and man as mirror to the Divine Names. These are all interrelated, but for the purposes of discussion it will be useful to treat them separately.

## Man the Microcosm

The idea Nursi propounds most frequently in the context of the vicegerency is that of man being a miniature version of the universe; that is, the microcosm. In his words, man is "an illuminated summary of the macrocosm, a tiny sample of the world,"[211] and, "whatever the pen of power has written in the great book of the universe, it has written its

---

[211] Nursi, *Rays*, 77; also *Words*, 442.

summary in man's nature."[212] By the same token, "As man is a small world, the microcosm, so is the world a large human being, the macroanthropos. Small man is an index and summary of the macroanthropos."[213] This may be explained as follows. Again in Nursi's words, "A human being is, quite simply ... a fruit of the tree of creation, and a seed of the world, for he contains samples of most of the realms of beings in the world. It is as if [man] is a drop filtered from the universe in extremely fine measure."[214] Accordingly, "the whole universe [is] turned towards man as a tree together with all its parts is turned towards its fruit."[215] In more explicit terms: "Most of the wisdom, aims, purposes, and benefits in the universe look to man," thus making him, "the center, pivot, and conscious fruit of the universe."[216] Thus, man is the aim and result of the universe, as well as being its "essence"[217] and seed. Nursi states too that it is in respect of the Muhammadan Reality that man is the "original seed" of the cosmos.[218]

While some aspects of the microcosm mentioned above look to the physical world, others look to other dimensions of reality. For example, Nursi argues: "Since man is a comprehensive index of the universe, his heart resembles a map of thousands of worlds. For ... man's heart in his essential being is the place of manifestation of innumerable cosmic truths, and is their means and seed."[219] Moreover, just as man is the fruit of the tree of the universe, so his heart, the fruit's seed, "is a most brilliant and comprehensive mirror to the universe's Maker."[220] Similarly, in the human heart are displayed "the works of all the Divine Names manifested on the pages of the macrocosm."[221]

---

[212] Ibid., 290, fn 1; *Rays*, 80.

[213] Nursi, *Flashes*, 118.

[214] Nursi, *Words*, 302.

[215] Nursi, *Flashes*, 135.

[216] Ibid., 456.

[217] Nursi, *Words*, 704; *Rays*, 588.

[218] Ibid., 238.

[219] Nursi, *Letters*, 518–519.

[220] Nursi, *Words*, 641.

[221] Ibid., 302.

## Man's Comprehensive Disposition

Clearly, it is owing to the comprehensiveness of his nature (*mahiyet-i camiiyeti*) that ontologically man is the microcosm, and moreover, was made vicegerent of the earth. Nursi explains this as follows:

> For by virtue of the diversity of man's abilities and the multiplicity of ways in which he can utilize things and the many sides of his knowledge, and his encompassing the universe with his five sens- es, external and inner, and especially his boundless conscience, he is a comprehensive copy [of the world] and locus of all the manifes- tations [of the Divine Names].[222]

Two aspects of this question may be mentioned here. In connection with his universal worship, Nursi describes man's many faculties, sens- es, and powers, by which on multiple cognitive and existential levels he may experience the Divine bounties associated with each, and so perform his fundamental duties of thanks, praise, and worship.[223] Another aspect of the comprehensiveness thus gained is the ability "to understand and take pleasure in all the Divine Names." That is to say, the Creator gave man a comprehensive disposition so that He might make known to him "the countless different manifestations of His Names."[224] Man thus becomes "a comprehensive place of manifestation," and from another point of view, "a point of focus of a thousand and one Names."[225]

## Man as Mirror of the Divine Names

A matter fundamental to Nursi's understanding of the human being, and indeed central to his whole system of thought, is the notion of man being merely mirror-like. This notion does not diminish man's existential sta- tus; that is, it does not relegate his existence to the realm of the imaginary. It stems rather from Nursi's conception of the human 'I' or conscious self, that the 'I' lacks actual existence and is merely like a unit of measurement or instrument or a mirror which, having no meaning itself, shows the

---

[222] Nursi, *Signs of Miraculousness*, 274.

[223] See Nursi, *Flashes*, 456–57; *Rays*, 76–77.

[224] Ibid., 77.

[225] Nursi, *Flashes*, 137.

meaning of others; that is, it is a means of knowing the Divine Attributes and Names.[226] According to Nursi, the 'I' in this sense is a part of the Trust, from the bearing of which the skies, earth, and mountains shrank, but which man was foolish enough to undertake. This conception of the 'I', which has its origin in Divine revelation, is the source of "sheer worship," for the person with such a consciousness "knows [himself] to be a slave (*abd*)" of God and claims ownership of nothing, not even himself. Thus, since man is "a conscious mirror of the Creator"[227] and "a comprehensive mirror to all [the Divine] Names,"[228] the conscious reflection of the Names is among man-the-vicegerent's "innate duties." Nursi offers fairly detailed descriptions of what these duties entail.[229]

## The Duties and Functions of Man the Vicegerent

Having outlined some main features of Nursi's conception of the world and of man, and noted some relevant aspects of his method of explicating these, we may look further at his interpretation of the vicegerency and its functions. These latter pertain to both the physical and spiritual worlds, and Nursi's descriptions of material aspects of the vicegerency in particular are reiterations of the classical interpretations, although his style and method of portrayal are almost certainly original:

1. *The Vicegerent's Duties of Reflection and Worship.* Many of the duties incumbent on the vicegerent as Nursi expounds them look directly to worship, and consist of such tasks as "studying and pondering over the Divine missives [that is, the natural world] written by the pen of power" and observing the acts of dominicality on the one hand, and consciously proclaiming "God's unity in the realm of multiplicity," heralding the Divine Names, and exhibiting the Maker's arts in the world, on the other.[230] It is through the performance of these and other "duties of worship in the mosque of the world" that man achieves "true progress"

---

[226] For detailed explanation of this question see *Words*, 557–569.

[227] Nursi, *Rays*, 173.

[228] Nursi, *Letters*, 431.

[229] See Nursi, *Rays*, 81–82; *Flashes*, 457–459; *Words*, 718–720.

[230] Nursi, *Mesnevî-i Nûriye* (İstanbul: Envar, 1994), 45, 222; *Words*, 90, 115, 329.

and becomes "a reliable vicegerent of the earth, worthy of bearing the Trust."[231]

Besides both witnessing the glorifications of God that all creatures, particularly animate creatures, perform through the manner of their creation and the Divine art and Names they display, in his capacity of vicegerent man both intervenes and participates in their glorifications, and he consciously represents them and offers their worship and glorifications at the Divine court, as part of his own universal worship.[232]

2. *Vicegerent in the sense of 'Ruler of the Earth'.* In many places where he is citing the attributes and functions associated with the vicegerency, Nursi points out that man "rules over the earth ... has disposal over creatures, and subjects most living beings, gathering them around himself."[233] Having been "entrusted with the regulation of all the vegetal and animal life upon earth,"[234] he is the "sultan" and "commanding officer" of animate beings,[235] and "the most active functionary empowered over the other inhabitants of the palace [of the universe]."[236]

3. *Vicegerent as Cultivator and Developer of the Earth.* Just as man has disposal over beings and has the ability to order them and utilize them according to his needs and wishes, so he has the capacity to develop the sciences and arts,[237] and to make material progress and build civilization. This latter question was discussed in a previous section. Moreover, with a view to the development of agriculture, Nursi calls man "the official charged with overseeing the income and expenditure, and the planting and cultivation of the gardens of the quarter of the earth in the city of the universe."[238]

---

[231]  See ibid., 138–139, 338–339.
[232]  Ibid., 100, 371, 442–443, 530.
[233]  Ibid., 115.
[234]  Ibid., 100.
[235]  Nursi, *Flashes*, 226; *Rays*, 233.
[236]  Ibid., 238.
[237]  Nursi, *Words*, 115.
[238]  Nursi, *Rays*, 238.

4. *Man as the Vicegerent or Deputy of God.* Apart from once in *Isharat al-I'jaz*, Nursi does not use this controversial epithet. Only in one place in the Eleventh Ray, discussing the duties he ascribes to man, does he, in qualified terms, describe man as "an inspector and sort of vicegerent (or deputy) of the Monarch of Pre-Eternity and Post-Eternity, under His close scrutiny, in the region of the earth in the country of the universe."[239] This is discussed in greater detail below.

## The Utilization of the Vicegerency in Proofs: Some Methodological Observations

Most of the relevant points concerning Nursi's method generally and his use, as with other concepts and subjects, of the vicegerency in his proofs of the tenets of faith have been touched on in the course of this chapter. Here, an attempt will be made to illustrate these points with a few examples.

Of the references Nursi makes to the vicegerency in sections of the *Risale-i Nur* proving one or more of the truths of faith, many concern some aspect of the resurrection and the hereafter, most often the question of preservation (*hafiziyet*), that is, the recording of men's actions and of all things, which is a manifestation of the Divine Name of *Al-Hafiz*. In such sections, Nursi proves his point by including among other evidences, mostly from the natural world, succinct descriptions of man's cosmic functions and his duties of worship, some of which are related to the lofty rank of the vicegerency. Since he was addressing the general population, Nursi conveys these ideas and inculcates key concepts through the frequent use of metaphors and other literary devices, examples of which have been given above. Of numerous such sections, the Seventh Truth of the Tenth Word may be taken as an example.

The Seventh Truth, one of twelve main sections which demonstrate the truth of the resurrection of the dead by depicting the evidences offered by the manifestations of various Divine Names, offers proofs for the Last Judgment based on evidences proceeding from the Names of Preserver and Guardian. Nursi begins by asserting that these Names preserve all

---

[239] Ibid.

things with the utmost order and balance and then asks if it would possible for them to neglect the deeds of man, who has been given the lofty
disposition of humanity, the rank of the supreme vicegerency, the duty
of bearing the Trust, and whose acts closely pertain to God's universal
dominicality. He then proceeds to describe the many acts of Divine preservation in the natural world and to demonstrate "the universality and
comprehensiveness of the law of preservation," in order to prove that
this could not be the case. Having cited these evidences, which constitute
the reasoning reflective thought that is a basic element of his overall method, he asks the same rhetorical question, this time showing the loftiness
of the vicegerency by citing others of its functions, hence demonstrating
the impossibility of man's deeds not being preserved and his not being
called to account at the Last Judgment.[240]

Another part of the *Risale-i Nur*, the Seventh Topic of the Eleventh Ray,
which describes the evidences for the resurrection of the dead provided
by around thirty of the Divine Names, cites, in the passage expounding the
name of Preserver,[241] again in the form of succinct phrases, twenty human
attributes and functions, some of which are related to the vicegerency and
have been quoted above.

Nursi uses the same form of argumentation to prove other tenets
of faith. For instance, in the conclusion of the Second Ray, which proves
Divine unity from various angles, among brief arguments for each of the
pillars of belief he argues that since even the seeds and fruits of the
commonest plant are clearly determined (*kader*) in respect of their
development, all the actions of man—"the result of the universe, vicegerent of the earth, the supervisor of all realms of beings and their
officer"—are within God's determining and regulation of beings, as well
as being recorded.[242] Other examples are in proofs of Divine unity,[243]
and of Divine power.[244]

---

[240] Ibid., 88–91.
[241] Nursi, *Rays*, 238–239.
[242] Ibid., 47–48. Also, *Words*, 485–486.
[243] Nursi, *Rays*, 588.
[244] Ibid., 631.

# How Original Is Said Nursi's Interpretation of the Vicegerency?

It will be useful to examine this question in three respects, the last two coinciding with Nursi's two main approaches to the concept of the vicegerency, set out above. The first concerns Nursi's exegesis of 2:30, describing the appointment of a *khalifa* on the earth in preference to the angels and their querying this because of the corruption and bloodshed he would cause.

## Exegetical Interpretations of 2:30 and Nursi's Views

From earliest times exegetes have advanced various ideas concerning the matters indicated in this verse. Nursi mentions many points that are found in the classical *tafsirs*; that is, he reiterates the interpretations of the classical exegetes, though without citing any sources or making reference to other verses in the Qur'an where derivatives of the word appear. His comments are mostly found in *Isharat al-I'jaz*, his only work of exegesis that is in traditional form. As regards sources for the brief overview that follows, only major *tafsirs* were consulted, since its purpose is to indicate points made by Nursi that restate classical interpretations and others that are most probably original.

One of Nursi's chief aims in the early period of his life, namely, the updating of the science of Qur'anic exegesis, was partly realized in his unfinished commentary, *Isharat al-I'jaz*, in which, while expounding the subtleties of the Qur'an's word-order in emulation of the great masters of Arabic grammar and rhetoric, especially 'Abd al-Qahir al-Jurjani (d. 471/1078),[245] he wanted, besides offering proofs for the essential truths of faith, to introduce his readers to some basic facts of science and to demonstrate that there is no conflict between the truths of religion and the findings of science, especially its disclosure of the cosmic order. He wanted too to disprove some of the basic tenets of materialism.[246] Thus, in the course of explaining points related to the word-order of verse 2:30, he

---

[245] See Nursi, *Signs of Miraculousness*, 8, 123, etc.
[246] See e.g. ibid., 164–169.

advances the view that the word *khalifa* suggests that previously to conditions on earth being "readied" for human life, the Earth was inhabited by intelligent beings, and he supports the idea by asserting that it is in conformity with "questions of science." He then cites "the most widely held [view] ... that these creatures were a species of jinn, but they spread corruption [on the earth] so were succeeded by mankind."[247] This interpretation of the word *khalifa*, which is in accordance with its primary root meaning of to succeed and replace, is cited by such authorities as at-Tabari[248] and ar-Razi,[249] who nevertheless ascribe it to the famous companion of the Prophet and exegete Ibn 'Abbas (d. 68/687), who is also imputed with having introduced *isra'iliyyat* or mythical stories into Islam. The Modernist scholar Muhammad 'Abduh also cites the view that the earth was previously inhabited by intelligent beings, but concludes that their being specified as jinns or similar beings is a foreign notion that has nothing in Islam to support it.[250] A variation on the above interpretation, one advanced by one of the earliest exegetes, Muqatil b. Sulayman (d. 150/767),[251] that man succeeded or replaced the angels on the earth, who had previously banished the warring jinns, is also alluded to by Nursi when he states that the earth was previously "under the supervision of the angels."[252]

As to whom the *khalifa* refers, Adam, or his righteous descendants, or all his progeny, who succeeded each other generation after generation (views all cited by Tabari[253]), Nursi favors the latter view, but in places refers to the vicegerent as ruler of the earth, and its cultivator and developer,[254] both also given by Tabari.

The second main interpretation of the term *khalifa*, that of Adam, or man generically, being God's *khalifa*, is one that Nursi does not uphold,

[247] Ibid., 267.
[248] Abi Ja'far Muhammad b. Jarir at-Tabari, *Tafsir at-Tabari, al-Musamma, Jami' al-Bayan fi Ta'wil al-Qur'an* (Beirut: Dar al-Kutub al-'Ilmiyya, 1420/1999), i, 236.
[249] Fakhr al-Din ar-Razi, *at-Tafsir al-Kabir aw Mafataih al-Ghayb* (Beirut: Dar al-Kutub al-'Ilmiyya, 1421/2000), i, 152.
[250] 'Abduh, 257–258.
[251] As cited by Wadad al-Qadi, 399–400.
[252] Nursi, *Signs of Miraculousness*, 267–268.
[253] Tabari, 237.
[254] See notes 52–57 above.

except for once in *Isharat al-I'jaz*, where he says, "[the function] of the Most High's vicegerent on the earth is to execute His ordinances and apply His laws,"[255] and once in qualified terms in the *Risale-i Nur*. This is striking considering its wide currency. However, investigation shows this to be a controversial and possibly acquired meaning. For as the author of a detailed study of early exegetical literature states: "... it is noteworthy that nobody endorsed [the *khalifa* being God's *khalifa*] at all, unlike the late exegetes like at-Tabari."[256] Another study goes so far as to claim that nowhere in the Qur'an, the Sunna, or narrations of the Companions is the *khalifa* referred to as God's *khalifa*.[257] Nevertheless, this interpretation subsequently gained wide acceptance. Such authorities as az-Zamakhshari (d. 538/1144) cited the term, stating that such a meaning was permissible and might also be ascribable to all the Prophets,[258] while ar-Razi (d. 606/1209–10) gave a source for a narration, Ibn Mas'ud, Ibn 'Abbas, and as-Suddi, saying, "God called him *khalifa* because he deputizes for God (*yakhlufu Allah*) in ruling those of His creatures that are answerable [to Him]," and he cited verse 38:26 in support of this.[259] Despite these authoritative statements, by way of refuting Ibn 'Arabi's alleged pantheism and his interpretation of the term, the Hanbali theologian Ibn Taymiyya (d. 728/1328) denounced the idea as *shirk*; that is, imputing limits to God's absolute Attributes by ascribing partners to Him.[260] Nursi, however, for whatever reason, appears to have avoided using the expression, although, as is shown below, he borrowed other terms from Ibn 'Arabi.

Among other points made by Nursi in his expositions of verse 2:30 that reiterate the classical *tafsirs* are, firstly, that God's informing the angels of man's vicegerency to provoke their query was to teach them, or His

---

[255] Nursi, *Signs of Miraculousness*, 274. This is close in meaning to citations in Tabari, 237, and Razi, 152.

[256] Wadad al-Qadi, 406–407.

[257] Jaafar Sheikh Idris, 'Is Man the Vicegerent of God?,' in *Journal of Islamic Studies*, 1 (1990), 100–101, 103.

[258] Mahmud ibn 'Umar az-Zamakhshari, *al-Kashshaf 'an Haqa'iq Ghawamid at-Tanzil* (Beirut: Dar al-Kutub al-'Arabi, 1407/1987), i, 124.

[259] Razi, 152.

[260] *Majmu' Fatawa Shaykh al-Islam Ahmad ibn Taymiyya.* Ed. 'Abd ar-Rahman ibn Muhammad ibn Qasim (Saudi Arabia, 1368), xxxv, 44–45; quoted in Jaafar Sheikh Idris, 104.

servants, consultation (*mushawara*),[261] and secondly, according to one interpretation, that the corruption and spilling of blood that the angels knew the *khalifa* or his offspring would perpetrate would result from excesses in his innate powers of anger and animal appetites.[262] On the other hand, apparently original to Nursi is a meaning he detected in the use of the word "place" when the angels asked, "Will You place therein?" He suggests that mankind being "placed" on the earth hints that man's origins, descent, and characteristics were not necessitated by nature, but were all "placed" by one who places.[263] In other words, he sees in this choice of word an implicit refutation of such ideas as those of the Naturalists and Evolutionists.

## Interpretations of the Teaching of the Names (2:31) and Nursi's View

In commenting on this verse, Nursi again restates many points found in the classical *tafsirs*, but in his linking the teaching of the names to the miracles of the Prophets as recounted in the Qur'an, as has been discussed above, he added a new dimension to this question, which in its looking to the development of science and mankind's material progress suggests the influence of the Islamic Modernists.

In elucidating the relationship of this verse with the previous one, Nursi makes a point found also in Razi, that while the explanation of the wisdom in the vicegerency given in the previous one was brief and concise, this verse gives an explanatory, detailed answer;[264] it indicates the cause of man's superiority over the angels, while the previous one merely alluded to his superiority. Although Tabari asserts, on grammatical grounds, that the names that were taught to Adam were the names of his progeny and of the angels, the great majority of the narrations he quotes state that they were the names of all things,[265] as Nursi also

---

[261] Nursi, *Signs of Miraculousness*, 265; Zamakhshari, 124; Razi, 152.

[262] Nursi, *Signs of Miraculousness*, 265; Razi, 156; also Ibn al-'Arabi, *Tafsir al-Qur'an al-Karim* (Beirut: 1399/1978), i, 35–37, cited by Mahmoud Ayoub, *The Qur'an and Its Interpreters* (Albany: SUNY Press, 1984), i, 79.

[263] Nursi, *Signs of Miraculousness*, 268.

[264] Ibid., 274; Razi, 161.

[265] Tabari, 252–253.

states. Nursi also cites the possibility that they refer to the myriad human languages.[266] Nursi stresses that Adam was preferred to the angels because of the knowledge that had been conferred on him on being taught the names: "It was knowledge that gave him superiority over the angels."[267] A similar emphasis is found in 'Abduh.[268] And as Zamakhshari points out, the angels questioned man's vicegerency because they did not know the benefits related to knowledge, the bases of all benefits, that were attached to the vicegerency.[269]

This brings us to an aspect of Nursi's expositions that is not found in the classical *tafsirs*: his offering fairly detailed descriptions of man, and of the vicegerent's innate disposition and faculties owing to which he was taught the names, and moreover by virtue of which, to quote, "he is a comprehensive copy [of the world] and locus of all the manifestations [of the Divine Names]."[270] These latter concepts and terms, which are clearly derived from Sufi sources, will be discussed in the following section.

As was noted above, the present author has not found to date any other commentator who links the teaching of the names and the vicegerency with the miracles of the Prophets and mankind's civilizational progress. The whole ethos of this interpretation, based on such notions as civilization, science, and material progress, is clearly modernist and has its roots in nineteenth-century European thought,[271] although as shown in a previous section Nursi attempts to seat these notions on spiritual foundations. Material progress and similar ideas are also stressed in the expositions of these verses of 'Abduh and other Islamic Modernists, though not in the context of the miracles of the Prophets.[272] Moreover, the idea

---

[266] A view advanced by some commentators. See Ayoub, 80.

[267] Nursi, *Words*, 433.

[268] 'Abduh, 261–263.

[269] Zamakhshari, 126.

[270] Nursi, *Signs of Miraculousness*, 274–275.

[271] Albert Hourani, *Arabic Thought in the Liberal Age 1798–1939* (Cambridge: CUP, 1986), 114–115, 167.

[272] 'Abduh, 260. See also 'Abd al-'Aziz Chawish, *Asrar al-Qur'an* (İstanbul: 1331/1912–1913), 115 ff. One scholar has pointed out that 'Abduh made a "novel interpretation" of the vicegerency, stating that God's vicegerent was charged with building civilization, with each individual being responsible. See Yvonne Haddad, 'Muhammad 'Abduh. Pioneer of Islamic Reform,' in *Pioneers of Islamic Revival.* Ed. Ali Rahnema

underlying Nursi's whole argument concerning this interpretation of the miracles of the Prophets, that as an aspect of its miraculousness or inimitability the Qur'an makes allusion on some level to all events and all things, had been previously propounded by Jamal al-Din al-Afghani,[273] the pioneer of the Modernists and mentor of Muhammad 'Abduh, who also favors the idea.[274]

## Ontological Dimensions of Man the Vicegerent

As was shown above, in including mention of the vicegerency in some of his proofs of the tenets of faith, the second main context in which he makes reference to it, Nursi generally does so together with various human attributes, by way of elucidating its elevated station and the duties and functions attendant on it. Three of these were singled out as summarizing his view: man as the microcosm, man's comprehensive disposition, and his being mirror to all the Divine Names. Here, indication will be made of the source of these ideas in Sufi literature, or at least of parallels therein, while noting divergences and differences.

At the outset it should be recalled that Nursi was always adamant that he was not involved in Sufism and that the way of the *Risale-i Nur* was not *tarikat* but *hakikat*; indeed, he argued that Sufism was inappropriate for the modern age since it was ill-equipped to reply to the intellectual assaults of materialism. Nevertheless, he acknowledged his great spiritual debt to 'Abd al-Qadir Jilani and Shaykh Ahmad Sirhindi, as well as to al-Ghazali and Jalaluddin Rumi, whom he said were among his "masters."[275] So, too, he makes several references to the famous Sufi poet 'Abd ar-Rahman Jami (d. 898/1492). However, Nursi included in the *Risale-i Nur* critiques of Ibn 'Arabi, which point out errors in his thought as he saw them, particularly in regard to the unity of existence.

---

(London: Zed Press, 1994), 46; quoted from Muhammad 'Abduh, *al-A'mal al-Kamila*. Ed. 'Amara (Beirut: 1972), iv, 135.

[273] See his article 'The Benefits of Philosophy,' as is pointed out by Nikki Keddie in *An Islamic Response to Imperialism: Political and Religious Writings of Sayyid Jamal al-Din al-Afghani* (Berkeley and Los Angeles: University of California Press, 1968), 114; also, 48, 64, 97.

[274] See Yvonne Haddad, 47.

[275] Nursi, *Emirdağ Lahikası* (İstanbul: Envar, 1992), ii, 220–221; also i, 215.

All that said, it appears that, in constructing a system of thought to meet the needs of the day, Nursi borrowed from the body of terms that has become associated with the thought of Ibn 'Arabi and his school, including those related to the vicegerency, sometimes attaching new meanings and sometimes retaining the basic ideas associated with the terms. A brief look at the concepts mentioned above will show this quite clearly.

The most immediately noteworthy are the concept of the microcosm and the comprehensiveness of man's innate disposition. The former was introduced into Islam, or at least given currency, by Ibn 'Arabi.[276] In both the substance of key concepts and the terms used to denote them, there are a number of parallels between the explications of Ibn 'Arabi and his school and Nursi, despite the vast differences in their objectives, approaches, and methods. The main point of similarity, and the crucial attribute that allows man to be vicegerent, is his comprehensive, mirror-like nature, by virtue of which he may reflect all the Divine Names manifested in the universe and "bring together all the realities of the cosmos,"[277] thus becoming the microcosm. While Ibn 'Arabi uses the term *jam'iyya* for comprehensiveness, Nursi uses *camiiyet*.[278] Above were listed some of Nursi's many expressions denoting this: man is "a comprehensive (*cami'*) mirror of all His Names;" he has "the most comprehensive (*cemiyetli*) capacity," and is "the most comprehensive fruit of the tree of the universe," and so on. Also similarly to Ibn 'Arabi, Nursi uses the terms "alem-i ekber" and "alem-i asgar" for the macrocosm and the microcosm,[279] and "insan-ı ekber" and "alem-i asgar" for the macroanthropos and man the microcosm.[280] Use of these terms was not restricted to Ibn 'Arabi's school, but is standard in works on Sufism.[281]

---

[276] See, 'Âlem,' in *TDVİA*, ii (1989), 360 by Süleyman Uludağ.

[277] William C. Chittick, *The Sufi Path of Knowledge: Ibn al-'Arabi's Metaphysics of Imagination* (Albany: SUNY Press, 1989), 286. Also Toshihiko Izutsu, *Sufism and Taoism: A Comparative Study of Key Philosophical Concepts* (Berkeley: University of California Press, 1983), 224 ff.

[278] Nursi, *Letters*, 431.

[279] Ibid., 275. Also Chittick, *Self-Disclosure*, 470–471.

[280] Nursi, *Flashes*, 28. Also Izutsu, 220–221.

[281] Chittick, *Faith and Practice*, 31. See e.g. Najm ad-Din Razi, *The Path of God's Bondsmen from Origin to Return*. Tr. Hamid Algar (New Haledon, NJ: Islamic Publications International, 1980), 109.

Among the key concepts of Ibn 'Arabi that Nursi does not subscribe to is that of the Perfect Man, who as "the perfect epitome of the universe" and locus of the manifestation of all the Names is the vicegerent of God.[282] That is to say, the vicegerency is "fitting only for the Perfect Man."[283] The vicegerency thus has a pivotal place in Ibn 'Arabi's system of thought, unlike in Nursi's. Similarly, Nursi is critical of the idea expressed by the Hadith, "God created Adam in His form,"[284] which is frequently quoted to justify views of the vicegerency, even by such authorities as al-Ghazali.[285] In connection with this, it should be noted that while, according to Ibn 'Arabi's interpretation, the vicegerency is the counterpart of *tashbih* (since, to quote Chittick, "asserting God's similarity and nearness is to recognize the human role in representing Him in the cosmos"[286]), Nursi's emphasis is on *tanzih*, or declaring God's incomparability with or dissimilarity to creatures, as an expression of man's servanthood or servitude (*ubudiyet*) of God.

Servanthood and Divine dominicality or lordship, two concepts that have been discussed in various contexts in this essay, again appear to have their origin with Ibn 'Arabi.[287] But with these, Nursi takes only the terms and reinterprets them in the light of his own thought.

Doubtless other parallels and differences related to the vicegerency could be found between Nursi and Ibn 'Arabi and his school, but it is hoped that the above is sufficient to demonstrate their influence on Nursi's interpretation, and especially on aspects of his view of the human being. So far as the present author has been able to ascertain, there is little emphasis on man as vicegerent in the works of Sirhindi and his school of *mujad-*

[282] Izutsu, 234.

[283] Ibn al-'Arabi, *The Bezels of Wisdom.* Tr. and introd. R. W. J. Austin (New York: Paulist Press, 1980), 56.

[284] See Nursi, *Emirdağ Lahikası*, i, 145–47. Hadith: *Bukhari*, Isti'dhan, 1, Anbiya', 1; *Muslim*, Janna, 28; quoted in *Kütüb-i Sitte.* Tr. and ed. İbrahim Canan (Ankara: Akçağ, 1990), x, 177.

[285] İmam Gazali, *İhya*, iv, 554; Chittick, *Self-Disclosure*, xxi, 205; Chittick, *The Sufi Path of Love: The Spiritual Writings of Rumi* (Albany: SUNY Press, 1983), 61.

[286] Chittick, *Self-Disclosure*, 399, n. 21; also xxi–xii.

[287] For example ibid., 198–9; Chittick, *Sufi Path of Knowledge*, 313; Chittick, 'The Perfect Man as the Prototype of the Self in the Sufism of Jami,' in *Studia Islamica* 49 (1979), 153; Izutsu, 110–115.

*didi* Naqshbandi Sufism, which are known to have been influential on Nursi; at any rate, the vicegerency does not hold the central place in Sirhindi's thought that it does in Ibn 'Arabi's.

## Conclusion

In conclusion, one may say that in expounding verses 2:30–31, which relate the story of the placing on the earth of a *khalifa*, Nursi reiterates many points found in the classical *tafsirs*, which are mostly derived from narrations from the Prophet and his companions, and that his views are firmly based on these sources. He does, however, augment the standard interpretations with other material, most of which appears to stem from contemporary concerns, namely, realization of the need to embrace science and secure material progress and civilizational advances. These questions clearly reflect the influence of Islamic Modernists, most probably 'Abduh, to whom he twice refers in his early works. Further influence may be seen in his looking to the Qur'an for solutions to the plight of the Islamic world, his seeking to develop new methods of exegesis, and his ascribing to the Qur'an infinite meanings and the capacity to address the needs of humanity in all historical periods. Nevertheless, although in expounding these verses Nursi does in some instances use science as a yardstick for judging the reasonableness of a narration (e.g. the Earth being previously inhabited by jinns), he does not emphasize reason ('*aql*), or free will, to the extent of 'Abduh and his followers.

Nursi's main originality in this question appears to be his conceiving of it within the context of the Qur'anic stories of the miracles of the Prophets, and his perceiving, in the Qur'an's recounting of these miracles, prescience of the final goals of human progress and encouragement to achieve them. Also original is his seating these material aspects of the vicegerency on a spiritual base, by linking science and progress to the Divine Names and presenting the vicegerency within the concept of servanthood of God (*ubudiyet*). In this way, too, he brings together two of the three branches of knowledge, of the cosmos and the Creator's attributes, that he posited as having been imparted to man with 'the teaching of the names.' The third, knowledge of man, he deals with in his proofs of the truths of faith, which include mention of the vicegerency.

The ontological dimensions of man that Nursi associates with the vicegerency and the influence on them of Ibn 'Arabi and his school have been discussed above. By reason of this influence, Nursi's interpretation of the vicegerency in this context cannot be said to be entirely original. However, his conception of it in terms of "duties" of worship, within a schema that presents the natural world as forming innumerable evidences for the truths of faith, is most probably original. The religious renewal and revitalization of faith that were Nursi's greatest concerns necessitated these approaches to the vicegerency.

# Chapter 5

## Sincerity and Wisdom in the Fully Human Person: *Ikhlas* in the *Risale-i Nur*

*Thomas Michel, S.J.*

## Building Unity through the Practice of Sincerity

About ten years ago, I gave a paper at a *Risale-i Nur* symposium held in Bonn, Germany. The paper was entitled "Nursi's View of Tolerance, Engagement with the Other, and the Future of Dialogue." In that paper, I tried to draw out the implications of Said Nursi's "rules for sincerity." In these nine counsels, found in the Twentieth Flash of the *Risale-i Nur*, Nursi's main concern is to affirm that the way to preserve and build unity within the Islamic *umma* is through the practice of sincerity. In the Twenty-First Flash, which I did not treat in my earlier paper, Nursi elaborates his teaching on sincerity; it is this advice on which I will focus in this essay.

Nursi sometimes noted among his disciples a sense of rivalry and competition. This troubled him, because such rivalry could easily lead, if left unattended and unchecked, to hard feelings, resentment, and divisive factions in the community. Nursi saw that while this tendency can be found among the students of the *Risale-i Nur*, it is even more evident in the broader Islamic *umma*. These divisive inclinations must be taken seriously for, in Nursi's view, disunity—along with ignorance and poverty[288]—represents the most serious enemy of modern believers; combat-

---

[288] *Münâzarat* (Ott. ed.), 433, cited in Şükran Vahide, *Bediüzzaman Said Nursi* (İstanbul, 1992), 95.

ing this triple enemy presents pious Muslims with their greatest social challenges.

The basis of Nursi's advice to his students is that the way to combat tendencies toward factionalism and rivalry is through the practice of sincerity. Because of the importance of these "rules of conduct," I will summarize them briefly here:

1. Act positively with love for one's own point of view but avoid enmity for other views; do not criticize the views of others nor interfere in their beliefs and practices.

2. Build unity within the fold of Islam by recalling the numerous bonds of unity that evoke love, brotherhood, and harmony.

3. Adopt the rule of conduct that the follower of any sound position has the right to say, "My outlook is true, or very good," but not "My outlook alone is true," or "My outlook alone is good," implying the falsity or repugnance of other views.

4. Consider that union with pious friends brings God's help and supports one's faith.

5. Recognize that error and falsehood will be defeated through unity among pious believers, which depends upon their ability to create a united and collective force to preserve justice and righteousness.

6. Defend truth from the attacks of falsehood.

7. Abandon self-centered egoism.

8. Get rid of the erroneous notion of self-pride.

9. Put an end to all petty feelings aroused by rivalry.[289]

Nursi's point is that differing points of view need not cause division, factions, and enmity within the community. If every Muslim is willing to admit that others also have part of the truth, even when they disagree with one's personal view, unity can be maintained despite differences of opinion. However, this can only be done if the believer is truly worshiping God with sincere intention. To this end Nursi cites the Qur'anic verse "We have sent down to you the Book with the truth (embodying it, and with nothing false in it); so worship God, sincere in your faith in Him, and practicing the Religion purely for His sake" (Qur'an 39:2).

---

[289] The Twentieth Flash, 'On Sincerity,' 203.

As a Christian, I find the advice contained in these nine rules valuable for several reasons. In its narrowest application, Nursi is guiding his disciples to avoid the kinds of self-aggrandizement and competition that can cause rancor and splits among the students of the *Risale-i Nur*. His advice has a broader application in calling Muslims to heal the wounds of disunity and enmity within the worldwide Islamic community. However, the value of Nursi's advice is not limited, in my opinion, to the followers of Islam, for it is the same tendency toward the egoistic defense of one's views, an intolerance of differences, and the judgmental criticism of others' views that has caused and exacerbated so many of the historical divisions and enmity among Christians. Moreover, Nursi's advice is also useful for building and maintaining unity in various Christian communities, as well as for preserving the purity of intention of any believer desiring to serve God.

The disunity brought about by a lack of sincerity has also characterized relations between Christians and Muslims down through the centuries, and I feel that Muslim–Christian relations at the present time could benefit from taking seriously and following Nursi's rules of sincerity. Rather than recognizing one another as two communities of believers who seek only to worship and love God sincerely, Christians and Muslims have too often regarded one another as enemies and rivals, making exclusive claims to truth and condemning each other's beliefs as false and repugnant. How much more positive and reflective of the loving God that both communities worship would their mutual relations be if they were to follow Nursi's Third Rule: "The follower of any sound position has the right to say, 'My outlook is true, or very good,' but not 'My outlook alone is true,' or 'My outlook alone is good,' implying the falsity or repugnance of other views."

It is significant that Nursi himself appended to his nine rules of sincerity a surprising footnote. It reads as follows:

> It is even recorded in authentic traditions of the Prophet that at the end of time the truly pious among the Christians will unite with the People of the Qur'an and fight their common enemy, irreligion. And in our day, too, the people of religion and truth need to unite sincerely not only with their own brothers and fellow believers, but also with the truly pious and spiritual among the Christians, tem-

porarily refraining from the discussion and debate of points of difference in order to combat their joint enemy, aggressive atheism.[290]

By linking his rules for sincerity with the Prophetic expectation of Muslim–Christian unity, Nursi is implying that the way to build unity between the two communities in our day is by promoting and following "sincerely practiced religion." Nursi is pointing out that the principles of sincerity not only indicate how Muslims should relate to one another, but also imply how Muslims should act toward sincere and pious Christians (and, I might add, to the way that Christians should act toward Muslims).

## Sincerity as Purity of Intention

One might ask what Nursi means by *sincerity*. Everyone knows the common understanding of sincerity as indicating "an honesty of mind, freedom from dissimulation or hypocrisy." More to the point, perhaps, is the data of personal experience, by which sincerity is universally recognized as being an affective and intellectual honesty, a lack of pretense to be other than what one is, a faithful correspondence between one's inner thoughts and emotions and their outer expression in word and action. A sincere person is not self-promoting, hypocritical, pretentious, two-faced, or devious. He is neither a flatterer nor a manipulator. In the words of Jesus in his Sermon on the Mount, the sincere person says "yes" when he means yes, "no" when he means no (Matthew 5: 37).

Nursi's use of the term goes much deeper than that derived from everyday parlance. When he writes of sincerity he is referring to the Qur'anic concept of *ikhlas*. This notion, which brings together the notion of "purity" with that of "dedicating, devoting or consecrating oneself" to something, is a key virtue in Islamic practice.[291] *Ikhlas* is an eminently interior disposition by which the faithful Muslim performs all external actions in a spirit of service directed solely toward pleasing the Divine Lord. In fact, the perfection of one's witness to faith can be gauged by the double standard of *ikhlas* (purity of intention) and *ihsan* (goodness).

---

[290] Ibid., note 7, 203.
[291] L. Gardet, *Encyclopaedia of Islam* (Leiden: 2006), Vol. III, 1059.

It is noteworthy that the brief expression of the Islamic creed found in the Qur'anic Surah 112, "Say: He—(He is) God, (Who is) the Unique One of Absolute Oneness. God—(God is He Who is) the Eternally-Besought-of-All (Himself in no need of anything). He begets not, nor is He begotten. And comparable to Him there is none", has been known in Islamic tradition as the Surah al-Ikhlas, that is, "The Chapter of Sincerity" or "The Chapter of Pure Religion."

The importance of *ikhlas* has been commented upon down the centuries by Muslim scholars, exegetes, and spiritual guides in every generation. The Sufi masters have been particularly fond of elaborating on this virtue, to the extent that in the minds of many Muslims, *ikhlas* is considered a "Sufi concept." In commenting on *ikhlas*, Nursi must repeatedly distinguish his own advice from that of the teaching of the Sufis. While acknowledging the beneficial value of the instruction of the Sufi masters, he notes: "I am not a Sufi, but these principles of theirs make a good rule for our path."[292] Nursi's approach differs from that of the Sufis because of his praxis-oriented approach, what he calls the "way of reality," in which he eschews contemplative speculation in favor of practical guidance for his disciples' life together. He states: "However, since our way is not the Sufi path but the way of reality, we are not compelled to perform this contemplation [of death] in an imaginary and hypothetical form like the Sufis."[293]

Because of its roots in the Qur'an and in the tradition of Islamic spiritual writing, Nursi's use of *ikhlas* can more adequately be conveyed in English by "purity of intention" or "pure religion" than simply by "sincerity." *Ikhlas* is the virtue of practicing all the acts of religion solely for God's pleasure rather than for any personal benefit that may accrue to them, whether that be prestige, pride, or the admiration of others. When one "worships God with sincerity" one's intention is pure and undefiled by base or irrelevant motives. Such a person is described in the Qur'an as follows: "And (in contrast, there is) among the people one, who sells himself in pursuit of God's good pleasure. God is All-Pitying towards His servants ..." (Qur'an 2: 207).

---

[292] The Twenty-First Flash, 216.
[293] Ibid., 217.

## Correspondence between Purity of Intention and Divine Wisdom

In the Twentieth Flash, Said Nursi instructs his disciples on the necessity for sincerity in order to overcome divisive tendencies and build fraternal unity in their community. If one accepts the principle that fraternal love and unity demand sincerity, some questions inevitably arise, such as: "Why is sincerity so important? How does one acquire this purity of intention? What obstacle might one encounter in seeking a pure intention in religious acts?" These are the topics treated in the Twenty-First Flash. So much importance does Nursi place on purity of intention in religious observance that he instructs his disciples to read the Twenty-First Flash once every two weeks.

According to Nursi, a pure intention is "the most important principle in works pertaining to the Hereafter." In his praise of the value of sincerity he resorts to the rhetorical device of personification. Purity of intention is like a spiritual mentor—the source of a believer's greatest strength, the firmest supporter of one's faith, and the believer's most welcome intercessor before God. Sincerity enables the most acceptable prayer one can make to God, the most effective means of achieving one's goal, and the shortest path to reality. One might compare Nursi's paean in praise of sincerity with the evocative description of wisdom in the prayer of Solomon in the Bible.

> And O my companions in the service of the Qur'an! You should know that in this world sincerity is the most important principle in works pertaining to the Hereafter. It is the greatest strength, and the most acceptable intercessor, and the firmest point of support, and the shortest way to reality, and the most acceptable prayer, and the most wondrous means of achieving one's goal, and the highest quality, and the purest worship. In sincerity lies much strength and many lights like those mentioned above. At this dreadful time, despite our being few in number and our weak, impoverished, and powerless state and our being confronted by terrible enemies and suffering severe oppression in the midst of aggressive innovations and misguidance, an extremely heavy, important, and sacred duty of serving belief and the Qur'an has been placed on our shoulders by Divine grace. For these reasons, we are compelled more than anyone to

work with all our strength to gain sincerity. We are in utter need of instilling sincerity in ourselves. Otherwise what we have achieved so far in our sacred service will in part be lost, and will not persist; and we shall be held responsible.[294]

God of my fathers, Lord of mercy! You who have made all things by your word and in your wisdom have established man to rule the creatures produced by you, to govern the world in holiness and justice, and to render judgment in integrity of heart:

Give me Wisdom, the attendant at your throne, and reject me not from among your children, for I am your servant, the son of your handmaid, a man weak and short-lived and lacking in comprehension of judgment and of laws.

Though one be perfect among the sons of men, if Wisdom, who comes from you, be not with him, he shall be held in no esteem.

With you is Wisdom, who knows your works and was present when you made the world, who understands what is pleasing to you and what conforms to your commands.

Send her forth from your holy heavens and from your glorious throne dispatch her that she may be with me and work with me, that I may know what your pleasure is. For she will guide me discreetly in my affairs and safeguard me. Thus my deeds will be acceptable, and I shall judge your people justly and be worthy of my father's throne.[295]

The correspondence between Nursi's understanding of purity of intention and the Biblical concept of wisdom as found in the "Wisdom Books" of Proverbs, Wisdom, Sirach, and Ecclesiastes lies in the believer's carrying out actions solely to serve and obey God. For Nursi, it is the purity of one's intention that guards the Muslim from performing his religious duties for any reason other than that of seeking God's pleasure. To be seen and admired by others, to try to show oneself more faithful or more assiduous than others, to take selfish satisfaction or pride in the praise given by others, and to denigrate the intellectual or spiritual achievements of

---

[294] Ibid., 212–13.
[295] The Book of Wisdom 9: 1–18.

others are all common temptations of religious people, even as they are destructive of community life. Nursi honestly and humbly admits that it was the sincerity of his students that saved him from such temptations in the past: "I have also to confess that through your heartfelt sincerity, you have saved me to an extent from the hypocrisy which used to flatter my soul under the veil of fame and renown."[296] He cites Prophet Yusuf (Joseph) in the Qur'an to show that no one is exempt from this universal tendency: "Yet I do not claim myself free of error, for assuredly the human carnal soul always commands evil, except that my Lord has mercy" (Qur'an 12: 53).[297]

Similarly, in the prayer recorded in the book of Wisdom, King Solomon acknowledges his human weakness and his constant need for the guidance and support that comes from God. It is true wisdom, of exclusively Divine origin, that teaches Solomon how he can serve God for God's sake alone. Solomon affirms that, unlike worldly and even devilish human cunning, true wisdom will guide him discreetly in his affairs and will safeguard his faith. Eternal wisdom that comes from God will enable one to render judgment "in integrity of heart." Solomon declares that even if one were endowed to a perfect degree with intelligence, power, and wealth, without wisdom that person would not be worthy of esteem. It is the wisdom that cannot be acquired through human effort but will be freely granted by God to His servants who ask him that will enable that servant to act with a pure intention and to judge with integrity.

## Rules for Obtaining Purity of Intention

The conviction in faith that a pure intention can only be realized with God's grace does not mean that human effort is useless or irrelevant. God gives gifts to those who actively seek them through right conduct. In this context, Nursi offers to his disciples some rules of conduct which they should follow in order to acquire sincerity:

1. The first rule is to do everything only to seek God's pleasure. Whether or not others approve of what one does or whether one is successful in attaining one's worldly goal, if that deed is per-

---

[296] The Twenty-First Flash, 215.
[297] The Thirteenth Flash, 124.

formed out of desire to please God, then one need not worry about human approval. "Once His pleasure has been gained and He has accepted an action, even if you do not ask it of Him, should He wish it and His wisdom requires it, He will make others accept it. He will make them consent to it too."[298] In short, performing one's actions purely in order to give due worship to God will free a person from temptations to pride in achievement, desire for adulation, or rivalry with fellow worshipers.

2. The second principle for obtaining purity of intention is not to criticize others. Nursi is aware that nothing is more likely to destroy unity among fellow believers than carping criticism. He holds that the students of the *Risale-i Nur* should regard one another as members of one body, who need and complement one another to achieve their common goal. "Each of the members completes the deficiencies of the others, veils their faults, assists their needs, and helps them out in their duties. Otherwise man's life would be extinguished, his spirit flee, and his body be dispersed."[299] In addition to the image of the human body, Nursi uses the metaphor of a complex piece of machinery whose smooth functioning demands the constant synergy of all parts.

Nursi envisions the students of the *Risale-i Nur* as forming a collective personality who together make up "the Perfect Man." The Perfect Man, or *al-Insan al-Kamil*—although the words do not appear in the Qur'an—had a long tradition of study and speculation in Muslim scholarship. The Sufi authors, and especially Ibn 'Arabi, ascribed key importance to the concept as a means of understanding the spiritual nature of the Prophets and *awliya'* (God's special friends). Derived from the idea that, in all creation, humankind has a special status and is given, uniquely, the task of manifesting God's Qualities through life and behavior, the Perfect Man is recognized primarily in the Prophet Muhammad, peace and blessings be upon him, but is also to be sought in those who have received the light of Muhammad.

---

[298] The Twenty-First Flash, 213.
[299] Ibid., 214.

For Nursi, the term has a special sense in that it is his disciples, the students of the *Risale-i Nur*, who collectively are called to live as the Perfect Man, displaying God's Qualities in all they say and do. Since the personal transformation that is brought about through the study of the *Risale-i Nur* is a grace not only given to the individual but oriented toward renewing the whole Islamic *umma*, the duty of the *Risale-i Nur* students demands unity and fraternal love among themselves. The complaining, fault-finding, and nitpicking that springs from lack of a pure intention thus becomes an obstacle to the Divine Qualities of compassion and love that should be manifested by the collective Perfect Man.

3. The third rule of conduct is to give preference to others, over against one's own inclinations, desires, and penchant for honors. One must not be self-centered, even in spiritual matters, but must be constantly more concerned about the state of soul of one's companions than about one's own condition. Nursi writes: "Choose your brothers' souls to your own soul in honor, rank, acclaim, in the things your soul enjoys like material benefits."[300] In preferring the other person to oneself, the student of the *Risale-i Nur* will find much strength and will gain the blessing and support of God's friends like Ali ibn Abi Talib and Ghawth al-A'zam ['Abd al-Qadir al-Jilani], who will "honor you with their miraculous wonder-working and wondrous vision of the Unseen because of this mystery of sincerity. They will offer you consolation in protection and applaud your service. You should have no doubt that this attention of theirs is because of sincerity."[301]

4. The fourth and final rule of conduct that Nursi offers is to imagine the achievements, the virtues, and the aspirations of fellow disciples to be one's own. In this way, one can glory in the triumphs of others, share in their hopes, and enjoy their good qualities and virtues, without succumbing to envy and a sense of competition. This fellow-feeling Nursi sees as the characteristic path of those who study the *Risale-i Nur*. He writes:

---

[300] Ibid., 216.
[301] Ibid., 215.

Forget the feelings of one's own carnal self and live in one's mind with one's brothers' virtues and feelings. The basis of our way is brotherhood, not the way between father and son or sheikh and follower. Our way is the closest friendship, which necessitates being the closest friend, the most sacrificing companion, the most appreciative comrade, the noblest brother. The essence of this friendship is true sincerity.[302]

In short, the way to build a deep friendship among the students of the *Risale-i Nur* is through the practice of sincerity. Nursi goes so far as to say that purity of intention is the essence of the friendship he wants to exist among his disciples.

Nursi concludes his treatment with two suggestions for attaining a pure intention. The first way to achieve sincerity is through a contemplation of death. Since it is worldly ambition which militates against a pure intention, the contemplation of death helps the believer put things in perspective. The world is transitory, the believer is a transient on this earth, yet people find themselves caught up in a web of petty rivalries, self-aggrandizement, and hypocrisy. By contemplating death, one can become aware that it is only God, who is imperishable, who is deserving of service and devotion.

The second way is to reflect on God's omnipresence and omniscience. Living consciously in the presence of the Compassionate Creator should make the believer aware that to be acting for others' approval is an unworthy attitude before God, who sees and knows all. To have one's attentions and emotions dominated by oneself or another companion when the Creator is present is actually a hidden form of *shirk*, that is, the sin of associating others in the worship due to God alone: "This is to flatter the ego and give high status to one's lower nature through attracting attention to oneself and public acclaim, driven by the desire for fame, renown, and position. This is a serious spiritual sickness which opens the door to hypocrisy and self-centeredness. It may be called a *hidden association of partners with God* and damages sincerity."[303]

---

[302] Ibid., 216.
[303] Ibid., 220.

## Conclusion

The main themes of this essay—sincerity and purity of intention and their relation to true wisdom, and the dangers of factionalism, hypocrisy, pride, and criticism arising from pride and carping criticism—come together in a remarkable passage in the Bible. I will conclude my paper with a quotation of that passage, taken from the Letter of James, to show how the spiritual advice given by the spiritual masters of Christianity and Islam so often coincide and complement one another. Clearly, James was dealing with the same dangers to the unity of the community as was Said Nursi, over a space of twenty centuries, and his advice is significantly similar to that found in the *Risale-i Nur*:

> Who among you is wise and understanding? Let him show his works by a good life in the humility that comes from wisdom. But if you have bitter jealousy and selfish ambition in your hearts, do not boast and be false to the truth. Such 'wisdom' does not come down from heaven but is earthly, unspiritual, demonic. For where jealousy and selfish ambition exist, there is disorder and every foul practice. But the wisdom from above is first of all pure, then peaceable, gentle, compliant, full of mercy and good fruits, impartial and sincere. Peacemakers who sow in peace raise a harvest of righteousness. (James 3: 13–18)

# Chapter 6

## Nursi's Divine Attribute Based View of Man and Its Link to Holy Spirit

*Yunus Çengel*

S ciences are based on observations, and progress by questioning. A major obstacle before the advancement of sciences is preconception, and its source is conjunction. A person who is accustomed to seeing two things always together eventually develops the idea that the two are parts of each other or that one is the source of the other. It is difficult to break this conditioning and mindset solidly entrenched over time and to prevent its shaping the mind.

Despite the major scientific developments in the twentieth century and the fact that this is the age of information, the nature of man continues to be a puzzle. Understanding the past behavior of human beings and predicting their future acts depends on having a good understanding of the human being and of human society, which resembles a big human being. If the behaviors of people and societies differ significantly from those predicted and we continue to be surprised, then we are still a long way from knowing people and societies.

In medicine, treatment becomes useless and cannot provide a cure for ailments when the diagnostics are wrong or incomplete. Likewise, in personal and social life, it is not possible to find effective solutions to personal and societal problems unless the nature of man is known correctly. Therefore, the starting point for finding solutions to the problems of people and societies and to provide lasting peace and happiness must be the understanding of the true nature of man. Otherwise, all the solutions offered and prescriptions written are bound to remain ineffective, and we will continue to be disappointed.

The past century has witnessed major developments in the biological sciences, and biotechnology has become one of the locomotives of the global economy. As a result, today we know the human body much better and diagnose and treat its ailments much more effectively. We are not far from the days when genetically engineered tissues and organs compatible with the genetic code of the person will be grown in labs. But it is not possible to draw the same rosy picture for the human spirit that manifests itself through behavior. That is, the sciences associated with the human body, or the material being of people, have pursued a fast pace and portend a bright future outlook, but the sciences associated with the spirit or non-material being of people have lagged behind. This picture shows clearly that sciences associated with the non-material being of people are largely underdeveloped, inadequate, and even invalid. The first thing that needs to be done is to try to understand the true nature of man correctly by stripping off any profound prejudices and misinformation. And this should be done on the basis of logical consistency, careful observations, and conformity with the current state of knowledge.

The primary mind-block of modern times is the preoccupation with matter, and the main mix-up is the presumption that the source of everything is matter. This materialistic idea, that forms the basis of the current scientific approach, is a belief and an ideology, rather than science. This approach, which views the human being basically as a bag of matter and looks for the source of the disposition, actions, and feelings of people in the interactions of matter, is far from understanding the human being. The Darwinian view asserts that man is an advanced animal species that emerged by evolution following a chain of random events.[304] It is unfortunate that this view is taken under a protective shield through the declaration that it is 'scientific' while other views are flatly rejected for not being based on observations and thus not being scientific. The highest point human beings can reach given the premise that man is viewed as an animal is that of being 'happy animals.' And this corresponds to the situation in which the body is in good health and comfort, its entire needs

---

[304] Charles Darwin, *On the Origin of Species* (London: John Murray, 1859).

are met, and all its desires are satisfied to the fullest extent possible. The validity of this 'prescription for happiness' for human beings is open to discussion on the basis of observations.

When viewed as physical bodies, there is indeed not much difference between human beings and animals. Compared to animals, human beings are much more intelligent, are interdependent, and trade goods and services to meet their needs. Therefore, the human being is often described as an 'intelligent animal', 'social animal', or 'economic animal.' Another noticeable difference between animals and human beings is that humans use tools and gather all necessary materials before starting something, which shows imagination. But the difference between people and animals is not limited to the above. For example, a person is concerned with the past as well as the future, and his or her range of interests and understanding is rather wide, to include all times and places. Physically, a person can live only at a certain place and in a certain moment; but mentally, emotionally, and in imagination, that person can travel both in time and space with no limitations, can receive pain or pleasure from both the past and the future, and can effectively live in a wide span of time spiritually. Therefore, unlike an animal, while living *bodily* a heaven-like life, *spiritually* he or she can be suffering a hell-like torment, with the pains of past life and fears for the future. Or, even when he is quite happy and comfortable, the pain of others, especially close ones, can, through empathy, spoil his current pleasure and cause him to weep. In Nursi's words:

> Man is connected with all living creatures, and in this respect is gladdened by their happiness and saddened by their pain. ... A person with conscience who feels sorrow and pity at the weeping of a motherless, hungry child, surely feels pleasure at a mother's compassion for her child, surely he is pleased and happy.[305]

Animals, on the other hand, do not empathize with their associates in pain, and continue to enjoy themselves as if nothing had happened and there is no future.

Materially, a person is just a point in the world, and the world is a point in the universe. That is, as far as his body is concerned, a person is

---

[305] Nursi, *The Rays*, Second Chapter of Twenty-Ninth Flash (İstanbul: Sözler, 2000; translation by Şükran Vahide), 654.

a mere dot within a dot. But through his meaning or spirit, his non-material faculties and emotions such as the mind, imagination, and heart, and his talents, that encompass everything, he is such a vast being that the enormous earth becomes only a point in his imagination. Both the pain and the pleasure a person receives through his non-material faculties—depending on their degree of development—are in proportion to their vastness. The magnitude of the difference between a human being and an animal lies not in matter but in non-matter.

As far as physical parts and organs are concerned, there is not much difference among people, and all are basically replicas of each other. Of course there is some difference in terms of bodily size, but the value of a person and the magnitude of the pain and pleasure a person gets in life does not have much to do with bodily size. The attribute 'great man' has no relation to the weight and height of a person. From the point of view of non-physical faculties, however, two people can be worlds apart. For example, while a mother who risks her life for her infant is lauded as a hero of compassion, a person who kills an innocent is reviled as a heartless wild beast. While distinguished intellectuals and scholars are given the royal treatment, the laymen receive the ordinary treatment. While a person with a strongly moral character inspires well-being in a community like a medicine, another person filled with greed or revenge can be a poison. In short, the difference between two people can be far greater than the difference between two different species of animals, and this difference is entirely in non-material qualities rather than matter. In the words of Nursi:

> Each and every member of humanity is like a species. This is because the light of thought and imagination gives such vastness to his aspirations that they will not be satisfied even by swallowing all times. The nature, self-worth, view, progression, pleasures, and pains of the members of other species are subtle, individualistic, limited, bounded, and momentary. But those of human beings are high, comprehensive, and everlasting.[306]

The most striking difference between human beings and animals is in the number of stomachs they have. There is one stomach in animals,

---

[306] Nursi, *Muhakemat*, Üçüncü Makale, 169.

but several in human beings. The familiar physical stomach that digests the food we eat when we are hungry is basically the same in both human beings and animals. The foods for this physical stomach are the variety of fruits, vegetables, and dishes, that turn the face of the world into an extravagant buffet. All the other stomachs of human beings are associated with their status as human beings, and all are non-matter or meaning. For example, the mind is a stomach, and its food is knowledge. The sense of loving is a stomach, and its food is love. Generosity is also a stomach, and its food is to give or to receive. All stomachs—physical or non-physical—shrink when they are subjected to deprivation. The hunger of all stomachs is pain, and their fulfillment a pleasure.

There is an upper limit for the size of the physical organs that are nourished via the familiar stomach. But for the non-physical organs or faculties, there is no such limit. Sometimes a single emotion like greed or animosity develops so much and establishes such deep roots that it dominates the person. All physical parts of the body are good, and serve a useful purpose. Goodness is also the rule for non-physical organs, which are sown as the seeds of abilities and capabilities into human nature. But the bringing up of these depends on how free will is used, and only those attributes that are watered and fertilized will properly be nurtured and grow. Others will remain dormant like a dry seed. The human body resembles the soil of a garden, but its value depends more on the value of the plants that grow on it than on the soil itself.

## Matter Based and Attribute Based Views

The materialistic view maintains that all things, including humans, are meaningless beings that consist of material bodies and are formed following a series of random events starting with the Big Bang. Nursi, on the other hand, expresses the thought that matter is just a veil spread over existences of meanings, and states that the real existence is the non-matter or meaning. It is not possible to understand the essence of the world of existence by viewing the universe as a pile of ink-tainted paper rather than as a book. According to Nursi, true enlightenment is going beyond the paper and the ink and understanding the inscriptions.[307]

---

[307] Nursi, *The Words*, Gleams, 527.

Nursi expressed a striking difference between the viewpoints of materialist philosophy and Qur'anic philosophy in the Twelfth Word, by likening the wondrous universe to a Qur'an inscribed with jewelry. In this pamphlet, Nursi talks about the creatures being verses of creation written with the pen of power (matter–energy) on the pages of universe, and states that every being is a meaningful letter on those pages. Also, he stresses the importance of looking at beings taking into account their maker, that is, from the perspective of *mana-i harfi* (other-indicative) and not *mana-i ismi* (self-indicative). According to Nursi, viewing beings from the perspective of *mana-i ismi*, or on their own account (like viewing a painting by Picasso as a mere painting, having no connection with Picasso), is ignorance rather than enlightenment.[308]

One of the most fundamental suppositions in sciences is the notion that the origin of everything is matter—an idea that dates back to Stoic times, and is regarded as an unquestionable scientific fact in modern times. Yet, it is remarkable that this notion is never tested, and therefore it is not even scientific. The Big Bang theory has also helped to propel this notion of an 'all-material' universe.

A basic requirement for scientific facts is that they should be consistent with observed phenomena and the existing scientific evidence, and pass certain tests. Yet the notion that everything is made of matter and matter alone fails even the simplest test. Two identical roses, one of them smashed to mud and the other not, are materially equivalent. But they are very different, all differences, like beauty, art, and order, being non-material, or 'meaning'.

We sense non-material things only when they manifest on matter, and naturally we think matter to be the source of everything. This prejudgment still forms the main platform on which sciences are built. Nursi rejected the one-dimensional view that the universe and everything in it are made entirely of matter (or energy) by stating: "the matter in which they got drowned did not even wet my toes."[309] According to Nursi, matter-energy is a manifestation of the Divine Name "All-Powerful" (*Al-Qadir*). All non-material attributes are reflections of other Divine Names.

---

[308] Ibid., Twelfth Word, 143–49.

[309] Nursi, *The Words*, Thirtieth Word, 568.

For example, life is a manifestation of the Divine Name 'Ever-Living' (*Al-Hayy*), the character is a manifestation of 'Divine Individuality' (*Al-Fard*), and utility and purposefulness are a manifestation of 'All-Wise' (*Al-Hakim*).

In this way, Nursi relates all beings to the Divine Names (*Esma-i İlahiye*), and thus to God:

> The reality of the universe and of all beings is based on the Divine Names. The reality of every being is based on one Name or on many. All sciences and arts are also based on and rely upon a Name. The true science of philosophy is based on the Name of All-Wise, true medicine on the Name of Healer, and geometry on the Name of Determiner, and so on. And in the same way that all the sciences are based on and come to an end in a Name, the realities of all arts and sciences, and of all human attainments, are based on the Divine Names. Indeed, one group of the most learned of the saints stated that the Divine Names constitute the true reality of things, while the essences of things are only shadows of that reality. They said too that even only on appearance, manifestations of the impresses of as many as twenty Divine Names may be seen on a single living creature.[310]

Nursi states that all beings are mirrors that reflect the Divine Names of God, and that the mirror that reflects the Names in the brightest and most comprehensive way is the human being. He also invites man to read himself:

> Man acts as a mirror to the Divine Names, the imprint of which are upon him. There are more than seventy Names the impresses of which are apparent in man's comprehensive nature. These have been described to a degree at the start of the Third Stopping-Place of the Thirty-Second Word. For example, through his creation, man shows the Names of Maker and Creator; through his being 'Most Excellent of Patterns,' the Names of Most Merciful and All-Compassionate, and through the fine way he is nurtured and raised, the Names of All-Generous and Granter of Favors, and so on; he shows the differing impresses of different Names through all his members and faculties, all his organs and limbs, all his subtle senses and faculties, all his feelings and emotions. That is to say, just as among the Names there is a

---

[310] Ibid.,Thirty-Second Word, 655.

Greatest Name, so among the impresses of those Names there is a greatest impress, and that is man. O you who considers himself to be a true man! Read yourself! Otherwise it is possible you will be a man who is either animal-like or inanimate![311]

This expression also explains the often misinterpreted hadith "God has created man in the image of the 'Most Merciful'" and its Christian counterpart "Man is created in the image of God."

Of course, these expressions can be used in reverse to discover God and His Attributes by making extensions of traits built into the human nature. For example, tracing the rays of compassion that stream out from compassionate beings, mostly mothers, will take us to the source, which is the 'Most Compassionate'. Likewise, the sense of justice we all feel is an indication that God is All-Just, and so on. Therefore, the carefully sorting out of the basic purified tendencies in human nature can be used as a compass to map out the Attributes of God, which is the source of all these immaterial glitters.

## Holy Spirit as Divine Attributes

In mainstream (Trinitarian) Christianity, Holy Spirit refers to some aspect or action of God, and not to a distinct entity outside God. In Eastern Orthodoxy, Holy Spirit is believed to proceed eternally from the God the Father (but not the Son). Thomas Michel defines Holy Spirit as "God's active, transcendent presence at the heart, not only of human nature, but of the whole created universe."[312] In the early stages of Christianity, some considered Holy Spirit an 'emanation' of God the Father. There are many Divine Attributes (aspects of God's Divine character or nature) such as all-just, most merciful, eternal, omnipresent, and omnipotent. In the second century, Athenagoras of Athens[313] wrote in his treatise *Plea for Christians* that the Holy Spirit was an "effluence of God, flowing forth and returning to God like a ray of the sun." The Spirit doesn't change, is present everywhere, and is intimately involved in all the doings of the Father and the Son.

---

[311] Ibid., Thirty-Third Word, Thirty-First Window, 719.
[312] Thomas Michel, *Trinity as Radical Monotheism*, 2009; www.thomasmichel.us.
[313] www.earlychristianwritings.com/text/athenagoras-plea.html.

The Nicene-Constantinopolitan creed which came out of the Council of Constantinople in 381 states:[314]

> We believe in the Holy Spirit,
> the Lord and Giver of life,
> who proceeds from the Father,
> who with the Father and the Son is worshiped and glorified,
> who spoke through the Prophets.

That is, Divine acts such as giving life are attributed to the Holy Spirit.

In mainstream Christianity, the Holy Spirit, Father, and Son make up a unified Godhead known as the 'Trinity.' While each 'personage' is distinct in function, each shares together in the same deity and each reflects the Divine Attributes of the one living God. The interpretation of Holy Spirit as Attributes of God might bring Islamic and Christian theologies closer.[315]

Nursi, like Athenagoras of Athens, who likened the Holy Spirit to the rays of the sun, also makes extensive use of the analogy between the sun and God. The sun, for example, is everywhere on earth with its warmth and light, but not with its existence-body. Therefore, the sun is very close to us and can even caress us with its light, but we are very far from it. It can affect us, but we cannot affect the sun. Any person can receive inspirations from God, and feel God's presence in his heart—which resembles a spiritual mirror upon which the unseen reflects—just like receiving sunlight on a properly oriented hand-held personal mirror having a 'personal sun' in it to interact with.

The sun analogy can further be extended to include the Son. A Prophet can be viewed as the moon that shines the light it receives from the sun on earth, with scriptures continuing spiritual illumination after the moon has set. The analogy of the sun, sunlight, and moon trio may open a window for an insightful interpretation of trinity. Also, the image of the sun in a mirror acts like a source of light, like the sun itself, but that image cannot claim to be a sun since its existence is dependent on the existence of the real sun in the sky. Nursi views all beings, including human beings, as the mirrors of the Glorious Sun, reflecting its attri-

---

[314] www.allaboutgod.com/holy-spirit.htm.
[315] en.wikipedia.org/wiki/Trinity

butes. But he cautions those image-suns not to confuse themselves with the real sun. The sun in the sky, for example, is practically eternal by nature as it is the source of light. But the suns in the mirrors are eternal as long as they continue to receive light from the real sun, since mirrors are capable only of receiving light and not of generating it. For example, God is eternal in essence. But human beings are eternal only because they are created as the mirrors of the eternal One, capable of receiving and reflecting the immaterial rays of the attribute eternity.

## A New Look at Beings

To shed some light on non-material things or meanings, we can conduct some simple mental experiments. Consider, for example, a 100-gram book consisting of 99 grams of paper and one gram of ink, and compare it to one gram of ink randomly spilled over 99 grams of paper. In terms of matter, there is no difference between a 100-gram book and 100 grams of ink-stained papers. If we send these two to a materials analysis lab for tests, both will come back with identical reports regarding their content. Considering that the 100-gram book and 100 grams of inked paper are identical so far as their materials are concerned, all differences between the two relate to meaning only, and thus are non-material. Therefore, what we call "meaning" in the case of a book is everything other than the paper and ink. A book, it appears, is a material being that consists of ink and paper, and is visible to the eye and touchable by the hand. But in reality, what makes the book a book are the meanings in it, and the material being of a book is nothing compared to its meaning, which is the non-material being. As a matter of fact, the e-books whose popularity has increased in recent years and which can be recorded in a little space on a CD or a flash-card employ neither ink nor paper. It appears that words can be written in any color and reorganized by electric energy converted to light on the face of a screen. It can even be said that what we call a book is a screen, a monitor, a sheath, or a binocular that makes it possible for the meaning to appear on pages. A book is characterized as being good or bad on the basis of the meanings it conveys to the mind and the heart—both non-material.

Another example that will be helpful in understanding the relation between matter and meaning is the rose. Let us take two roses that are completely identical, and smash one of them until it turns to sludge. Then let us ask if there is any difference between the two. Most likely, such a question will be considered absurd, and it will be said that a rose cannot be compared to a pile of sludge. However, if the rose and its sludge twin are sent to a chemistry lab for analysis, the lab report will state that materially both are identical. Thus, materially, there is no difference between a rose and the sludge of its smashed twin. But the two are obviously different, and the difference between them is entirely meaning, since it is not matter. (I don't suppose anyone will even think of giving a smashed rose instead of an actual rose to a loved one thinking that materially they are the same.) This means, every attribute and quality that the sludge does not have is related to meaning, and the value of rose's matter is virtually nothing compared to the value of its meaning. In other words, what makes the rose a rose is not its matter, but rather, the meaning that transcends that matter. 'Rose' is a sort of meaning-bearer, and rose is the first thing that comes to mind when one wishes to send pleasant meanings. The person who receives the rose actually receives the pleasant meanings sent, not its matter, and absorbs meanings and rejoices via the senses—unless, of course, it is received by one who sees nothing other than matter, and is unaware of meaning, like a donkey or a cow. The striking difference between human beings and animals is the hundreds of such feelings and the associated non-material stomachs. In other words, animals have only one stomach whereas humans have hundreds of them, and all but one are associated with meanings. Therefore, to live to eat is, in essence, to resign from humanity.

The thing that makes a rose beautiful is obviously not the beauty in its atoms, since the nitrogen or hydrogen atom in a rose is completely identical to the one in a smashed rose—just as carbon atoms in graphite and diamond are identical. Since what is not in its parts cannot be in the whole (the conservation law), the beauty of a rose must be emanating from outside rather than from its material—just like a diamond's fascinating glitter originating from a source of light outside. The special trait of roses and other beautiful things is their ability to receive and reflect this beauty—just as the special trait of diamond is its ability to receive and scatter light in a glamorous way. And this necessitates the existence of widespread beauty and thus a layer of beauty, which has nothing to do with matter (and thus time) in the universe. Even the ancient Romans and Greeks must have felt this meaning, so that they sanctified this layer as Venus or Aphrodite, "the goddess of love and beauty."

As a final example, let us consider a housefly. Like those of all other living things, the basic building blocks of a fly consist mainly of hydrogen, oxygen, nitrogen, and carbon atoms, which are made up of electrons, protons, and neutrons like all other elements. In other words, all beings, dead or alive, consist of atoms (or electrons, protons, and neutrons), and the cement holding these basic building blocks together is the force. Now let us put a dead fly with its live twin side by side, and compare them. Materially, these two flies are identical since no mass is gained or lost by death. Further, if the live fly stands still, it is rather difficult to distinguish it from the dead one. Thus we can say that every difference between the dead and living beings—life, sight, hearing, order, beauty, consciousness, love, etc.—is immaterial and thus meaning.

## Life

There is no such component as life in the atoms or molecules (or the particles or waves they are made of) of which all living organisms are made. Considering that what is not in the parts cannot be in the whole, life has to be non-matter and thus meaning, and thus it is not subject to the limitation of time and space. There must, then, exist a vast non-matter "life" layer in the universe emanating the light of life, and everything that is capable of receiving this light of life—whether it has a material body or not—is alive.

Observations show that the common feature of all living things is to contain water in their bodies. Therefore, the search for extraterrestrial life is conducted by seeking water. But water is not the source of life, and cannot be. This is because there is no such thing as life in a water molecule that consists of two hydrogen and one oxygen atoms, and the claim that water is the source of something that it does not have is absurd, just like the false claims that the diamond is the source of the light it scatters or that the television set is the source of images on its screen. Likewise, the currently prevailing scientific view that life is chemical reactions is also baseless, since no chemical reaction has ever produced life, and thus it is not even scientific.

Following a logical approach on the basis of common observations, we can state that there is general agreement that there exists something called 'life' which distinguishes animate beings from inanimate ones. Also, it is well-established that the building blocks of living cells are proteins, and proteins are made up of amino acids (20 of them) that are composed of hydrogen, oxygen, nitrogen, carbon, and to a lesser extent, sulfur atoms. But these atoms and the forces that chemically bond them to each other do not have life as a component. They are lifeless. Thus one must conclude that life shines on matter, but there is no evidence that life originates from matter.

The view that life emerges out of nowhere and shines on matter is also reiterated by Nobel Prize winner Loretta Robert Loughlin, who asserts the notion that the unknowability of living things may actually be a physical phenomenon.[316] In a US public service broadcast interview about the origin of life, Andrew Knoll of Harvard University expressed the hopelessness of trying to understand life by stating "I imagine my grandchildren will still be sitting around saying that it's a great mystery."[317] The current state of understanding, and the references to the future, serve to attract more attention to Nursi's notion that matter is not the source of life and that life is a manifestation of the Divine Name *Hayy* (The Possessor and Giver of Life).

## Free Will

In the material universe that started with the Big Bang, everything is subject to physical laws, and consequently the actions of all beings—whether alive or not—are predetermined. According to this philosophical view, called 'determinism,' there cannot be any such thing as 'free will,' as this would be a violation of the laws of physics. Besides, there is no such component as 'free will' in the building blocks of matter. Yet, the existence of 'free will' is a scientific fact, since its presence can be observed, dem-

---

[316] Robert Laughlin, *A Different Universe – Reinventing Physics from the Bottom Down* (New York: Basic Books, 2005), 173.
[317] www.pbs.org/wgbh/nova/origins/knoll.html.

onstrated, and tested. In the inanimate world the physical laws govern fully, and the reaction of an inanimate being in response to a specific action can be predicted with precision beforehand. But this is not the case for animate beings that possess free will. Even this observation alone is sufficient to shatter the notion of an all-material universe. Also, if it were not for the non-material dimension of free will, the future would have been known with certainty, and people would have been like robots with no consciousness. Moreover, they would not be responsible for their acts—like a malfunctioning robot not being held responsible for the damage that it may have caused.

The question of immersion in matter has caused difficulties even for some prominent thinkers. Albert Einstein, for example, became a devoted determinist because of his firm belief in physics, and argued that even human beings cannot have free will:

> A person's actions were just as determined as those of a billiard ball, planet, or star. ... Human actions are determined, beyond their control, by physical and psychological laws. ... Everything is determined, the beginning as well as the end, by forces over which we have no control. It is determined for the insect as well as for the star. Human beings, vegetables, or cosmic dust, we all dance to a mysterious tune, intoned in the distance by an invisible player.[318]

Discussions of free will have caused deep divisions among philosophers, and the matter is far from being resolved. The existence of free will is incompatible with the notion of an all-material universe, and admitting its existence is certain to punch holes in materialism. The existence of free will can be proved easily by a simple thought experiment—such as leaving two physically identical people in two identical rooms with identical furnishings, and observing them act differently, or dropping two identical people, one dead and the other alive, into a river, and observing their behavior. The motion of the dead body in the river can be predicted precisely by physical laws, but this is not the case for the live body. This is sufficient proof that the notion of existence being made up of matter and natural laws only runs counter to the facts.

---

[318] Walter Isaacson, *Einstein - His Life and Universe* (New York: Simon & Schuster, 2007), 391.

On the basis of these and similar observations it can be asserted that free will does not emanate from a physical body; it transcends the physical body and reflects through it—like the light from an external source transcending the diamond and then reflecting from it. When the matter is viewed from the 'Attributes' point of view, free will appears as the reflection of the Divine Name *Al-Murid* ('The One Who Wills') on living beings that possess consciousness, just as 'life' is a reflection of the Divine Name *Al-Hayy* (The Possessor and Giver of Life).

## Physical Laws

Laws and rules are the foundations of order and peace in the entire world, and this is also the case in the universe. For example, if just the law of gravity is relinquished, everything will start flying around, and there will be complete chaos. The laws of a country reflect the general will of the people who live in that country, and the natural laws in the universe reflect a universal will that rules over the universe. The police force in a country enforces the law, and makes sure that people abide by the laws. In the universe, this is done by natural laws and principles—like gravitational force ensuring that everything obeys the law of gravity.

Laws are not of matter, and thus they are not subject to limitations of time and space. As such, they rule everywhere, but they are not anywhere. As Einstein put it, "a spirit is manifest in the laws of the universe."[319] The total obedience of every particle of matter to laws of nature and the manifestation of laws by their appearance in matter, perpetuated the presumption that the origin of laws, like the origin of force, is matter. In the basic building blocks of matter (particles or waves), there is no such thing as "*law*" as a component—just as there is no material component of laws in the bodies of law-obeying people. We can even say that the law of gravity will continue to exist even if all matter in the universe disappears, and Fourier's law of heat conduction will still apply even if there is no conduction of heat (as in the case of the whole universe being at the same temperature). This is like the income tax law remaining applicable over an entire country even if there is no income generated in a particu-

---

[319] Ibid., 388.

lar year, since the law is not part of the income or of the people who generate it.

In his book *A Different Universe*, the 1998 Physics Nobel prize recipient Robert Laughlin argues that most physical laws do not have their origins in the microscopic word, but rather, simply emerge or appear in the macroscopic world out of nowhere: "The most fundamental laws of physics—such as Newton's laws of motion or quantum mechanics—are in fact emergent. They are properties of large assemblages of matter, and when their exactness is examined too closely, it vanishes into nothing."[320] In other words, physical laws do not originate from the matter that they govern, they simply emerge out of nowhere—that is, somewhere other than the material universe. After examining some primitive organizational phenomena such as weather phenomena, Laughlin asserts:

> We are able to prove in these simple cases that the organization can acquire meaning and life of its own and begin to transcend the parts from which it is made. What physical science thus has to tell us is that the whole being more than the sum of its parts is not merely a concept but a physical phenomenon. Nature is regulated not only by a microscopic rule base but by powerful and general principles of organization.[321]

And:

> Physical law cannot generally be anticipated by pure thought, but must be discovered experimentally.[322]

These are powerful statements that assert, on the basis of observations, that the whole is more than the sum of its parts made of matter–energy originating from the Big Bang universe. Nursi points this out as follows: "Yes, there exists an attribute in the assembly that does not exist in the component."[323] The 'extras' in the whole must, then, be non-matter or meaning, and must be coming from 'non-matter universes' that Nursi

[320] Robert Laughlin, *A Different Universe*, back cover.
[321] Ibid., Preface, xiv.
[322] Ibid., xv.
[323] Nursi, *Muhakemat*, Üçüncü Makale, 146.

labels as 'Divine Attributes.' In Christian thought, 'Holy Spirit' fulfills the same mission.

## Character and Divine Individuality

Atoms, which are the basic building blocks of elements, are made up of electrons, protons, and neutrons, and there are over a hundred elements in nature—some naturally occurring and some artificially made in labs by fusion. The characteristic difference between these elements is the number of protons in their nucleus. For example, a hydrogen atom contains proton 1, carbon 6, iron 26, and gold 79. But all protons are the same—just like the grains of rice in a bag. If, when tightly wrapped, 6 grains of rice become a bean instead of a 6-grain rice stack, 26 grains become a corn, and 79 grains become a hazelnut, there is something curious going on. Or, if 6 white men become a single giant black man when tightly wrapped, and he then turns back to 6 white men when the rope is removed ... Even more peculiar, if two engineers turn into a medical doctor when tightly wrapped, and three engineers turn into a lawyer ... We will probably give up.

The characters of carbon, iron, and gold are very different from each other, and it is clear that this character does not originate from the protons themselves. This is because the protons possess the character neither of carbon, nor of iron, nor of gold. It also appears that it is quite possible to convert carbon or iron into gold—all we need to do is to split the carbon or iron atoms as we split uranium atoms in nuclear power plants, and recombine the released protons into groups of 79.

Similarly, if we mix two hydrogen atoms with one oxygen, this becomes a gas mixture with the properties of both components. But when the hydrogen and oxygen atoms combine with a chemical bond, we obtain "water" with completely different properties. Considering that the force that provides the chemical bond does not possess the properties of water or any other compound, one is justified to ask the question, 'Where does the character of compounds such as water come from?' It seems that there is a common non-material layer of individualism that is the source of character, and that the Name 'Divine Individuality' (*Fard*) shines on all beings.

## Love and Compassion

There is probably no doubt about the presence of love and different kinds and degrees of love in the universe. Nursi, like many others in the Islamic and Christian traditions, sees love as the core of creation: "Love is the cause of the universe's existence. And it is the bond of the universe."[324] The noblest and the purest of all loves is compassion, which are above all material and non-material interests. The presence of common motherly compassion in the universe is confirmed by observations, and the phrase "mother nature" is an expression of it. Nursi draws attention to this compassion that exists even in wild animals, and to the source of these common glitters of compassion:

> [Mercy] makes the hen-birds search out the food and bring it their wingless, frail chicks in the nests at the tops of trees. He subjugates the hungry lions to her cubs, so she does not eat the meat she finds, but gives it to them.[325]

The food for the emotion of compassion is giving and receiving compassion; that is, loving and being loved without any preconditions and without expecting anything in return. Therefore, there is no place for compassion in the materialistic philosophy that is based on material interests and pleasures. In the end, compassion, which is noblest feeling, is confused with lowly physical attraction or lust, and this mix-up is presented as science. Compassion shines the brightest in mothers, and turns them into statues of embodied compassion. Yet there is no such component as 'compassion' in the cells, the basic building blocks of living things, and thus compassion must be non-matter or meaning. If something is not originating from the parts, it must be coming from somewhere else. Therefore, there must exist a vast non-material layer of 'compassion' in the universe that is beyond time and space, and the most compassionate beings are those who, like a diamond, receive and scatter the rays of compassion emanating from that layer most intensely. According to Nursi, this apparent universe of compassion is a reflection of the Divine Name 'Most Compassionate' (Ar-Rahim):

---

[324] Nursi, *The Words*, Twenty-Fourth Word, 367.
[325] Nursi, *The Rays*, Fifteenth Ray, 581.

The existence and reality of a boundless mercy is as clearly apparent in the universe as the light of the sun. As certainly as light testifies to the sun, so this extensive mercy testifies to a Most Merciful and Compassionate One behind the veil of the Unseen.[326]

He also asserts: "The compassion of all mothers is but a flash of the manifestation of Divine Mercy."[327]

## Generosity

Among the traits most loved in people are generosity and courtesy. Everyone likes to receive gifts and bounties, and gets pleasure proportionately. The pleasure has a momentary material dimension, which is also the case for animals, and a timeless non-material dimension that is specific to human beings. For example, the greatest pleasure in a box of chocolates given as a gift is not the temporary pleasure that occurs in the taste buds while the chocolates are being eaten, but rather, the permanent pleasure that occurs in the heart while the gift is being received, which carries with it meanings like love, thought, and appreciation, and renews itself as it is remembered and as the memory is stirred with thought. Otherwise, rushing to open the box and attacking the chocolates inside is animalism. A bouquet of roses is probably nothing more than an instant of eating pleasure for a cow. But the same bouquet of roses is an endless pleasure for a human being because of the meanings it carries—although it offers no material pleasure to the taste buds. Not being aware of this major dimension of humanity, and spending a lifetime chasing after temporary physical pleasures as animals do, is deprivation and a waste of human traits.

When viewed from a materialistic angle, giving without receiving anything in return is against the interest of the giver, and thus it is a foolish act. And this is totally against the materialist philosophy, which views the purpose of life as 'self-interest' and the basis of relations as 'mutual interest.' Generosity or altruism, as it is known in scientific circles, has long been a topic of discussion among scientists because it is not in line with evolutionary theory, which suggests that altruism should not exist. Accord-

---

[326] Ibid., 582.
[327] Nursi, *The Words*, Seventh Word, 43.

ing to the theory, individuals with genes that provide advantage—such as being self-serving—will out-produce others and gradually change the characteristics of the whole group. Therefore, in the presumed evolutionary race, the stingy ones who helped themselves should have gotten ahead, and the generous individuals should not have stood a chance of enduring. But as it turns out, the generous ones managed to subsist and not perish, and evolutionary scientists are working hard to resolve this puzzle, with no hope in sight.[328]

On the surface, it looks as if the one who gives is at a loss and the one who receives is making a gain. But beneath the surface, there is a spiritual pleasure called 'the pleasure of giving,' that generous people receive as they give. Generosity is one of the noblest feelings in people. The food of this feeling is to give without expecting anything in return. This non-material stomach is nourished and grows by giving, and it becomes an endless source of pleasure for the person. The pleasure that the giver gets out of this human trait is probably far greater than the sum of the pleasures of the receivers. For people with a well-developed sense of pleasing others or a large stomach of humanity, giving and making others happy, even if it is merely with a pleasant word or a smile, is a source of permanent pleasure and happiness. In the attribute-based view, this universe of generosity is a reflection of the Divine Name 'Most Generous' (Al-Jawad).

## Knowledge

Nursi attracts attention to the 'knowledge body' (vücud-u ilmi) of beings, which can be viewed as the luminous matrices of beings interwoven with rays of knowledge, in addition to their material bodies. Observations confirm that from a subatomic particle to a galaxy, everything has a non-matter spirit-like robust 'knowledge body', and everything appears to be knitted with knowledge (like a biological cell and a cellular phone). A scientific study is merely an attempt to put together the 'knowledge bodies' of beings correctly in their entirety. This is done by observing the glimpses of knowledge emanating from beings, and by seeing the authentic form of the ray of knowledge with the mental eye, and describing it

---

[328] Adrian Bell et al., World Science, Oct. 13, 2009. Originally appeared in the Oct. 12, 2009 edn of the journal Proceedings of the National Academy of Sciences.

for others to see. The mass of a cell, for example, is about one billionth of a gram. But the knowledge that exists in a cell has already filled volumes of books. Therefore, the 'material body' of a cell is nothing compared to its 'knowledge body.' The cell is like the materialized form of knowledge.

The fact that everything is made with knowledge shows that there is a common invisible 'ray of knowledge' that penetrates into everything—just like the glitters of light from a diamond showing the presence of a source of light around. But there is no such component as 'knowledge' in the basic building blocks of beings. Therefore, knowledge has to be non-matter and thus meaning since there is no doubt about the existence of knowledge and what is not in the parts cannot be in the whole. If something is not originating from the parts, it must be coming from somewhere else. Therefore, there must exist a vast non-material layer of 'knowledge' in the universe from which emanates the invisible light of knowledge. Unlike ordinary light, this ray of knowledge can be sensed with the non-material mental eye rather than the ordinary bodily eye. Nursi relates this luminous universe to the Divine Name 'All-Knowing' (Al-Alim):

> All the evidences for knowledge are evidences also for the existence of the All-Knowing One. Since it is impossible and precluded that there should be an attribute without the one it qualifies, all the proofs of knowledge form a powerful and completely certain supreme proof of the Pre-Eternal All-Knowing One's necessary existence.[329]

## The Five Senses and More

In addition to the five senses such as sight, touch, and smell, that are related to matter, people have countless senses such as justice and motivation, and even a sixth sense that is not related to matter directly. When we perceive the environment and beings, we usually rely on the five primary sensory organs such as the eye and the ear, and the brain, which is the center to which all five sensory organs are connected. As a result of limiting the world of existence to matter, we tend to view the five senses as the making of matter, and other senses as the manifestations of interactions of matter. As a result, we call the brain the 'miracle organ', and

---

[329] Ibid., 615.

admit that we understand little about the operation of this amazing organ. Actually, what we do not understand is the truths of beings, and not the brain. The mystery of the brain is not due to its matter, but rather, to its use as a black box in which we hide all our inconsistencies and ignorance.

Now let us consider the process of seeing. On the basis of the simple observation that we see when our eyes are open and do not see when they are closed, we quickly draw the conclusion that 'it is the eye that sees'. But this is no different than for a person who depends on glasses for eyesight and sees only with glasses to say that 'it is the glasses that see'. (Besides, we can see in our dreams quite clearly with our eyes closed.) Those who take a more holistic approach also consider the nerves that transmit the signal to the vision center in the brain, and claim that seeing occurs in a wondrous way at the vision center in the brain. That is, seeing just happens out of nowhere. Here the brain is used as a black curtain to cover up our ignorance. In other words, the brain is turned into a black hole that gobbles up information and does not allow even information to escape. But what is called the 'vision center' in the brain is nothing more than the end-point of the sight nerves coming from the eyes. The basic building blocks of the entire brain, including the vision center, are simply the elements like carbon and hydrogen, or their components electrons, protons, and neutrons. That is, whatever is in wood is also what is in the brain. And the electric signal that occurs in the brain as a result of the flow of the charged particles is no different from the electric current in the processor of a computer.

There is no such component as 'eyesight' in the atoms or molecules of the eyes and the brain, and what is not in the parts cannot be in the whole. If it is, it must be coming from somewhere else. Eye and brain consist of atoms like carbon, hydrogen, and oxygen. The seeing ability of the eye and the brain is no more than that of a slice of bread, which is made of basically the same atoms. The cells that make up the eye–nerve–brain trio does not contain a material component called 'eyesight', and thus vision—whose existence is undeniable—must be non-matter and thus meaning. Then, there must exist a vast 'vision' layer in the universe, which is beyond time and space, giving off the light of 'vision', and like a diamond, everything capable of receiving this light of vision is a seeing being. According to Nursi, the immaterial vision world is a manifestation of the Divine Name 'All-Seer' (Al-Basir).[330]

The loss of eyesight when a fault develops in the eye or the vision center of the brain does not show that these organs are the source of vision—just like the glasses not being the source of vision for wearers of glasses. That is, the eye–nerve–brain combination is for eyesight what glasses are for the eye. It seems that what is called the 'vision center' is simply the manifestation point of the immaterial eyesight attribute in the brain. In other words, the vision center in the brain is the welding spot of the body and the sense of seeing of the spirit, and the cross over from matter to non-matter.

Likewise, all perfumes and pleasant-smelling flowers are made of atoms like hydrogen, oxygen, and carbon, and there is no 'smell' component in any of these atoms. The hydrogen atom in water is the same as that in a flower, and all atoms are made of electrons, protons, and neutrons. Then we should ask, 'Where in the perfume or flower is the smell?' Interestingly, even bad-smelling things are made of the same atoms. It seems that smell manifests itself on matter, is transmitted with matter, but is not matter. Therefore, smell must be non-matter or meaning, and each molecule has a certain ability to receive smell and to reflect it. But the source of smell is not the arrangement of the atom—just as the source of the glitter of a diamond is the light coming from outside and not the arrangement of carbon atoms in a crystalline form. The cause of deception here is what Nursi calls conjunction (iktiran), which is the emergence of two things together and the thinking that one cannot be without the other: that is, that when one goes so does the other, and thus a person is conditioned to think that one is the source of the other.[331]

Similar things can also be said about taste. For example, all fruits, from oranges to apples, are made of the same atoms. But the taste has nothing to do with the atoms in the fruits. That is, oxygen or hydrogen do not have a particular taste of their own, and water, which is a compound of these two elements, does not have an intermediate taste. Therefore, no one can predict the taste of an organic molecule by looking at the atoms

---

[330] Nursi, The Rays, Fourth Ray, 70–97.
[331] Nursi, Mesnevi-i Nuriye (İstanbul: Envar, 1996), 173.

in its structure. It appears that taste is also a meaning that reflects differently on different arrangement of atoms—yet independent of the atoms themselves—and the taste of a substance can only be known by experimenting. A chemist who comes across salt for the first time in his life can predict many chemical properties of the salt by examining its atomic structure. But he cannot say anything about its taste by simply examining the sodium and chlorine atoms that make up the salt, since taste is not rooted in matter; it rather reflects on matter.

## Diamond: Its Matter and Glitter

What the word 'diamond' brings into one's mind is not the material of it, but its lively colorful, enchanting glitter that flatters the eyes and hearts. In fact, the basic structural element of diamond is carbon, which is known by its matt black color, absorbing almost the entire light incident on it (and thus the black color). The reason behind the diamond's charm is not the value or the amount of its dense material, but its ability to take in a translucent world (the world of light) outside and to scatter its rays. Thus, the most precious diamond is not the largest and the heaviest one, but rather the one with the greatest clarity, purity, and perfection, and thus the one with the best light-scattering ability. That is, it is the diamond that exhibits the glitter of light best while remaining virtually invisible, to the point where someone who looks at the diamond sees only the array of fascinating beauty displayed by light, and does not notice its raw material, carbon.

Everyone knows that the source of a diamond's fascinating glitter is not its material, but the light that comes from an external source. That is, those captivating glitters are not emanating from the carbon atoms, the building blocks of diamonds, but from an external source like the sun or a lamp. This can easily be proved by taking the diamond into a dark room. It will be observed that all the glitter will disappear, and even the diamond itself can no longer be seen. It appears that what makes the diamond a diamond and gives the diamond its beauty, charm, and fascination is the light incident on it. A diamond without the light is like a dead corpse without the soul.

Attempting to explain that the source of light that seems to be coming off the diamond is something external may be stating the obvious and may even look ridiculous, since no one would claim otherwise. However, this simple observation is of great importance since it may serve as a ladder to climb to important phenomena that are hard to reach. To begin with, let us ask the following question: If there existed no darkness in the universe, and light sources such as the sun were not visible—that is, if there existed abundant light everywhere all the time—how would we explain the light constantly coming off the diamond, which would shine continually? Would we still easily say that the light comes from an external source that we cannot see, or would we claim that the source of those charming glitters is the diamond itself? Considering how shortsighted people are in general and how they take things at face value, the answer is not going to be easy this time. In this case, since we would not be aware of an all-encompassing spread-out light layer, we would claim that those glittering lights come from the diamond itself without a second thought, even if we did not understand how. And in so doing, we would have fallen into a deep illusion and would constantly struggle with dilemmas and deadlocks. For example, we would see that a single carbon atom (or a group of carbon atoms arranged as graphite) does not glitter, and would seek an answer to the fundamental question "How can a feature that does not exist in its basic structural elements exist in its whole?"

While some researchers examine the carbon atom in its finest detail and try to understand from where in the atom the light originates, others, who realize that the light-emitting diamond and non-emitting graphite differ not in the atoms but in their arrangement, would search for the secret of light in the bonds between the atoms rather than within the atoms themselves. And as evidence they would point to the variation of emitted light with the changes in the shape and cut of the diamond. In the end, many contradictory and confusing theories would be proposed, and while some theories would be rejected, others would be accepted, at least on a temporary basis, for lack of better ones. And these fundamentally wrong searches would be introduced as exact sciences, and those involved in these research projects as scientists. Any suggestions about searching for the origin of light outside the diamond would be judged false or unscientific by these researchers whose minds are curtailed by their eyesight, and would not be given any consideration. This prejudiced approach would build a wall on the path of the sciences rather than opening a pathway, and would block their progress. When we look at the history of science, we see that the greatest breakthroughs in the world of science have resulted when unorthodox approaches that run counter to the established ones have been taken—like Einstein's divesting himself of the hard rules of classical mechanics a century ago and proposing the theory of relativity.

In the light of the discussions above, we may express the diamond as follows: diamond = carbon + light. That is, what makes the diamond a diamond is light—more correctly, its ability to take in and scatter out light. It is interesting that the diamond's vicinity is also filled with light, but we do not even notice that all-encompassing but invisible being. It is present everywhere is space, but we can see light only via things like diamonds that receive and scatter it. Hence, it could be said that a substance made of carbon is diamond if it reflects light, and graphite otherwise. The most magnificent diamond is the one that reflects the light in the most fascinating way in accordance with the laws of optics. Therefore, in cutting and processing diamonds, the main factor taken into consideration is the light and the ability to reflect light. The first requirement for becoming a diamond craftsman is to know light and its characteristics well.

It appears that the reality of diamond and the secret behind its captivating glitter can only be understood when the presence of an all-encompassing world of light is noticed, and the diamond is viewed as a compatible composition of the worlds of carbon and light. This simple observation would play a key role in our trying to understand the true nature of beings, and deeply affect our perception of the environment and our understanding of creation. Light, which is an electromagnetic wave, serves as a good step toward understanding non-matter since matter is characterized by occupying space, and hundreds of electromagnetic waves (waves from cell phones, TV signals, radio waves) exist at the same point in space apparently without occupying space.

## The Body and the Spirit

The materialist philosophy views the human being, like all other beings, as a collection of different kinds of matter, and denies the existence of anything other than the nearly one hundred trillion cells that make up the human body. That is, in terms of basic building blocks, the human being is whatever a pile of soil is. The human being, like all other beings, consists of matter (or energy) only, and is subject to physical laws. This view also forms the foundation of the determinist philosophy. Upon decomposition of these cells after death and becoming part of the soil, a person ceases to exist.

Every difference between a live person and a dead one—life, seeing, hearing, consciousness, knowledge, free will, love, pain, pleasure, imagination, dreaming, individuality, greed, generosity, art appreciation, sense of justice, and the desire for immortality—is non-matter. The collection of all these non-material attributes that are beyond time and space is called meaning or the spirit. The materialist philosophy views these meanings as the outcomes of the manifestations of material interactions (whatever that means). Nursi, on the other hand, views meaning or the spirit as the kernel and essence of being, and matter as the shell or clothing. Death is simply the departure of this essence of human being from the body shell:

> In the course of life, the spirit gradually changes its body-clothes, and at the time of death, it is suddenly undressed. It has been established through certain conjecture, indeed, through observation, that the body subsists though the spirit.[332]

Those who view existence to consist of matter only and thus deny the existence of the spirit are also aware of the existence of a meaning that transcends the body and its non-material attributes. But they take the easy way out and give all the attributes of the spirit—such as to express preferences or to give orders—to the brain. Consequently, they are obliged to attach to the brain, which is no different materially from a piece of meat, a hard-to-comprehend, extraordinary status approaching divinity.

The brain is simply the control center of the human body—just as the pilot's cabin is the command center of the huge body of an airplane. All parts of an airplane are connected through wires to the pilot's cabin, like the network of nerves in the human body being connected to the brain, and they receive all the commands from there. But the thing that is in full command of the airplane and makes the necessary decisions is the pilot, who is not of the same kind as the cabin, and has attributes like conscious-

---

[332] Nursi, The Words, Twenty-Ninth Word, 535.

ness, sight, hearing, and free will, that do not exist in the material of the airplane. When pilots go on strike, all airplanes are still fully equipped with everything including the command center, but they remain grounded. Just as it is impossible to understand the true nature of a flying airplane by insisting on denying the existence of a pilot (or remote operator if remote-controlled) and attributing all wondrous acts to the command center in the pilot's cabin, so too it is impossible to understand the true nature of human beings by insisting on denying the existence of a spirit and attributing all extra-material wondrous traits like life, consciousness, imagination, sight, and free will to the material of the brain sealed in a dark thick shell.

The highest level that a human being, when viewed as something that consists of matter, can aspire to become is a highly advanced robot. A robot that is a technological wonder can walk, perform certain chores very well, take orders, and see its vicinity mechanically. It can even laugh loudly with a mechanical sound. But it cannot feel anything. Even if it is loaded with a library-full of knowledge, it cannot know anything, and it cannot be aware of what it is doing.

Even if a robot might have a state-of-the-art processor, it cannot have consciousness. It cannot suddenly be hit with ideas. It cannot love or get angry at other robots, and it cannot make plans to destroy the robots it does not like. A robot cannot enjoy the beauty of a flower, and cannot desire to see new places. It can play the best music and even do the job of an orchestra, but it can never know the joy of listening to a beautiful sound. It cannot show compassion by embracing a smaller robot. It cannot get a taste of the energy or the fuel it is consuming. It cannot feel pity for another robot and attempt to help it of its own accord. It cannot comprehend anything happening around itself; it cannot rejoice at good news and become sad at bad news. It cannot know what depression is. It cannot worry about becoming old someday and being taken to a robot cemetery to be discarded. It cannot know what longing for immortality is. It cannot think about the past and be concerned about the future. It cannot daydream or dream at night. It cannot laugh at funny things.

A robot can be loaded with a huge amount of information in a few minutes and can learn a foreign language in an instant, but it cannot enjoy learning new things, it cannot get amused, and it cannot perform a critique.

It cannot generate new knowledge and it cannot take the initiative so as to try new things for which it is not programmed. It can communicate with another robot, but it cannot carry on a casual conversation which is an enjoyable exchange of warm feelings—even if it has the most advanced electronic processor there is.

That is, a robot cannot have any features that make humans what they are. This is because none of these traits originates from matter. All the differences between a human being and a robot which is equipped with all the wondrous features of the human body are non-matter or meaning. And the entirety of all these meanings that transcend the body, just like the penetration of light into the diamond, is the spirit. The 1998 Nobel Physics Laureate Robert Laughlin expresses the meaning that transcends the body as follows:

> If a simple physical phenomenon can become effectively independent of the more fundamental laws from which it descends, so can we. I am carbon, but I need not have been. I have a meaning transcending the atoms from which I am made.[333]

Body subsists through the spirit, and it is the spirit that gives the body true value. The spirit is non-matter and thus beyond space and time, and as such it is not subject to any of the restrictions to which matter is subject, like the physical laws. The starting point for the understanding of the true nature of man will be the stripping off of the matter we are buried in, and the turning of our attention beyond matter.

## Conclusion

The source of the positive sciences is observation. In the fifth century BC, on the basis of simple observations, Empedocles stated that everything is made up of air, earth, water, and fire, and this theory dominated the sciences for many centuries. However, since the seventeenth century, re-questioning of the universe and the discovery of the elements have caused a serious leap in scientific advancement, and many new branches of sciences have emerged. Today, we know that everything is made up of a hundred or so elements, and every material thing can be expressed as a

---

[333] Robert Laughlin, *A Different Universe*, xv.

combination of those elements. This initiative has also resulted in the discovery of many chemical compounds and the development of modern chemistry.

The *idée fixe* of the modern scientific community is the deeply rooted preconceived notion that the source of everything is matter (or its equivalent energy), and this causes barriers and deadlocks in the sciences on the path of progress. The scientific community should recognize and openly declare that there are no such things as force, willpower, life, consciousness, sight, love, beauty, etc. in the basic building blocks of matter, regardless of whether they are particles or waves, and that something cannot exist in the whole if it is not present in its parts. It is about time the current, single-layered view of the universe as being made of matter or energy was seriously questioned, and a multi-layered view of the universe—that all beings consisting of numerous independent immaterial layers of force, willpower, life, consciousness, sight, love, beauty, etc. as well as matter or energy—was seriously considered. The proposed view is fully consistent with observations, which is the primary source of the sciences. The philosophical discussions of the sources of these layers are no different from the discussions of the source of matter and energy prior to the Big Bang. In ancient Greek philosophy, the sources of these layers were attributed to Gods such as Venus, Eros, and Hermes. For positive scientists, the approach can be akin to "Eat the grape and don't worry about the vineyard." To Nursi, the sources of all non-matter features can be the Divine Names or Attributes of God. Therefore, for the followers of Abrahamic tradition, to understand beings is to understand the Divine Names or the Holy Spirit, and thus to understand God.

Newton's questioning of the fall of an apple opened a new age in physics. The impact of the answers to the questions raised here will probably not be any less. It is hoped that articulate researchers who manage to divest themselves of prejudices and preconceived ideas entertained for hundreds of years will observe and show that the universe is not just one- or two-, but multi-layered. And only one of those layers is associated with matter, to which we are confined. Current discussions in scientific circles about multi-universes or multiverses are a step in the right direction.

The reality of diamond can be understood only when it is noticed that the origin of its glitter is a light source outside it and not the carbon atoms themselves or the bonds connecting them. The reality of television can be understood only when it is noticed that the origin of various channels of video and audio is the dozens of broadcasts surrounding the TV set, and not the TV set itself; that is, when it is realized that the television is only the receiver of the broadcasts, not the source of them. Likewise, the reality of beings, especially the human beings, will be understood only when it is realized that the origins of numerous immaterial glitters such as life, consciousness, art, and beauty that shine on matter are the numerous immaterial layers or parallel universes, and not the material universe itself that we know of. The approach of separating beings into their fundamental matter and non-matter layers and of putting things into their rightful places will provide a breakthrough in terms of scientific approach.

# Chapter 7

## Man's[334] Struggle with Mortality and His Quest for Rediscovering God: Finding Spirituality in Generation Y

*Mahsheed Ansari*

In the post-Enlightenment period, when God is long considered to be 'dead' and we are the ones claiming to have killed him,[335] mankind is still left unfulfilled in his battle with mortality. The search for meaning and purpose in life continues in Generation Y.[336] Even the *killing of death* has not resolved the battle with mortality.[337] In an era when his contemporaries were killing God, religion and even death itself, Bediüzzaman Said Nursi (1877–1960) emerged inimitably to defend belief, faith, religion, and God.

This essay closely examines the works of Said Nursi as a case study, and also as an example through which we can understand the practical,

---

[334] The word 'man' has been used to refer not only to adult males but also to human beings in general, regardless of gender. I have maintained the use of this term throughout for consistency; it is intended to include both males and females unless otherwise stated.

[335] P. Robert and F. Nietzsche, 'Nietzsche: Thus Spoke Zarathustra', *Cambridge Texts in the History of Philosophy* (Chicago, IL: University of Chicago Press, 2006), ix.

[336] Andrew Singleton, Michael Mason, and Ruth Webber, *Spirituality in Adolescence and Young Adulthood: A Method for a Qualitative Study* (Routledge).

[337] Joseph Jacobs, *The Dying of Death*. Jacobs talks about the practical disappearance of the thought of death as an influence directly bearing upon practical life. "There are no skeletons at our feasts nowadays" (1899-264). See also J. A. Walter, *The Revival of Death* (Routledge, 1994). Walter posits that 1700 books have been written on the topic of dying and death.

as well as the philosophical, dilemma that faces human kind: mortality and death. Human patterns of thought and behavior in the modern world will be examined in conjunction with Nursi's understanding of human nature and behavior as evidenced in his exegetical interpretation the *Risale-i Nur* (Treatise of Light). Nursi's unique methodology is evident in the *Risale-i Nur* as he uses both ontological reasoning and observations of the world and human life to solve the dilemma of mortality. Unlike his predecessors Saint Anselm of Canterbury in the eleventh century and René Descartes in the seventeenth century who sought to prove the existence of God ontologically,[338] Nursi believed that proving the existence of God was vital, since he believed that God is the answer to mortality. Nursi's onto-logical explanations of the existence of God are examined in this chapter with particular emphasis on the eleven aspects of Divine Unity from the Twentieth Letter. This essay will attempt to resolve this 'battle with mor-tality' that faces modern man, with a specific focus on Generation Y.

In the following discussion, I will first outline the definitional under-standing of Generation Y in order to delineate contemporary man's nature, essence and self. I will then discuss the relevant behaviorist theories that outline the essential needs and nature of humans in order to search for the current "prognosis" of the dilemma of mortality that faces man. The final section of the paper uses the methodology of behaviorist theorists as the basis for examining the eleven Aspects of Divine Unity in order to outline Nursi's ontological discussions of God—the Eternal *Al-Baqi* that he claims fills the existing gap in human nature.

## Defining Generation Y

In order to understand the context and the nature of "man's" struggles with mortality, a critical comprehension of Generation Y is necessary, in order to decipher contemporary man's struggles and problems. It is logi-cal to state that every generation is different in terms of the ways in which it sees the world and responds to it; each is raised in different his-torical, political, economic, cultural, and social circumstances. In this

---

[338] St Anselm (*c.*1033–1109), English philosopher and theologian, born in Italy, Archbishop of Canterbury 1093–1109. Feast day, April 21. See also 'St Anselm', *Stanford Encyclopedia of Philosophy*, September 2007.

chapter, 'Generation Y' is used widely to refer to those who were born in the period from the early 1980s to the early 1990s. The people of Generation Y are also known as Millennials, Echo Boomers, or the Backpack generation.[339] They are further defined demographically, and are influenced by or reside in Western cultures.[340]

Generation Y persons are often characterized as being 'demanding, impatient and bad at communicating'—a generation of 'individuals' who are mostly self-driven.[341] They have variety and choice available to them, and are exposed to a myriad organizations and spiritual disciplines, and to the world of the Internet.[342] Despite their easy access to technology and various electronic entertainments substituting for their social environment, Generation Y persons seemingly are still alone. Similar research conducted in Australia and America has described them as "directionless, lacking community ties and meaningful participation in communal life. They prefer informal, non-traditional methods of belief and fulfilment."[343]

Even though Nursi lived well before Generation Y, he understood that the 'killing of God' and religion had left man's conscience (*wijdan*) to search for a point of support and assistance in the face of his innumerable aims, wants, and needs.[344] However, Nursi maintained that it was a human being's inability and impotence, together with his nature (*fitrah*) and conscience (*wijdan*) in achieving these wants and innumerable needs, that makes him look to the necessarily Existent One for a solution.[345]

Overall, even though religion and faith are routes by which young people can find meaning and purpose in living and existence, the variety of prevalent opinions has resulted in religion becoming another item for sale in the market of spirituality. This lack of a clear concept of the Divine has arguably made the young people of Generation Y confused, estranged, detached, and lost. In addition, according to behavioral psychology, the

---

[339] Mark McCrindle, *Understanding Generation Y* (Australian Leadership Foundation, 2004), 55.

[340] Ibid., 55.

[341] Ibid.

[342] Ibid.

[343] Barbara Doherty, *Generation Y and Religion*, Dawn's Early Light, April 12 2005.

[344] Bediüzzaman Said Nursi (trans. Şükran Vahide), Thirty-Third Window of the Thirtieth Word, *The Words* (İstanbul: Sözler 1992).

[345] Ibid.

diagnosis of Generation Y would fall into the category of "identity crisis due to a lack of belonging." Subsequently, they have been left in a state of purgatory, aimless in their battle with mortality.

## Deconstructing Man in Generation Y

Emerging studies show that the young people of Generation Y are individually motivated and self-driven.[346] In order to understand man's condition further, it is important to deconstruct him on an individual basis and ascertain the modern characteristics of his nature.

In the world of modern man, his 'global village' has equipped him with the finest technology, and fingertip access to all types of information and knowledge (e.g. via the internet). He can easily contact close or distant relatives through various media; yet, even with his technological access and his opportunities, he is more bewildered, estranged, and lonely than ever before. This 'global village' has robbed him of his own village, and has parted him from his family and relatives—those who traditionally used to constitute the real sources of knowledge and wisdom.

Philip Hughes recognizes that the estrangement and individualization of our young people has come about as a result of a reduction in family size as well as through the systematic dissolving of the nuclear family. Focus and emphasis have thus been placed on the individual needs of a child rather than on the family as a whole. This change, he claims, has been one of the greatest contributors to the 'individualism' that pervades contemporary Western culture.[347]

Nursi affirms the individualization of our society, claiming that Western (when Western culture is referred to, it is understood that we are talking about modern culture) culture has made the modern man *khod bin* (self-centered) by placing emphasis on the 'self', which he claims has resulted in his inner world's demise:

> The man, who is entrapped in the self-centeredness of his soul, can in no way actualize such perfection and hence cannot attain happiness at all …

---

[346] Philip Hughes, *Putting Life Together: Findings from Australian Youth Spirituality Research* (Fairfield Press, 2007), 22.

[347] Ibid.

The reason is that such a man due to never ending demands and desires of his soul, becomes addicted to praise, glory and fame which he claims that he deserves for the deeds without realizing the Real agent that lies beyond all these achievements.[348]

Thus the reality of man's struggles in the modern world is an inner struggle. It is not just that he is left estranged and lonely in this 'global village'; his battle is also very internal, affecting his heart and mind.

## Psychological State of Generation Y

Man's inner struggle with mortality has taken a psychological turn in Generation Y. In today's world of Generation Y, consumerism has changed the patterns of social cohesion. A complex and excessively material lifestyle has replaced simplicity and modest living.[349] These simple mediums have been replaced by a mechanical revolution, which has dehumanized and depersonalized our world and living. Our simplicity has been tarnished by the confusion created by multifaceted and disproportionate amounts of advertising, media, entertainment, fast food outlets and other mediums which preoccupy minds and numb sensory, emotional, and cognitive faculties.[350]

Additionally, people are always in a dichotomous state of mind and are constantly waging an inner battle with their own selves. Individuals, therefore, find it more difficult to differentiate between delusion and reality when searching for meaning, purpose, and immortality. Thus, as a result of consumerism, the ties that bind society have changed drastically; we now deal more with machinery and technology than with humans.

In the midst of this disparity between the world and their selves, the young people of Generation Y want and need spiritual fulfillment that can be attained only through immortality. Channeling this innate need has been challenging in modern times, where the 'rational mind' has 'killed'

---

[348] Ibrahim M. Abu-Rabi, *Islam at the Crossroads: On the Life and thought of Bediüzzaman Said Nursi* (New York: State University of New York Press), 2003.

[349] McCrindle, *Understanding Generation Y*, 55.

[350] Ibid.

God[351] and killed 'death' itself; nevertheless, man is still left in a psychological state of confusion and uncertainty about his self and life. Being overwhelmed and surrounded by multiplicity, he is still seeking ways to satiate his most innate need—the need for immortality.

Dissatisfied man is seeking immortality through other avenues in his modern world. He seeks it through loved ones, children, a successful career, fame, power, money, or even material possessions. Thus modern man has killed God, but created many new gods for himself in order to fulfil his innate desire for a sense of belonging and attachment which is the essence of worship and love of God.

## Generation Y and Developed Patterns and Behaviors

One reason outlined for man's ongoing battle with mortality in the modern context of Generation Y is his inability to fulfill his need for immortality. Man's fundamental needs for *belonging*, *significance*, and *attachment* have also been left unfulfilled. As the behavior management theorist Albert Adler has written,[352] belonging, significance, and attachment are essential needs of human beings. Although people are naturally drawn to the good and adapt to naturally accepted norms, if these needs are not met, Adler states, people turn to the negative in order to satisfy all these needs.[353]

---

[351] P. Robert and F. Nietzsche, 'Nietzsche: Thus Spoke Zarathustra', ix. Nietzsche, Friedrich Wilhelm (1844–1900), German philosopher. He is known for repudiating Christianity's compassion for the weak, exalting the 'will to power,' and formulating the idea of the *Übermensch* (superman) who can rise above the restrictions of ordinary morality.

[352] Adler's 1912 book, *Über den nervösen Charakter* (The Neurotic Character), defines his earlier key ideas. He argued that human personality could be explained teleologically, separate strands dominated by the guiding purpose of the individual's unconscious self-ideal to convert feelings of inferiority to superiority (or rather completeness). The desires of the self-ideal were countered by social and ethical demands. If the corrective factors were disregarded and the individual overcompensated, an inferiority complex would occur, fostering the danger of the individual becoming egocentric, power-hungry and aggressive or worse. Common therapeutic tools include the use of humor, historical instances, and paradoxical injunctions. See also A. Adler (ed. H. L. and R. R. Ansbacher), *The Individual Psychology of Alfred Adler* (New York: Harper Torchbooks, 1956).

[353] Adler, A. *The Individual Psychology of Alfred Adler.*

We are living in times in which Generation Y children are raised in childcare centers that cannot care enough for them, and it will be so for generations yet to come. Babies are from a very early age often raised with minimal or no direct love, compassion, and emotion on the part of their mother and father. Thus, from an early age, the three essential needs, those for belonging, attachment, and significance, which are essential for the bonding of a child, are displaced and disrupted. As a result, children do not bond with their parents as they should.

Children growing up in these times can be deprived of learning from knowledge sources and bases; thus, in order to satisfy their essential needs for belonging, attachment, and significance they look for substitutes. Cyberspace has become increasingly attractive,[354] with many teenagers spending hours online, disconnecting themselves from their family and friends. Their time on the Internet leaves them with limited abilities to cope with meaningful relationships later in life, or leaves them open to unhealthy relationships.[355] Thus the socializing agents of the past generations are nonexistent, and there are gaps in the social education of children, which have left more and more families and individuals estranged from their communities, families, and their own selves.

Today, young people immerse themselves in the 'e-world' of cyberspace, the internet, Facebook, My Space, Twitter, and other virtual outlets of entertainment as they seek substitutes for the addressing of their real needs. This lack of direct nurturing from parents has resulted in babies losing their attachment to parents and finding, as behavior management theorist Albert Adler states, other and often negative substitutes in the form of drugs, alcohol, cults and gangs.

Many statistics show that Generation Y is also characterized by excessive alcohol consumption, and overuse of illegal drugs such as marijuana, meth-amphetamine and cocaine. Although these trends were also seen in Generation X, the numbers have accelerated in this generation, alongside an ever-increasing incident rate of self-harm behavior, suicide

---

[354] ezinearticles.com/?Teenagers,-Computers-and-Internet&id=304743
[355] youthdevelopment.suite101.com/article.cfm/teens_and_cyber_safety

attempts and deaths.[356] The USA has topped the list for drug abuse in a recent set of national statistics.[357]

These factors have added to their indifference toward the world around them, be it local or global. The excessive individualism of Generation Y is the main cause of this indifference to others, making issues such as Iraq and Afghanistan subject to a decision-making tool of merely political choice, with little or no regard afforded to the quantity of loss of human life (whether one or a million). Such issues would only be of concern to this generation if their personal interests were directly affected.

## Nursi on the Nature of Man

In this modern context, particularly that of Generation Y and its struggles, it is necessary to examine the nature of man from the perspective of Said Nursi in order to further comprehend man's real nature and his ultimate needs and wants ontologically, and in order to ascertain the reality of Generation Y, including their divergence from or concurrence with other generations.

Through the use of ontological reasoning, Nursi explains the *existence of the Divine being* in order to shed light on man's nature and his need for the immortal.[358] In presenting an argument for the existence of God in the Twentieth Letter, Nursi explains in a teleological fashion the evidence for order, ease, artistry, and design in nature, claiming that this necessarily points to the existence of an Eternally Existent One.[359]

It is evident from the *Risale-i Nur*'s logical explanations of nature and man that man's essence is his spirit and that man's spirit is immortal.[360] Suffice to say, Nursi makes a compelling argument, stating with evidence and proof that it is an innate faculty of human nature to seek and desire immortality.[361] Nursi further expounds, in a logical fashion, all the aspects

---

[356] Hughes, *Putting Life Together*, 27.

[357] Ibid.

[358] Ontological studies are the branch of metaphysics dealing with the nature of being. See also *Ontology: A Resource Guide for Philosophers*.

[359] Nursi, *The Letters* (Turkey: The Light Inc., 2002), 265.

[360] Nursi, *The Words*, 521.

[361] Covering the various compelling arguments is beyond the scope and capacity of this paper; however, some evidence will be briefly outlined. Said Nursi, in the

of man's nature. He says that from the perspective of the Divine, man is created and designed for eternity. Man's potential abilities and inner faculties point to and are designed for an eternal existence and realm. Therefore, God has endowed mankind with these eternal faculties and has made him vicegerent on earth by giving to him the supreme Trust.[362] Thus, man's inner faculties such as heart, mind, and spirit, as well as the subtle emotions of compassion, justice, and love, are all designed in such a way that their purposes will not be met in this ephemeral realm of temporary existence and therefore the meeting of them requires a permanent eternal abode:[363]

> The subtleties inscribed in the book of man's heart, the senses written down in the notebook of his intellect, the equipment contained in his essential character, are all turned towards Eternal Bliss they have been given to man and fashioned in accordance with this ultimate goal for example if one servant and illustrator of the intellect called 'the imaginative power' is told 'you can have a million years of life and rule over the world, but in the end you shall become nothing', it will react with sorrow instead of pleasure unless deemed by vain fancy and the interference of the soul. The greatest of transient things therefore cannot satisfy the smallest faculty of man. It is then this disposition of man, his desires extending to eternity his thoughts that embrace all his thoughts that embrace all of creation and his wishes that embrace the different varieties

---

Twenty-Ninth Word, examines four angles or sources and proves beyond doubt the immortality of the spirit. Firstly, Nursi proves subjectively and asks the reader to examine him- or herself to perceive the immortality of his or her own spirit, stating that in the course of occupying the body the spirit causes the body to change considerably, yet self-evidently remains constant. Thus Nursi claims that, although the body is ephemeral, it does not affect the spirit's permanence, nor spoil its nature, even though the spirit is completely naked at death. Secondly, Nursi proves objectively that it is a sort of empirical judgment which has been formed through repeated observations and numerous occurrences of events. Thus if a single spirit continues, all spirits must continue existence. So also is man's spirit a "commanding law" and the spirits of the dead too dwell in the Inner and Spirit Worlds. See Nursi (trans. ŞükranVahide), Twenty-Ninth Word, *The Words* (İstanbul: Sözler, 1992).

[362] Nursi, *Words*, 100.

[363] Ibid.

of eternal bliss that demonstrates he has been created for eternity. This world is like a hospice for him a waiting-room for the Hereafter.[364]

In the Third Flash, Nursi penetrates to the essence and core of man's nature and shows the real wants and needs of man, thereby providing a salve for his endless wounds arising from separation and ephemerality. Firstly, he asserts that man's nature connects him to all things; therefore, he harbors love for all things and suffers at their departure. Thus, uttering with conviction *Ya Baqi Antal Baqi* ("O The Enduring One, You are The Enduring One"), Nursi claims that this severs all attachments to transitory things and true love for an Eternal Being envelops in the human self.[365] This 'state' enables man to see the stamp of transitoriness on temporal beauties and loveliness, thus Nursi claims that when uttering and calling The Enduring One, man is reminded that if He exists, all exists! Further, Nursi asserts that human nature is created for intense love and again, through the faculty of imagination, he shows the need for immortality, and instructs the reader to see how immortality is sought in all the beloveds. Thus, if there were no imagined immortality, there would be no love for or praying for eternity.[366]

According to Nursi, man, who in composition is infinitely weak in essence and in meaning, is the fruit of the Tree of Creation and the reason for the creation of the mystery of life and existence; however, man seeks eternity because he is from the eternal. He wants, seeks, and yearns for eternity, but the reality of his mortality and the inevitability of death bring pain and no fulfillment to his essence and core.

As a result, man's complex and subtle inner abilities are left unused and paralyzed. Man's spirit, mind, and heart suffer from atrophy. Thus, as Nursi exclaims "expensive diamonds are traded for crystals made of glass."[367] These factors can bear some grounding in an understanding of Generation Y and its ontological characteristics.

[364] Ibid.
[365] Nursi (trans. Şükran Vahide), *The Flashes* (İstanbul: Sözler, 1992).
[366] Ibid., 29.
[367] Nursi, *Words*, 39.

## The Biggest Wound To have Afflicted Humanity

According to Nursi, the wound that has affected man has been brought about in the modern age by materialistic and postmodern philosophies. Materialist philosophies deny or misrepresent the immortality of man's spirit or soul, the angels, and the end of the world and the life of the Hereafter. As a result, no reasonable alternative solution or answer is provided to heal the wounds from which modern man has been suffering.

Materialism, the environment in which Generation Y is being nurtured, has a tendency to consider material possessions and physical comfort more important than spiritual values. Materialist philosophy is the doctrine that nothing exists except matter and its movements and modifications. It is also the doctrine that consciousness and will are wholly due to material agency.[368] It is from out of this mindset that philosophers like Friedrich Nietzsche, who claimed that "God is dead," made existentialist claims about religion and the nature of God.

Nietzsche's infamous statement "God is dead" is found in his book *Das fröhliche Wissenschaft* (The Gay Science), and later in *Also sprach Zarathustra* (Thus Spake Zarathustra), and the phrase has become very well-known. The idea is stated in the section of *Das fröhliche Wissenschaft* entitled 'The Madman' as follows:

> God is dead. God remains dead. And we have killed him. How shall we comfort ourselves, the murderers of all murderers? What was holiest and mightiest of all that the world has yet owned has bled to death under our knives: who will wipe this blood off us? What water is there for us to clean ourselves? What festivals of atonement, what sacred games shall we have to invent? Is not the greatness of this deed too great for us? Must we ourselves not become gods simply to appear worthy of it?[369]

This " killing of God," as Gabriel Vahanian argues in his book *The Death of God*, has made modern secular culture lose all sense of the sacred, so

---

[368] The philosopher Mary Midgley, among others, argues that materialism is a self-refuting idea, at least in its eliminative form. While some critics hold that matter is an ill-defined concept, it is not clear that substitutes, such as Spirit or Hegelian *Geist*, fare any better.

[369] Robert and Nietzsche. 'Nietzsche: Thus Spoke Zarathustra', ix.

that it is lacking any sense of the sacred meaning of the Divine, with no transcendental purpose or sense of Providence.[370] Vahanian concludes that for the modern mind "God is dead." Also, in Vahanian's vision, a transformed post-Christian and postmodern culture is needed in order to create a renewed experience of deity.[371] Generation Y finds itself amid this new trend in human experience, yet its search for meaning and understanding continues.

## An Answer to Materialists and Materialistic Philosophy

Nursi claims that materialist thought has stupefied everyone in this age. It has been able to plant doubts in their minds concerning even the most evident matters, such as the immortality of the spirit. Nursi is extremely confident and convincing in his approach to the immortality of the spirit. At the conclusion of the First Fundamental Point of the First Aim of the Twenty-Ninth Word, he explains the reality of the material life and the importance of the spirit and spirit-world, or the inner world of meanings. In direct response to materialist philosophies that give ultimate prominence to material existence and life,[372] Nursi responds that true living and life are not material, but rather of the spirit and inner world:

> As may be established empirically, matter is not essential so that existence may be made subject to it, and be dependent on it. Rather, matter subsists through a meaning, and that meaning is life, it is spirit. Also, as may be established through observation, matter is not the thing served so that everything may be ascribed to it. It is rather the servant; it renders service to the process of the perfection of a truth. And that truth is life. And the fundament of that truth is spirit.[373]

Nursi claims that "an eternal beauty requires an eternal admirer that will accompany that beauty, that perfection, that mercy on the endless road to eternity, it will be immortal."[374]

---

[370] Gabriel Vahanian, *The Death of God: The Culture of Our Post-Christian Era* (New York Times: Braziller, 1961).

[371] Ibid.

[372] Nursi, *Words*, 541.

[373] Ibid., 542.

[374] Nursi (trans. Şükran Vahide), *Traveling towards Eternity* (İstanbul: Mega Basim, 2003), 219.

Thus, materialist philosophy has reduced the noble composition of man in a reductionist way to mere matter; has replaced all the aims and sublime purposes of his life and his noble duty with the meeting only of certain economic and material aims and objectives; and has robbed man of his real identity as a vicegerent and trustee of God. Thus, as is stated in the *Risale-i Nur*, rather than helping man to reach his highest peak of perfection and state of being, modern materialist forces have cut off his only hope and true source of salvation, that is Almighty God, the necessarily existent and Eternal One.

As a result, man has, for the past few generations, lived in his lowest base (animal) self. His mind and intellect have been numbed and bamboozled by fast-paced technology and he has been preoccupied by the hypnotic and excessive advertisements that are thrown at him from every media outlet on a daily basis, leaving him in a hopeless state of paralysis. He is therefore lost, confused, bewildered, lonely, and deeply hurt. All his fine composition and inner faculties have long been dead. Thus the biggest dilemma of modern man, and in particular of Generation Y (this being one of the most affected groups), remains mortality, which he witnesses every day. He sees his loved ones dying, the death of plants, trees, and nature and the world, and finally, the death of his own self. This is very tormenting and is like a hell, as Nursi posits. Thus, the only cure and aid for wounded, sick, and lost man, according to Nursi, is the light of belief in God as a Supreme Being, alongside the high morals and purposes of religion that would give him hope, vision, purpose, meaning, and an answer to his perception of mortality, shedding immense light into his dark, desolate world.

## Rediscovering God through the Light of Belief

Accordingly, modern man and the estranged Generation Y should not be in a state of struggle. Ontologically and teleologically, Nursi has made a case for belief in God as "a salve to innumerable wounds caused to man by modern times and the tyranny of extreme philosophies."[375] Indeed, the modern world seems to be nurturing and breeding humans that are in a state of amnesia owing to a lack of belonging and identity, and to per-

---

[375] Ibid.

sonality disorders arising from a lack of direction in life and lack of under-standing of the reason for the existence of life. As a further exacerbation of the condition, the persons of Generation Y are constantly hurt by the torments of their living mind, heart, and intellect, the pain of separation, and, particularly mortality, and death.

The consequent option for this lonely, lost, confused and melancholy generation is a firm belief in the "Eternal Existent Being," and by recon-necting with Him and rediscovering this link they may be led to a newly founded immortality in God. Further, if faith is embedded in the intellect and affirmed by the heart and spirit, man can be reassured that he need not struggle with mortality or death. As Nursi states, "his own very spirit is immortal, which connects Him directly back to God."[376]

Agreeing with Nursi, Ali Ünal states that in a physical world, time and space create the thick walls of our worldly dungeon. If we remain con-fined within them, we can never find happiness or lead a happy life. We can find spiritual satisfaction only through belief in God Almighty and our aspiration to reach Him and thereby gain eternal happiness in the other world.[377] Ünal's notion of the worldly dungeon echoes the research con-ducted on Generation Y and its current realities, making his recommenda-tion of a "newly founded faith" an attractive alternative to the present reali-ty, thereby fulfilling Generation Y's quest for a meaningful existence.

Nursi also stresses the benefits and the fruits of belief in God:

> Belief in God is creation's highest aim and most sublime result, and humanity's most exalted rank is knowledge of Him. The most radi-ant happiness and sweetest bounty for jinn and humanity is love of God contained within knowledge of God. The human spirit's purest joy and the human heart's sheerest delight is spiritual ecstasy con-tained within love of God. All true happiness, pure joy, sweet boun-ties, and unclouded pleasures are contained within knowledge and love of God.[378]

---

[376] Nursi, *Words*, 533.

[377] Ali Ünal, 'Humanity between the fall and ascension', *Islam and contemporary Issues* (Turkey: The Light Inc., 2006), 130.

[378] Nursi, *Letters*, 265.

For man, being connected to a Creator—the Eternal One—draws out his anguish and pain, that arise from the realization of his mortality and finiteness. According to Nursi, man's intellect and rational thought become a source of torment for the individual through a realization and knowledge of his impotence, which expounds his dark world. Through the light and radiance of belief, man is illumined; his mind, heart and soul gain light from the Eternal Light. This radiance comes as a result of his belief, trust, and reliance in God. As he develops through the stages of his belief and climbs the stairs of witnessing, his essence is brought to peace as it feeds via the connection established directly to the source of The One and True Eternal God.

Nursi also outlined the believer's state of humanity and the benefits of belief, and also the state of humanity whilst in disbelief:

> People who do not recognize their Owner and discover their Master are miserable and bewildered. But those who do, and then take refuge in His Mercy and rely on His Power, see this desolate world transformed into a place of rest and felicity, a place of exchange for the Hereafter.[379]

Here Nursi is echoing the many difficulties he faced in his own lifetime, such as exile and torture, but nevertheless he remained defiant in his ego and extremely *mutawakkil* (trusting to and entreating God, and happy). Thus, by rediscovering God with sound reasoning and proofs to satisfy the bewildered mind, and by harnessing the strength of the truths of belief as outlined by Said Nursi in the Twentieth Letter, man may find cures and antidotes for the wounds of the heart and spirit. Mankind today, and in particular Generation Y, can gain true purpose and a meaningful existence, and can be elevated by realizing his sublime duty and real nature and thus finding true and everlasting happiness.

## Nursi Uncovers the Divine Remedies, Providing Quick Healing

As a result of the wound opened by materialist philosophies and the continual battles and struggles of man as evidenced in Generation Y, an

---

[379] Ibid.

urgent and rapid remedy is needed to heal the deep wounds of modern man, especially in his solitary battle with mortality and in his quest to find God.

Nursi, in the eleven aspects of the Twentieth Letter and the following phrase, provides direct cures and antidotes for the illnesses suffered by modern man. The aspects directly address man's condition, and positively meet his basic fundamental needs of *belonging, attachment,* and *significance,* with the good news arising from faith and belief:

> There is no god but God, He is One, One having no partner. His is the Kingdom and to Him belongs all praise; He alone gives life and makes to die; He is living and dies not; in His hand is all good. He is powerful over everything, and unto Him is the Homecoming.

In the First Station of the Twentieth Letter with its eleven phrases, Nursi makes affirmations pointing to the Divine Unity which carry glad tidings to modern man, and offer cures which each contain spiritual pleasure. Thus belief in God raises man to the presence of the Divine by giving him a place where he may belong (even if other belonging has been severed), an attachment to hold on to (other attachments have caused him pain), and significance, by making him addressee and vicegerent, raising him from his lowest base self (*khod bin*) *nafs ammarah* to the high station of *Khuda bin* (God-centered), making him a true human (*al-insan al-kamil*).

Nursi uncovers the mystery of mortality by emphasizing the need to know and connect to God. In these eleven phrases, he does not only directly address the fundamental needs of man for belonging, attachment, and significance, but beyond. He also addresses different *hals* or states of being; thus each phrase opens a window to the spirit, which Nursi claims is immortal, and brings it to a particular state, or reality, by connecting it to the Divine,[380] thus healing all the illnesses of the self. The eleven phrases are as follows:

1. With the phrase "There is no deity but God" (*La illaha illallah*) an inexhaustible source of help for the human spirit is provided. This mighty phrase thus acts like a 'connector' attaching man to a point of support, showing and making known the Creator to

[380] Nursi, *Words*, 561.

him.[381] It is meant to save the heart from desolation and the spirit from suffering through constant uplift and continual felicity, thereby meeting all three of the basic fundamental needs in this beginning phrase.

2.  With the phrases "He is One" and "One having no partner" (*Wahdahu*) an instant ability to focus and a state of unity are attained. This is most useful, especially for modern man, who suffers constantly from the many complexities of modern life that put him into a state of confusion. Nursi explains that this confusion, and an overwhelming feeling, occurs because man is connected to most species in the universe (*wahdahu*); this gives him refuge and delivers him from confusion with the assurance that God is One. For humanity this command resolves everything, for finding Him means that you obtain whatever you wish and are liberated from interminable indebtedness and innumerable fears.[382]

3.  Explaining 'His is the Kingdom' (*La Hu al-Mulk*), Nursi provides a correct understanding of the individual and the reality that all is owned, governed, and ruled by the Almighty One; thus, do "not think you own yourself."[383] This phrase saves you from being over-possessive. It also saves you from feeling dependent and reliant on others. As if assuring modern man directly, Nursi concedes that man should not suffer and worry aimlessly but should rely on the power and compassion of the One who owns everything, thus saving 'man' yet again from fear of poverty and indebtedness to others. By attaining trust in the Almighty, man gains immense freedom by relying on His power. As the behavior and choice theorist William Glazer emphasizes, freedom is another fundamental need of man,[384] which this phrase has met.

4.  With the phrase 'To Him belongs all praise' (*Wa lahu'l-hamd*) Nursi claims that God alone is deserving of praise, by connecting all praise and bounty to its Eternal Source. Knowledge of this

---

[381] Nursi, *Letters*, 265.

[382] Ibid.

[383] Ibid.

[384] On William Glazer see C. George Boeree, *Personality Theories: Alfred Adler and Others* (1965).

'inexhaustible treasury' that never ceases gives great joy to the spirit, and furthermore fulfills man's need for significance, survival, and love. By reflecting on this phrase man recognizes the true bestower of bounty and opens the doors to spiritual enjoyment and ecstasy.

5. With the phrase 'He alone gives life' (*Yuhyi*) Nursi again provides a sense of purpose and relief, knowing that life is from Him and that all its aims and results point to Him. It also brings relief from heavy responsibilities. We are told that life comes from Him. Only thus, by doing one's duty, is immortal life secured, a relief for the spirit and a source of great joy.

6. The announcement that God 'makes to die' (*Yumit*) answers one of the greatest dilemmas of humans—death. Nursi relates that death is not annihilation, non-existence or eternal separation from your beloved; rather, it is a discharge from the duties of this life, a change of abode from your transient home to your eternal one and a release from the burden of service to a place where you will be united with all friends, a door to union and everlasting happiness.[385] This announcement is the greatest news for the human soul that is tricked by a mind that it will be extinct upon death. It reassures man that his spirit is immortal and that thus his end will be also. This phrase alleviates the pains arising from death, loss, and separation.

7. As regards the phrase 'He is living and dies not,' while the last phrase gave light by exposing the real giver of death, this phrase further satisfies man's need for immortality, along with the phrase 'His Eternal life is free from any trace cessation or ephemeral worry or grieve at disappearance of the mirrors to the Divine for his manifestations and reflections are continuous thus this phrase relieves the spirit from pains of separation, the knowledge of "He never leaves" states when you find Him, you find everything'.[386]

8. The phrase 'in His hand is all good' (*bi-yadihil khayr*) again takes man from being *khod bin* (self-centered). Even while acknowl-

---

[385] Nursi, *Letters*, 266.
[386] Nursi, *Letters*, 267.

edging man's good actions and deeds, it puts him in his place and humbles him by assuring him that only God possesses all good things and guides man to good acts and deeds. This phrase also gives hope to man, by stating that all good acts will be recorded and presented like the seeds of last spring: as with these, so too with the results of your deeds.

9. The phrase 'He is powerful over everything' empowers a weak-spirited individual, who may feel powerless in the face of problems and overwhelmed at being misused by others exercising power over him.[387] It reminds him that anything is possible, and that it is as easy for the Divine Being to create the spring as to create a flower.

10. The phrase 'unto Him is the Homecoming' pronounces the reality that the end of all good, and of all aims and purposes in life, is God. By uttering *wa ilayh al-masir* modern man, who often lacks vision and foresight and who feels lost and aimless in the multiplicity of life, gains the good news that all things have their end in Him.[388] This phrase answers the sighs of man, who asks of his end and asks of his ultimate end. The answer given not only gives a vision and purpose, but a beautiful picture of a beautiful end assuring man that, at cessation of this temporary abode of examination and trial, he will be honored with an Eternal abode, and he will not go into nothingness and dissolution but will enter the peaceful presence of the Beautiful One without any veils. Thus man is designed for an abode of unity and not separation.[389]

11. Belief gives a conclusion to everything. Thus, whatever our life here, it has an end-result with a purpose, the conclusion being at the court of an All-Just One. Therefore true justice, forgiveness and all beautiful ends are with God, thereby giving closure to man's need for finality and foresight.

In this way, Nursi's eleven aspects of the Twentieth Letter address mankind's fundamental needs for belonging, attachment and significance,

---

[387] Ibid., 268.
[388] Ibid.
[389] Nursi, *Letters*, 269.

thus giving man an identity as the fruit of the Tree of Creation[390] and a significance as one 'created in the best of forms' and having an immortal spirit.[391] The eleven aspects, in fact, go beyond and address the subtle states of man and how they can be remedied. Thus man finds a remedy for his illness in misbelieving himself to be only mortal by discovering a true and affirmed belief in the Divine One of Reality, to whom "everything bears a sign pointing to the fact that He is One."[392]

Man reaffirms within himself that he belongs to the beautiful and merciful One and that through all things he is connected to Him. Finally, man receives a boost of self-empowerment, and gains significance, by knowing that he has been the 'trustee' and appointed vicegerent of the Almighty Creator.

The eleven aspects address the human selfhood or *ana* and man's need for immortality, establish Divine Existence and man's connectedness to God, and, finally, provide remedies for the psychological and emotional, behavioral, and spiritual illnesses of man.

## Conclusion

This essay has closely examined the works of Said Nursi as a case study, and also as an example, to understand the practical, as well as philosophical, dilemma that faces human kind: mortality and death. The human patterns of thought and behavior in the modern world were compared in some respects with Nursi's understanding of human nature and behavior drawn from his exegetical interpretation the *Risale-i Nur* (Treatise of Light).

Overall, the author attempted to raise awareness that man's innate, his deepest, need, and thus his happiness, is immortality. The discussion conceded that the very nature of man as observed in his patterns of behavior and multiple pursuits indicates the search for an enduring reality. By means of a special focus given to Generation Y and the complexity of this generation's 'global village' environment, the chapter attempted to high-

---

[390] Ibn Sina (980–1037), Persian physician, the most famous and influential philosopher-scientist of Islam. He was particularly noted for his contributions to the fields of Aristotelian philosophy and medicine.

[391] Nursi, *Words*, 319.

[392] Ali Bin Abi Talib.

light the fact that human beings continue to want permanence and to find answers to the deep questions within their hearts and minds. Via the case study treating *Risale-i Nur*, the chapter argued that life in its universal manifestation is indicative of an Enduring Creator. Man's answer, and his healing of the many ills of his self, can come about only through this one point of recourse, as Said Nursi affirms with a compelling argument in the Twentieth Letter.

Furthermore, the analysis of the behavior theorists such as Alfred Adler, in conjunction with the characteristic behaviors of Generation Y alert us to a gap arising in the emotional and psychological needs of our Generation Y and, evidently, the ensuing generations. The gap has increased more in this era, particularly, as mentioned above, owing to existentialists' theories and doubts about Divinity being more prevalent in the works of contemporary philosophers, which have shaped and are still influencing modern social modes of lifestyle and living.

Nursi not only displays an honest understanding of human nature in the current context as we know it: he also, further, demonstrates a true understanding of man's spiritual quest for an Eternal One, and makes a fine connection between the Creator and the Creation. Only with belief in God can the heart and mind settle to its serenity; therefore, the quest, remedy, answer and destination begin with the knowledge of His necessary existence across every generation, a reality which is especially acute for the bamboozled Generation Y.

# Chapter 8

## Nursi on the Problem of Theodicy

### Zeki Sarıtoprak

T he problem of evil is a question of whether reconciliation can be made between the Most Just God and the existence of evil in this world, a practice known as theodicy. This problem has occupied the minds of many, including Muslim philosophers and theologians. Where some Western philosophers have found difficulty reconciling a Just God with suffering in the world, a group of Muslim thinkers, namely the Mu'tazilites, denied any relationship between the creation of evil and God. On account of this approach, they claim that human beings are the creators of evil, not God. God, in their view, is exalted above being the Creator of evil. In mainstream Sunni theology, the problem is discussed on the basis of the Islamic understanding of God. Therefore, in order to understand the problem addressed by theodicy, it is necessary to elaborate on the Islamic concept of God, and some characteristics of human nature. The formulation of this problem goes as follows. God is all-powerful and all-loving; still, there is suffering. These two statements are apparently irreconcilable. In other words, the existence of evil is incompatible with the existence of an all-powerful God. I shall discuss this subject from an Islamic theological perspective, with special emphasis on examining Nursi's view on the subject and how he approaches the concept of suffering and Divine justice.

According to Muslim theologians, the statements that God is all-powerful and all-loving, and that there is suffering, are reconcilable and there is no contradiction between them. The seeming contradiction arises from a limited human perception of events rather than from their real aspect.

Human beings are by nature obsessed with appearances, are character-istically selfish, and look at an event and decide about its ugliness on the basis of their own judgments. Because of these characteristics of humans, their judgments about any event are, generally speaking, based on those aspects that concern them only. Elaborating on this quality of humans, Bediüzzaman Said Nursi says, "In fact, if the goal of the creation of any-thing relates to the human being as one, it relates to the Creator as one thousand."[393] In other words, for every creature, the Creator has thousands of goals; only one of these goals concerns the human being. Therefore, to judge only according to the aspect that concerns human beings may be considered a misjudgment. Similarly, the famous Sufi theologian and jurist Abu Hamid Muhammad al-Ghazali (d. 1111) coined the famous statement, "In the realm of possibility, there is none more beautiful than this realm." This statement of al-Ghazali would, almost six hundred years later, be related to the ideas of the German mathematician and philosopher Got-tfried Wilhelm Leibniz (d. 1716). Perhaps al-Ghazali built his idea on the Qur'anic verse which says, "Such is He, the Knower of the Unseen (of all that lies beyond sense-perception) and the witnessed (the sensed realm), the All-Glorious with irresistible might, the All-Compassionate: He Who makes excellent everything that He creates; and He originated the creation of humankind from clay ..." (Qur'an 32: 6–7). Most commentators on the Qur'an have elaborated on this verse. For example, the famous Ottoman commentator on the Qur'an Mahmud al-Alusi (d. 1854), in interpreting this verse, says the following: "The Almighty God beautified every creature of his creation. That is because every creature is brought together in the way which wisdom requires and is necessary for its good. That is why all crea-tures are beautiful. Although their level of beauty may differ, as the Qur'an relates, "Surely we [God] have created human [beings] of the best stat-ure" (Qur'an 95: 4).[394] In interpreting the Qur'anic verses 32: 6–7 Nursi says, "In everything, even in the things that appear as the ugliest, there is an aspect of real beauty."[395] He divides beauty into two: there are directly beautiful things and indirectly beautiful things. The indirectly beautiful

---

[393] Bediüzzaman Said Nursi, *Sözler* (Izmir: Isik, 2002), 302.
[394] Shihab al-Din Mahmud bin Abdillah al-Alusi, *Ruh al-Ma'ani*, ed. Mahir Habbush (Beirut: Ar-Risala, 2010), vol. 21, 137.
[395] Nursi, *Sözler*, 301–303.

things are those that are beautiful because of their results. Accordingly, some events are apparently ugly, but under that apparent curtain of ugliness there is amazing beauty and order.[396] According to these principles that Nursi presents, one should not make a judgment on the basis of the apparent aspects of events. For example, when one looks at apparently ugly, or harmful, events, one should think of the eventual positive results that may come from those events. In comparison to spring, winter is cold and unfavorable; however, when one thinks of the beautiful flowers of spring that lie underneath the snow of the winter, one can understand the beauty of the event, though it appears to be cold and unfavorable. This is true even for earthquakes or diseases, beneath which there may be blossoming spiritual flowers. Owing to a strong trust in the judgment of God, Sunni theologians did not find the existence of apparently ugly things problematic. Within Islamic theological discourse, however, the Mu'tazilites, who are known also as rationalist theologians, have elaborated on this subject.

It may be argued that one of the main reasons why the problem of evil has not been discussed extensively in the Sunni Islamic tradition lies in its understanding of God and its approach to the realm of creation. First of all, the realm of creation is a reflection of the Divine Names. God has ninety-nine Names, and even more are mentioned in the Qur'an. All events that occur are considered the reflections of these Divine Names. God intervenes in the realm of creation in every moment. There is no such idea in Islamic theology as "God has created the world to be a mechanism that takes care of itself." Every name of God has a different reflection in this realm. For example, the name Al-Qayyum (The Sustainer) is reflected in the sustainability of the universe. This is not to say that the universe is self-sustaining, but that it is sustained by God. For example, if there were to be even one second of absence of that Divine Name Al-Qayyum, there would be a collapse in the universe. Similarly, the Divine Name Al-Jamil (The Beautiful) is reflected in the beauty of creation. Even so, the beauty of any part of creation is only like a drop of water in the ocean of the Divine Beauty. The Name Ash-Shafi means "The Healer," but to heal requires sickness or disease. Even apparently ugly things like disease become a reflection of the Divine Name, so that healing may occur. Thus all the Names of God can be seen in the visible realm through contemplation of their

---

[396] Ibid.

reflections. The Qur'an encourages people to contemplate the reflection of the Divine Names.

In Islamic theology, God has power over everything. There is no such thing as the realm of creation not being under the control of God. Scholars such as Harold Kushner, author of the book *When Bad Things Happen to Good People*, claim that God is not all-powerful. God wishes to intervene, but "His hands are tied." Kushner expresses his main idea as follows: "If we can bring ourselves to acknowledge that there are some things that God does not control, many good things become possible."[397] From an Islamic theological perspective such an understanding of God is problematic, because nothing can be outside the control of God. Although God is in control of everything, God leaves something to the free will of human beings. A Qur'anic verse says, "And that human has only that for which he labors" (Qur'an 53: 39). This verse clearly indicates the importance of human action as a reason for some things coming into existence, and such an action, from an Islamic theological perspective, is an act of prayer. If one wants to have a harvest, one must sow seeds. Without the sowing of seeds, expecting a harvest from God is going against the Divine will and rules because God's dealings with the realm of humanity is through the realm of causality. Causes are parts of the Divine law in the realm of creation. They should not be considered the real maker, because the real maker is God; but also they should not be omitted, because they represent steps necessary for the existence of things. The analogy of light may help here. When we enter a room in order to turn off the light we need to flip the light switch. If we do not flip the switch the darkness will continue, but the mere flipping of the switch cannot be considered the only cause of the light in the room. In order to have the light we need the electrical system of the building, and even the hydro-electric system of the state, and perhaps of the country. Without all of these, that light cannot exist in that room. It is true that without the switch being flipped the light will not come, but flipping the switch is not the main cause of the light.

According to this analogy, human beings are responsible for their actions, and in order to receive positive things they need to act, but their action represents only one step in the reception of positive things in this

---

[397] Harold Kushner, *When Bad Things Happen to Good People* (New York, NY: Harper Collins, 1981), 45.

realm. Therefore, if God wishes to intervene no one can prevent God's intervention. According to Islamic theology, God occasionally halts the law of nature for the sake of proving the truthfulness of His Messengers. This is what is called the miracles of the Prophets. Other than these extraordinary, exceptional cases, the Divine laws in nature are unchangeable and human beings are required to follow these laws. For example, pollution may cause the destruction of nature, and the destruction of nature may bring about some disasters which result in the suffering of human beings. We may know the reason for the suffering in some cases, but in many cases we may not be able to know. That is to say, there are in the sight of God many reasons that human capacity may not be able to grasp, and therefore, without us knowing those reasons, any judgment we might make about calamities and unfavorable events would be inaccurate. The general principle of Islamic theology maintains that everything is under the control of God. If God wishes, He can stop a storm in the entire ocean with the prayer of one child. Sometimes He does.

A major departure from the Islamic theological approach came with some philosophers, such as Pierre Bayle (d. 1706), who, discerning suffering in the Creation, thought that this was a sign of a lack of justice in the universe. Leibniz's response to Bayle is much more compatible with mainstream Islamic teachings: he claimed that evil things and suffering on earth and the justice of God may be reconciled. As Leibniz responded to these Western philosophers, so too did Sunni philosophers respond to claims that God is not a God of justice. Whatever God creates is beautiful. There is an overwhelming concept of justice in this world, but in the Islamic understanding this world and the other world complement each other. So, if something is not finished in this world it does not mean that there is no justice. Said Nursi invoked this principle as evidence for the existence of the afterlife. His argument is that since God is the Most Just and there is a remarkable balance happening within the universe, some criminals who die before receiving their sentences or punishment will be punished in the afterlife as a result of their worldly criminal actions. This is not because God cannot fulfill justice on earth, but because God wishes to postpone something for the afterlife. For God this life and the afterlife are not separate things, because for God, time is not. God is timeless; yesterday, today, and tomorrow are the same. Theologically speaking, there is not any doubt about the justice and the power of God.

Both the holy texts of Islamic and those of Christianity are in agreement that the realm of creation, being created by God, is beautiful. "God saw everything that God had made, and, behold, it was very good" (Genesis 1: 32). Similarly, the Qur'anic verse says, "He makes excellent everything that he creates" (32: 7). In the following, I shall elaborate on this beauty and on how apparent ugliness may be perceived in Muslim theology. Since my approach will be from an Islamic perspective, I will not go into the details of Western thought on the subject.

Etymologically, the word 'theodicy' is made up of two Greek words, 'theos,' which means God, and 'dike,' which means justice. The word 'theodicy' literally means 'the justice of God.' The term was originally coined by Gottfried Wilhelm Leibniz. Before Leibniz, the Muslim Mu'tazilites, in order to reconcile God and the existence of evil, established the principle of justice as one of their major doctrines, claiming that to do what is best for people is compulsory for God. In other words, God *must* do what is best for people. The Sunni tradition, by contrast, does not accept any way of indicating that there is anything that it is compulsory for God to do. God always does what is good and best, but to say God *must* do, in the Sunni tradition, is to limit and confine the power of God by laying upon God certain requirements. In the Sunni understanding, God is utterly above being compelled to do anything.

A verse of the Qur'an gives a hint of the Sunni tradition's approach to the subject of theodicy. The verse says, "It may well be that you dislike a thing but it is good for you, and it may well be that you like a thing but it is bad for you" (2: 216). This verse suggests that every event has two phases. One is the appearance phase, which may sound evil but in reality may not be evil. The other phase is the unseen aspect which shows the reality of the event. Therefore Sunni scholars have coined the saying "The creation of evil is not evil, but the acquisition of evil is evil." In other words, the entire creation of God is good and beautiful. It becomes evil for individuals when they misuse or distort it.

The Islamic concept of God differs considerably from many Western philosophers' perspectives on God. In Islamic theology, God sees, knows, and controls everything at every moment. As human beings, we are unable to understand and encompass God's nature and His Attributes thoroughly, because God does not look like anything in the world of creation. "There is nothing whatever like Him" (Qur'an 42: 11). His existence is demonstrated through the Qur'an and the created world of nature. The Prophet himself, who is the closest to God, in his supplications frequently would say, "Lord, we have not known you as you deserve." Muslim theologians and mystics would say the same of the Prophet. Our understanding of God, then, is incomplete. We know God through God's actions in the realm of creation. God is the Creator (*Al-Khaliq*) and the Sustainer (*Al-Qayyum*). The Qur'anic verse says, "God, there is no God but Him. The Most Living, the Eternal, neither slumber nor sleep overtakes Him. Unto Him belongs whatsoever is in the heavens and whatsoever is on the Earth" (2: 255). As is mentioned above, the Qur'an presents natural phenomenon as reflections of the Divine Names. It also presents some natural disasters as punishments for certain actions of human beings. The relationship between human beings and God is the relationship between the Creator and the created. The duty of the created is to worship and show thankfulness and pray to the creator constantly. According to the Qur'anic narrations, many nations have passed and those who have denied God's existence and disobeyed Him were punished for those behaviors. The events that the Qur'an mentions by name as punishments for certain nations are known. For example, the Qur'an narrates the story of the owner of a garden who woke early to harvest his fruits because he did not want to share his produce with the poor. His garden was subsequently destroyed by a fire (68: 17–27). The Qur'an also speaks of the stories of historical nations such as Aad and Thamud which also did not listen to their Prophets and were punished (51: 41–45). It also speaks of the people of Noah, who denied Noah and were punished (11: 36–54). The main characteristic of those people who were punished in the past was that they denied the signs of God. Although in the Qur'an we see that God punishes people for their denial of God's message, God is also the Most Compassionate and Most Merciful. Owing to God's compassion and mercy, many punishments are postponed until the afterlife. In the afterlife, God chooses whether to forgive wrongdoers or uphold these punishments. A Qur'anic verse says, "If God were to take people to task for whatever wrong they commit (and accumulate to their account), He would not leave on earth any living creature. But He grants them respite to a term appointed (by Him). When the end of their term falls (He treats each as He wills, according to his just deserts), for surely He sees His servants well" (35: 45). Therefore God is the Most Just and at the same time the Most Compassionate.

Some calamities are warded off because of the prayers of believers. The Qur'anic verse says, "My Lord would not care for you were it not for your prayer" (25: 77) Therefore, it is the duty of believers to supplicate God and to ask God forgiveness for their mistakes. Prayer has a great effect on the delaying of calamities. In Islam there is great space for prayer, not only five daily prayers, but constant prayer while walking, driving, and sleeping. There are certain prayers for each. Prayer can stop the consequences of evil actions. Therefore, in the mornings and in the evenings, the Prophet used to make certain supplications and prayers, besides the required daily prayers. One of the prayers is the prayer of Job in the Qur'an. Job says, "Lord, calamity has touched me and you are the most merciful of the merciful" (21: 83) One may ask God's mercy regarding any calamity or disaster or one may repeat the prayer of Jonah, who left his community out of fear that calamity would come upon him. Apparently this was against the Divine will, so he prayed, "There is no deity but You, O God, you are exalted. I was among the wrongdoers" (21: 87). The Prophet of Islam used to say the following prayer in the mornings and the evenings: "In the name of God, who, through His name, nothing can harm on earth or in heavens, and He is the One who hears everything and knows everything." Prayer is essential for human beings in making communication with God and in confessing their weaknesses and their vulnerability to calamities.

Human beings may know the causes of certain calamities, but there may be many calamities and disasters whose causes are known only to God. Because of this, there may be some events known as calamities, but which are actually aimed not as punishment, but as aids to people's development, either spiritually or materially. It is an over-quick decision to interpret every calamity as a punishment. If the main reason is not known, the doors to various interpretations are open. Calamities upon individuals, societies, nations, and regions may all have different reasons and causes. Theologically speaking, if a calamity is considered a punishment for certain criminal actions, in this case it is comparable to a government's decision to punish a person who has committed a crime against society or the government. Let us think of a criminal who has killed many people. To capture such a criminal, the government makes certain efforts and takes certain measures, but these measures may also negatively affect some innocents. In order to do justice for those innocents, the government compensates their suffering and eventually it captures the criminal. Theologically speaking, when calamities come, if they are aimed at punishing certain criminals who have committed crimes against the Divine, humanity, or the realm of nature, many innocents may also suffer as a result of those calamities. The compensation that they will receive in the afterlife is so great that their suffering becomes nothing in comparison to that compensation.

According to Nursi, God is the only creator. In Nursi's own terms, "God did not create the universe based on the engineering of human beings' small minds." Nursi argues that God's creation looks on the entire result and not on individual results. Since the creation is not evil, even if some event appears evil, as human beings we construe the event as an evil for ourselves because of our misuse of free will. Here Nursi gives the example of fire or rain. Fire is, essentially, good; we use it for heating, cooking, and many other things. But fire can burn someone's house or someone's body. For that person it becomes evil, but in essence it is good. Similarly rain, essentially, is good, but if someone leaves his windows open and his house is flooded, that person construes rain as being for himself evil, although it is not in essence evil.

In a different argument, Nursi uses the Qur'anic concept of the test. The Qur'an clearly states that human beings will be tested. The verse says, "We will certainly test you with something of fear and hunger, and loss of wealth and lives and fruits (earnings); but give glad tidings to the persevering and patient" (2: 155). Another Qur'anic verse says, "He Who has created death and life, so that He may try you (and demonstrate to yourselves) which of you is better in deeds. And He is the All-Glorious with irresistible might (Whose will none can frustrate), the All-Forgiving (Who forgives many of His servants' sins so that they learn from being tested)" (67: 2). As these two verses clearly indicate, in the Qur'anic language life is a test, and when people remain patient they will receive a great reward for every calamity or suffering that they face. For those who are criminals, the suffering is a mere punishment, but those who are innocents and are affected by such calamities and sufferings will be greatly honored in the afterlife. To clarify this further an analogy may help. If someone comes to you and takes your ten dollars and gives you one million dollars in return, you would be considered lucky rather than a loser. Similarly, when someone's house is destroyed in a disaster, if this person is innocent, according to the Islamic theological perspective they will receive a palace in Paradise which will be better than this house—probably more than a million times better. Again, this is because in the Islamic teaching nothing is lost forever; everything is calculated and accounted for. Through such a test, human beings' patience and trust in God are put on trial. If people are successful in this, their reward will be doubled. Also, such a test increases people's spiritual capacity. For example, some events wake people up from certain lazy and monotonous lifestyles. Here Nursi gives the example of two birds, an eagle and a sparrow. The eagle attacks the sparrow and the sparrow is thus able to improve its capacity for survival. So the attempts of the eagle to attack the sparrow help with the development of the sparrow's capacities. Similarly, illnesses or sicknesses may attack human beings, but all these trials help with the development of their various capacities, particularly their spiritual development if not always their physical development. Disasters or sickness, then, may sound bad or ugly, but in reality there are some beautiful results in the end.

Also, in Islamic teaching, in this life people work hard to gain eternal bliss. The Prophet of Islam uses the term "farm" for this world. Therefore when people encounter certain calamities and sicknesses they can imagine that God will reward them for this, and that their afterlife will be much better. God knows people better than people do, and it is the duty of human beings to trust in God, to be patient, and to be pleased with whatever God decides. Fighting against God is meaningless according to Islamic teaching and is also a transgression against the Divine will. Nursi says, "it is like fighting with a broken arm," which would only make the arm worse.

The Divine plan is always good. Whatever God creates is good. His creation is inclusive and encompassing. In Islamic theology, God is the Most Compassionate, the Most Merciful. This Qur'anic verse clearly states that God does not do wrong to any of His creation. Whatever he does is just. "And it has never been the way of your Lord to destroy the townships unjustly while their people were righteous, dedicated to continuous self-reform and setting things right in the society" (11:117). That is to say, if the number of people who are acting for justice and righteousness is considerably greater than the number of those who are acting to destroy and bring evil, then according to the Divine principle that town, in the sight of God, does not deserve to be destroyed. Therefore, in such cases God's mercy encompasses everyone. Because the town is not destroyed, those who are denying God also benefit from the Divine mercy. Their physical body survives because of God's provisions—water, food, etc. To enlarge upon this analogy, one may think of our planet as a global village for humanity. If all people on earth deny God, there is no longer meaning in the rotation of the planet around the sun, a movement designed by the Divine to subjugate the planet of Earth to human beings for their benefit. In this respect the Earth can be compared to a factory, whose existence the owner will no longer maintain when it ceases to produce any product that he regards as satisfactory in meeting the purpose for which it was designed. He will replace the factory with something else. Similarly, according to Nursi, this entire planet is working as a Divine factory, in which human beings are the most valuable workers. The products of this factory are thankfulness (*shukr*), praise (*hamd*), and exaltation (*tasbih*). If these products are not produced by the workers and the factory, the Owner will have no reason to maintain the factory and will replace it with another one. That is why it has been accepted as a principle in Islamic theology that a general calamity comes as a result of a general mistake. In conclusion, one can argue that according to Nursi's understanding, what we see as calamities are not always negative, and may contribute to positive results that change the ugly aspect of the disasters. Since God is the Most Just, and never does wrong to His creatures, whatever is seen as apparently ugly or unjust is far from reflecting the reality of their own events. The realities of the events are connected through thousands of purposes to the Divine, and they are all beautiful and just. Therefore, when human beings make judgments about certain events, it is necessary to look at the event in all its aspects, and not just look at those aspects which concern human beings.

# Chapter 9

# Nursian Perspective on Social Change: Top Down or Bottom Up?

*Hasan Hörküç*

S aid Nursi does not present any "normative" picture of Islamic society. He discusses in detail only those problems which seemed important from his moral point of view and which related to the time in which he lived, the rest being covered by powerful general statements. Perhaps here we can see another parallel between Nursi's *Risale-i Nur* and the scriptures upon which Nursi modelled himself. As far as society is concerned, the Qur'an deals in generalizations. It does this because the question of social structure is tied to time and place, and what is suitable for seventh-century Arabs will not be suitable for twenty-first-century urban dwellers. In modelling himself on the Qur'an, Nursi may have been taking this into consideration.

The first section of this chapter attempts to unfold an understanding of Nursi which holds that each age has particular social and moral needs, and emphasizes Nursi's views as to the importance of the individual's interpreting the Qur'an in this regard, since for him a morally based, humane society should consist of self-aware individuals. The section takes a closer look at Nursi's understanding of the individual, society, and the "collective personality", and discusses whether individualism or personal relations strengthen the collective personality. The second section deals with Nursi's conception of social change. It discusses the moral principles and values that Nursi upheld in his attempt to found a humane society—respect, love, sincerity, compassion, and communal brotherhood—in order to evaluate the phenomenon of social change based on a culture of belief.

I shall also briefly review issues relating to social change in order to establish whether, in the understanding of Nursi, Islam is a universal panacea or not. I will also seek to clarify whether the Nursian way of thought tackles particular issues individually, and therefore whether its formula is descriptive or prescriptive, and whether change in Islam comes from the top or the bottom. Herein lies the key difference between Nursi and his contemporaries. While Nursi was of the opinion that society evolves from individuals, his contemporaries were involved with revolutionizing and radicalizing the masses.

## Social Change: Top Down or Bottom Up?

To evaluate the phenomenon of social change, it is necessary to relate it to the time in which it takes place and the source on which it is based. Social change is a process which operates over time. Living as he was in a modern age in which scientific advances and developments promoted nihilistic and modernistic ideas, according to which there is no longer a need for God and religion in social life, Nursi advocates Islamic principles as being the only solution to the problems of social life: a solution which, unlike other religious scriptures at the time, properly takes into account scientific advances.[398]

In many places in his writings, Nursi emphasizes the differing needs of the time. According to Mardin, "In the most general sense, Said Nursi is aware that his time, the time of modernity, bears a special mark. He sees the three concepts which characterize these times as *malikiyet* (private property), *serbestiyet* (freedom), and the growth of science."[399] This influences all his interpretations of the Qur'anic verses, including his decision to abandon the classical method of verse-by-verse (atomic) exegesis in favor of a thematic interpretation of the Qur'an using selected verses to explore his diagnosis. Nursi points out that each age has par-

---

[398] See and compare with Ibrahim Ozdemir, 'A Study of the Views of Bediüzzaman Said Nursi and J. P. Sartre on Existence and Man,' in *Fifth International Symposium on Bediüzzaman Said Nursi, The Qur'anic View of Man, According to the Risale-i Nur* (İstanbul: Sözler, 2000).

[399] Serif Mardin, *Religion and Social Change in Modern Turkey: The Case of Bediüzzaman Said Nursi*, ed. Said Amir Arjomand (Albany: State University of New York Press, 1989), 172.

ticular needs and characteristics and that Qur'anic knowledge includes all these needs. According to Nursi, in this age of neglect misfortune has changed its form and affected religion and one's involvement with religion.[400] It was therefore his main goal to maintain the healthy state of people and society in this world. Religiously based moral conduct is the issue with which he deals throughout his interpretation.

It is important to note Nursi's pluralistic approach to interpretation in order to grasp the issue of social change.[401] According to Nursi, there is not just one truth: understandings of truth may be many, and can take different forms according to time and place. According to Nursi even sacred laws change over time. Indeed, in one age different Prophets may, and have, come. There have even been different Prophets and laws in the same continent in the same century.[402] In this context, Nursi's approach to interpretation is, according to Voll, pluralistic. Voll writes: "In terms of Qur'anic commentary, Said Nursi argues that the verses of the Qur'an reflect the vastness of God's message and depths of meanings." In addition:

> As the Qur'an of Miraculous Exposition expresses truths through its explicit, clear meanings and senses, so it expresses many allusive

---

[400] See Bediüzzaman Said Nursi, *The Flashes* (trans. Şükran Vahide) (İstanbul: Sözler, 1995), 27.

[401] Just to mention here that during the past decade, pluralism has been one of the most contemporary issues among the Islamic reformers, among whom are Abdolkarim Soroush, Mohsen Kadivar, Ayatollah Muhammad Mojtahed-Shabestari in Iran, Sheikh Rashid Ghannouchi from Tunisia, and Fethullah Gülen of Turkey, whereas Nursi dealt with the issue nearly a century ago, at the beginning of the 20th century. For more information on Nursi's discourse on pluralism, see Hasan Hörküç, 'New Muslim Discourses on Pluralism in the Postmodern Age: Nursi on Religious Pluralism, and Tolerance,' *American Journal of Islamic Social Sciences* 19, no. 2 (Spring, 2002). Also see Hasan Hörküç, 'Reconsidering Islamic Pluralism in the Contemporary World,' *Fountain*, April–June 2003.

[402] However, it is worth mentioning here that according to Nursi, with the coming of the Prophet of the end of time, man as it were advanced to the stage at which all the human peoples could receive a single lesson and listen to a single teacher and act in accordance with a single law. He considered that no need remained for different laws, neither was there a necessity for different teachers. However, he also states that, because human beings were not all at exactly the same level and did not proceed via the same sort of social life, the schools of Islamic law became numerous. For this and more see Bediüzzaman Said Nursi, *The Words* (trans. Şükran Vahide) (İstanbul: Sözler, 1992), 500–501.

meanings through its styles and forms. Each of its verses contains numerous levels of meanings. Since the Qur'an proceeds from all-encompassing knowledge, all its meanings may be intended. It cannot be restricted to one or two meanings like man's speech, the product of his limited mind and individual will. It is because of this that innumerable truths contained in the Qur'an's verses have been expounded by Qur'anic commentators, and there are many more which have not been expounded by them.[403]

Therefore, according to Voll, "This openness to many different levels of understanding reflects a pluralism that is not a relativist position, but rather emphasizes the importance of the role of the individual in the interpretation."[404] Elsewhere, Nursi argues that the phrases of the Qur'an are not restricted to a single meaning; rather, since the Qur'an addresses all levels of mankind, its phrases are like universals or wholes which comprise meanings for each level. Every Qur'anic commentator, every adept, mentions one part of the whole.[405]

In short, Nursi was of the opinion that Islam needs to be rethought in accordance with the needs of the age, and the Qur'an needs to be reinterpreted according to the spiritual and moral needs of man. In his understanding, this necessitated the writing of the *Risale-i Nur* and the reforming of society, starting with individuals. Thus, faith-based morality stemming from individuals was Nursi's main concern. According to Nursi, the moral society is predicated on the evolution and growth of belief among its members.

---

[403] As quoted in John Obert Voll, 'Renewal and Reformation in the Mid-Twentieth Century: Bediüzzaman Said Nursi and Religion in the 1950s,' *The Muslim World* 89, nos 3–4 (1999): 255–56. In this respect Nursi states elsewhere that time is a great interpreter; if it determines its limits, it cannot be gainsaid. That is, when a matter becomes clear in the course of time, one cannot object to it. Moreover, if the judgment is based on derived evidence, the source of the derivation shows the reason for the judgment. As quoted in Thomas S. J. Michel, 'Muslim–Christian Dialogue and Co-operation in the Thought of Bediüzzaman Said Nursi,' in *A Contemporary Approach Towards Understanding the Qur'an: The Example of Risale-i Nur* (İstanbul: Sözler, 1998), 559.

[404] Voll, 'Renewal and Reformation in the Mid-Twentieth Century,' 256.

[405] See Bediüzzaman Said Nursi, *The Letters* (trans. Şükran Vahide) , second (revised) edn (İstanbul: Sözler, 1997), 386.

Nursi believed that, at this time, duties in three areas—belief and religion, social life and the *Sharia*, and public law and Islamic politics—were all in need of a renewer of great stature. But for him the most important thing was to conserve individuals' belief. He believed also that the *Risale-i Nur* itself had been given the duty of renewing belief and preserving society from distractions: that is, of fulfilling the first of the three sets of duties.[406]

Before turning to Nursi's understanding of the individual, society and social change, it should be mentioned here that Nursi claimed that the only formula for the social and scientific, and the material and spiritual, progress of the East (of which Islam was a part) was not philosophy (negative) or reason (atheistic), but the heart and religion. In his view negative philosophy and reason, which have been a tool for irreligion, do not embrace all of humanity, but look to material needs.[407] Religion, however, with its universal principles, can satisfy man's desires, which stretch to eternity. The need of people for religion is, Nursi thought, greater than their material needs, which consist of their livelihoods.[408]

---

[406] See Şükran Vahide, *The Author of the Risale-i Nur: Bediüzzaman Said Nursi* (İstanbul: Sözler, 1992), 258–60.

[407] See and compare with Hassan Hanafi, 'The Origin of Modern Conservatism and Islamic Fundamentalism,' in *Islamic Dilemmas: Reformers, Nationalists and Industrialization the Southern Shore of the Mediterranean*, ed. Ernest Gellner (New York: Mouton, 1985), 100–2. Many philosophers make declarations about the so-called 'decline of the West', describe the phenomenon, attest to it and warn against it. According to Hanafi, such ideas as Sheler's reversing of values, Husserl's bankruptcy of soul, Nietzsche's, Heidegger's, Sartre's total nothingness and Bergson's matter creator of God (which are some nihilistic ideas) have their conservatist and spiritual philosophies reacting to this in the Muslim world as 'inside' witnesses from the West. See and compare this with 'Why Did the Great Promise Fail?', together with 'The End of an Illusion', Fromm, *To Have or to Be*, 11–17. Contemporary psychology has finally started to consider a new inspiration, something of a 'Freud is Dead movement'. According to Braden, led by Abraham Maslow a new group of psychologists defines Freudian psychology as preoccupied with pathology; it is primarily a sick psychology, or a psychology of sickness. See, for this and more, in 'Humanistic Psychology' William Braden, 'The Pearl of Great Price,' in *The Private Sea: LSD and the Search for God* (www.druglibrary.org/schaffer/lsd/braden.htm).

[408] See Wahbi Zuhayli, 'The Qur'an's Universality and Bediüzzaman Said Nursi,' in *A Contemporary Approach Towards Understanding the Qur'an: The Example of Risale-i Nur* (İstanbul: Sözler, 1998), 215.

## The Individual, Society and Collective Personality

According to social psychologists, any study of social change involves both persons and groups:

> As the basic constituent of any society the person is essential but ambiguous, for one can turn inward in a self-centered manner; hence it is important to add that any resolution of the social problem requires that the individual be endowed with moral values. Further, these are not simply functions of external circumstances; indeed the ideological effort to construct in these terms a "new socialist man" proceeded to destroy the inner person. Hence, there is need for an inner reconstruction that includes one's emotional life as well as intellect and will, and which must be reflected further in the values which guide one's options and the culture which emerges as the complex of values and virtues of one's people.[409]

It is in this perspective that Nursi's concept of individual and society will be analyzed in this section. The individual is the basic constituent of any society, and so will be considered together with Nursi's elaboration of the collective personality.

Veldhuis, in his book *Realism Versus Utopianism*, writes that the moral and political confusion of our age must, according to Niebuhr's diagnosis, be partly due to a misunderstanding of human nature:

> Because people do not know themselves, they come to cherish unwarranted expectations or to acquiesce too soon in existing situations. By overlooking some aspect of humanity they tend either to overrate or to underestimate man and his possibilities. Both tendencies are equally dangerous.[410]

According to some sociologists, at the end of the nineteenth century and the beginning of the twentieth, humanity was in great crisis. Man's

---

[409]  See online version of eBook, George F. McLean, 'Preface: The Value Base of Civil Society,' in *Civil Society and Social Reconstruction*, ed. George F. McLean (Washington, DC: Council for Research in Values and Philosophy, 1997), displayed in www.crvp.org/book/Series01/I-16.htm

[410]  Ruurd Veldhuis, *Realism Versus Utopianism? Reinhold Niebuhr's Christian Realism and the Relevance of Utopian Thought for Social Ethics* (Assen, The Netherlands: Van Gorcum, 1975), 24.

alienation from his fellow man and from nature was more apparent than before. He became selfish and dependent on approval, and started feeling insecure, dissatisfied, bored and anxious. More importantly, his disbelief in the Hereafter made him more distracted. The modern age has therefore rightly been called the age of anxiety or of individuality.[411]

Nursi's unique approach toward the individual and society, and his solutions to the problems besetting an age of anxiety and individuality, will be considered first; the "collective personality" will be considered later in this section. According to Mardin, whoever gathered around Nursi, whether aged mystical seekers or those of the younger generation who had received a secular primary education were deprived of a resource which operated at a deep individual level, namely the Islamic teachings. Mardin observes that the positivistic world view promoted by Kemalism and the early republican governments clashed with people's understanding of Islam, and thus Nursi had a fertile ground on which to sow his ideas concerning the total involvement of the individual in Islam as a solution for the tensions generated in the individual.[412] In this regard, Nereid writes: "After the Kemalist takeover, all religious brotherhoods were closed down and each individual was thus left on his own, to loneliness."[413] Nursi's role here was to fulfill the needs of individuals, who in the end form society. The question here is whether Nursi was in favor of individualism in the time of modernity or not. According to Mardin, "Neither Said Nursi nor the idiom he is trying to revive have anything good to say for individualism. Rather they bank on the *gemeinschäftlich* aspect of interpersonal relations."[414] Nursi's *gemeinschäftlich* concern for society puts forward the idea that individuals are socially united, and related to their families, relatives and neighborhood by moral values based

---

[411] See and compare with Erich Fromm, *The Sane Society* (London: Routledge & Kegan Paul, 1956), 270, 4 respectively. Also see, for man's alienation and mental health in capitalist society from the seventeenth to the twentieth century, Fromm, *The Sane Society*, 191–209. Another useful source in this regard, considering health and pathology and commenting on religions, values and peak experiences, is Abraham H. Maslow, *The Farther Reaches of Human Nature* (Arkana/Penguin, 1993).

[412] See Mardin, *Religion and Social Change in Modern Turkey*, 179.

[413] Camilla Trud Nereid, *In the Light of Said Nursi: Turkish Nationalism and the Religious Alternative* (London: Hurst, 1997), 31.

[414] Mardin, *Religion and Social Change in Modern Turkey*, 12.

on Islamic teachings. In this sense, Nursi's discourse is personalistic and not individualistic.[415]

Unlike his contemporaries, Nursi argued that the human as an individual has a core purpose. Nursi puts individuals at the center of his new discourse. In doing so, since the Qur'an focuses on man, he addresses individuals in particular and society in general. According to Mardin, Nursi's belief is that "Since Adam was the first man to be taught the name of Allah, which embraces all of his other Names (theophanies), the concept 'descendants of Adam' is [that] through which society should be apprehended."[416]

Nursi locates the problem afflicting the Muslim world at the level of the individual. His solutions started with reforming and transforming the individual. He tried to renew self-confidence of the individual through psychological renewal based on stressing faith.[417] According to Nursi, the human being as the "Divine vicegerency" has a mission, the first task of which is to recognize and to know God and to worship Him. Life is a test: man has to earn eternal happiness and deserve heaven. To do this he has to show and perfect his abilities through the capacities which he has been granted by his creation. According to Nursi, in this sense each individual has a universal human role that transcends natural, social, and cultural boundaries.[418] Man has to experience this life, this world and everything relating to it. He has been given the capacity to rise to the highest of the high, and also to descend to the lowest of the low.[419]

Discussing the process of modernizing the social structure, Mardin argues that Nursi succeeded in making faith something that was cultivated by truly autonomous individuals. He regarded Islam as the external,

---

[415] See, for more details, in 'A Personalistic View of Society' and 'Personalism and Ethics' in ibid., 163–171.

[416] Ibid., 167.

[417] See for more information M. Hakan Yavuz, 'The Sufi Conception of Jihad: The Case of Said Nursi' (paper presented at the Peace, Jihad and Conflict Resolution, Georgetown University, Washington, DC, available in www.iiit.org/iiitseminar/AMSS,%20IIIT,%20ISESCO%20Seminar.htm, November 2–3, 2002).

[418] See for more in this concern in Abd al-Aziz Barghuth, 'The Place of the Theory of Knowledge in the Vicegerency and Civilizational Process in the Thought of Bediüzzaman Said Nursi,' in *A Contemporary Approach Towards Understanding the Qur'an: The Example of Risale-i Nur* (İstanbul: Sözler, 2000), 21.

[419] See Nursi, *Words*, 319–331.

ideological "canopy" beneath which the internal thrust would come from individuals. He writes: "The importance of this internalization followed logically from the personalistic system, for where there are no holistic conceptions of society to work with – other than 'Islam' – then the end one pursues is not to change society as a whole but the individual and his 'heart'." Also, Mardin argues that it was this idea that Nursi seems to have had in mind when he shifted from politics, which had occupied him in the first period of his life, to the conversion of individuals, when he appeared as "New Nursi."[420]

The principle of community in Islam is the opposite of that of individualism, which implies that man (as an individual) is the center and measure of everything. According to the Islamic view of community, everybody has an awareness of being personally responsible for all others.[421] In the Islamic tradition, every individual is responsible for what he has done. In this sense Nursi never was individualistic. For Nursi, it is in the nature of man to have a place in the framework relating to the vicegerency. Each individual has to be equal to conveying its meanings, aims, and message to people.[422]

In many of his writings Nursi either starts or finishes by saying: "I have written down my own observations, according to my own understanding, and for myself," or, "I mostly address firstly my own soul." This shows that Nursi's addressee was man himself rather than society.[423] In

---

[420] See Mardin, *Religion and Social Change in Modern Turkey*, 165.

[421] See 'For an Islam of the 20th Century' by Roger Garaudy, available online. The text is an English translation of the report presented by Roger Garaudy, at the request of the Muslim Community of Andalusia, at the First International Congress of Muslims of European origin held in Seville from 18 to 21 July 1985.

[422] See and compare with Barghuth, 'The Place of the Theory of Knowledge in the Vicegerency and Civilizational Process in the Thought of Bediüzzaman Said Nursi,' 21. Also, according to Barguth, in Nursi's thought it was a time when the man bearing its mission has drawn away from the Divine revelation, which comprises the standpoint, project and method of man as regards belief, action, conduct, and culture. See for more details Barghuth, 'The Place of the Theory of Knowledge in the Vicegerency and Civilizational Process in the Thought of Bediüzzaman Said Nursi,' 21.

[423] See Bediüzzaman Said Nursi, *The Rays* (trans. Şükran Vahide) (İstanbul: Sözler, 1998), 123; also Dursun, 'Bediüzzaman Said Nursi as the Representative of Social Opposition,' 318.

the most important part of his writings, the treatise called *The Supreme Sign*, Nursi, in the form of a traveler, questions the universe about his Maker. He wrote the work for himself.[424] This treatise represents Nursi's view of man's relation with the cosmos and its interconnection with the idea of the Creator, harmony, peace, and prosperity. He questions the universe as an individual man and observes it as a traveler.[425] This is a common theme in the *Risale-i Nur*. Nursi takes man as an individual and attempts to educate him. In this regard Mardin states:

> Two characteristics may be underlined which I believe are relevant to an understanding of what is "truly" religious in Nurculuk: one is the centrality of the symbolic store in a person's involvement in religion. A second is the malleability of the set of religious symbols at an individual level.[426]

Elsewhere, Mardin states in this connection:

> Personalism in the sense in which we see it used by Said Nursi has a number of further connotations. Since Adam was the first man to be taught the name of Allah, which embraces all of his other Names (theophanies), the concept "descendants of Adam" is the conceptual unit through which society should be apprehended. A speculation of Bediüzzaman which is related to this trend of thought is his assertion that one should remember that one of the Names of God (through which the phenomenal works is activated) is *Farid*, or "The Individual" (BSN, 271). Thus even individuality has as its referent, the Divine and not the person's make-up or characteristics.[427]

According to Nursi, the chief concern of Islam was the strengthening of the individual's belief, leading him to seek belief-based solutions to every question relating to life.[428]

---

[424] See Vahide, *The Author of the Risale-i Nur*, 252.
[425] See for the treatise called 'The Supreme Sign' Nursi, *Rays*, 123–200.
[426] Mardin, *Religion and Social Change in Modern Turkey*, 21.
[427] Ibid., 167.
[428] In this regard see for more details Ahmed Davutoğlu, 'Bediüzzaman and the Politics of the 20th Century Islamic World,' in *Third International Symposium on Bediüzzaman Said Nursi: The Reconstruction of Islamic Thought in the Twentieth Century and Bediüzzaman Said Nursi* (İstanbul: Sözler, 1995), 301.

Mardin argues that the transformation Nursi underwent from the "Old" to the "New" Said also transformed his discourses, which centered on three 'second orders'. These were "a conceptualization of social relations as personalistic, a folk cosmology with imagistic moorings, and an allusive, obscure, highly metaphorical rhetoric."[429] In a time of social and psychological unhappiness and distraction, Nursi's solution appealed, in the first step, on a psychological level and aimed to increase Muslim spirituality by transforming it from "imitative belief" into "certain belief", which he believed to be the key to eternal life, and to social happiness in this world.[430] Nursi seeks to revive society through the promotion of self-aware individuals endowed with firm belief. Thus, according to Mardin, "the personalistic element explains some aspects of the religious strategy of Said Nursi, i.e. his special emphases on changing man's inner world as the touchstone of a revitalized Islam."[431]

Nursi never defines individualism or personalism in his writings. As Mardin argues, however, the issues Nursi addresses are more rightly termed personalistic. Nursi developed a methodology which he thought would create the good society by fostering "collective personality."[432] This is what he felt to be necessary in the modern age, that the students of the *Risale-i Nur* should renounce all the demands of the ego and transform their 'I's into 'We' – that is, give up egotism and work for the collective personality:[433]

---

[429] Ibid., 163.

[430] See Vahide, *The Author of the Risale-i Nur*, 251.

[431] Mardin, *Religion and Social Change in Modern Turkey*, 165.

[432] For Nursi, numerous things take on the form of a collectivity and if such a collectivity fuses and becomes a unity, it will have a collective personality. He exemplifies this as follows: "consider the plane-tree in front of my room here, a mighty word of the mouth of Barla and the tongue of this mountain: see how many hundreds of tongues of smaller branches there are on the three heads of the three main branches of its trunk. Study carefully how many hundreds of words of well-ordered and balanced fruits it has, and how many hundreds of letters of well-proportioned winged seeds; just as you hear and see how eloquently it praises and glorifies the All-Glorious Maker, the Owner of the command of *'Be!' and it is*, so too the angel appointed to it represents its glorification with numerous tongues in the World of Meaning. Wisdom necessitates that it is so." See Nursi, *Words*, 179.

[433] See for more details Vahide, *The Author of the Risale-i Nur*, 263–266.

This time is not the time for egotism and the personality for those who follow the path of reality (*ehl-i hakikat*); it is the time of the community (*cemaat*). A collective personality emerging from the community rules, and may persist. In order to have a large pool, the ego and personality, which are like blocks of ice, have to be cast into the pool and melted ...[434]

The individual, so Nursi thought, can live his religion alone. He maintains that

in early times the social collectivity and its collective personality had not developed as it has at the present and the idea of the isolated individual was predominant; the extensive attributes and wide-scale actions of the community, therefore, were ascribed to the persons who led them.[435]

The present time, however, is the time of social collectivity. The importance and value of individuals must accord with collective personality.[436] In this sense, Nursi's fundamental fear was that the "I" in a Muslim's life would take over.[437]

According to Nursi, in the age in which he lived, an individual, even one of the greatest spiritual stature, could not successfully combat the awesome collective personality of irreligion based on the materialist philosophy of the century, and could not completely remove the doubts caused by unbelief and misguidance. A collective religious personality, Nursi thought, is a necessity in order to combat the collective personality of irreligion.[438] According to Vahide, this consciousness of a joint or corpo-

---

[434] As quoted in ibid., 264.

[435] Nursi, *Rays*, 101.

[436] See Davutoglu, 'Bediüzzaman and the Politics of the 20th Century Islamic World,' 303.

[437] See Mardin, *Religion and Social Change in Modern Turkey*, 168. Elsewhere in this regard he maintains: "In any event, the service of the Qur'an around which we are gathered does not accept the 'I', it requires the 'we.' It says: 'Don't say "I," say "we."'" Nursi, *Letters*, 497.

[438] See Vahide, *The Author of the Risale-i Nur*, 264. Also see Sener Dilek, 'The Risale-i Nur's Method and Aim,' in *International Symposium on Bediüzzaman Said Nursi: The Reconstruction of Islamic Thought in the Twentieth Century and Bediüzzaman Said Nursi* (İstanbul: Sözler, 1992), 127.

rate personality is one of the distinguishing marks of Nursi's *Risale-i Nur*, and Nursi himself offered the finest example of it by always putting this collective personality before himself.[439] Nevertheless, Nursi does not see himself as a subject who states propositions about an external entity "society" without taking into account his personal involvement in it; for him society is, as Mardin states, not an "It" but an "I."[440] For Nursi there is no society as an abstract "it:" society is something in which individuals take part. Nevertheless, Nursi urged the forming of groups and communities (*cemaat*), and considered it to be the time of communities or social collectivities.

Along with the principles of belief, Nursi endeavored to strengthen the psychological infrastructure of the individual, and to develop a secure social system through the socialization of the individual in a balanced, individuals-based society.[441] In this context Nursi tries to develop social collectivity, making individuals self-aware of themselves first, and then, secondly, aware of society. Through his writings Nursi undertook to renew the belief of Muslim individuals, and to re-form a community or group of these individuals, rather than re-establishing the political structure of the Islamic world. His endeavor may be seen as reviving belief and forming community with this spirit.[442] Mardin states:

> A summary of findings concerning the sociological imagination of Said Nursi would emphasize one main point: Bediüzzaman does not have a holistic understanding of society: he sees society as made up of persons. But here we have to emphasize another feature which runs counter to this first finding: these persons are not real but "virtual" persons. They are defined not as individuals but as positions

---

[439] See for more details in Vahide, *The Author of the Risale-i Nur*, 260. Another point of interest which should be mentioned here is Nursi's statement in relation to socio-politics that for him, however great a genius an individual is, even a hundredfold genius, if he is not the representative of a group and if he does not represent the collective personality of a group, he will be defeated in the face of the collective personality of an opposing group. See Nursi, *Letters*, 554.

[440] See Mardin, *Religion and Social Change in Modern Turkey*, 170.

[441] See and compare with Davutoglu, 'Bediüzzaman and the Politics of the 20th Century Islamic World,' 298.

[442] See ibid., 301.

or roles that those persons would fill. The "Good Society" is one where this pyramid of roles—derived from the Quran—is constituted.[443]

Mardin argues that Nursi's ideas have their own holistic dimension: "They are not those of a society viewed as a machine but those of a community interlinked with ties of personal obligation. And at still another level, rules for the control of bodily expression."[444] However, even though it is true that the roles of individuals and interpersonal relations "complete the pyramid," nevertheless, contrary to what Mardin has written, in Nursi's understanding *persons* are not virtual, but actual.[445] For instance, Nursi maintained the view that it was a barbaric principle of present-day society that for the sake of society an individual might be sacrificed, or that for the sake of a nation a society's rights might be dispensed with. According to Nursi, the pure justice of the Qur'an does not spill the life and blood of an innocent, even for the whole of humanity. The two are the same, in the view both of the Divine Power and of justice. But through self-interest, man becomes such that he will destroy everything that forms an obstacle to his ambition, even the world if he can, and will wipe out mankind.[446] In this context, then, Nursi's individuals are very much actual. Mardin himself states that *insan* (man) was more important than *erkan* (orders).[447] It is clear that Nursi's main concern was man, not society.[448] This makes man actual rather than virtual. In addition, even though some of Nursi's ideas may have their own holistic dimension, this is not the case where society is concerned.

While his contemporaries were busy using Islam as a vehicle of protest, Nursi sought to reform society in the direction of drawing power away from individuals in order to form a collective personality so that

---

[443] Mardin, *Religion and Social Change in Modern Turkey*, 171.

[444] Ibid., 13.

[445] See and compare with 'Sense of Identity-Individuality vs. Herd Conformity' in Fromm, *The Sane Society*, 60–63.

[446] See Bediüzzaman Said Nursi, 'Seeds of Reality,' in *The Letters* (İstanbul: Sözler, 1997), 549, and Nursi, *Letters*, 75.

[447] See and compare with Mardin, *Religion and Social Change in Modern Turkey*, 166.

[448] See and compare this with Giddens when he writes: "society is not a creation of the (pre-social) individual but exists 'prior' to him and moulds him ..." Anthony Giddens, *Studies in Social and Political Theory* (London: Hutchinson, 1977), 285.

he could achieve his ultimate aim of building a good society based on belief, and was never involved with such political hostility or with revolutionary activities.[449] In conclusion, then: Nursi attempted to reactivate Islamic teachings in society via autonomous individuals, and harnessed interpersonal relationship within the so-called "collective personality" in order to mobilize and revitalize Islam.

## Personalism, Individualism and Collective Personality

Nursi expressed some moral virtues and re-established Islamic injunctions in order to found a humane and good society. In so doing he re-emphasized values and principles which sprang from the Qur'an. According to Nursi, the disease which afflicted the very 'heart of the nation' was its laxity in religion. A cure would come, he claimed, only with the revival of religion in the hearts of the masses.[450] Unlike most of his contemporaries, Nursi did not blame external forces. Muslims themselves had a great share in the situation of political, economic, and social backwardness. The eradication of their historical identity afflicted the minds of Muslims, who did not even realize the change taking place within themselves. This was, in a sense, self-criticism. As a result of the alienation from society of Islamic values, Muslims did not even realize what they had lost. Nursi attached great importance to his diagnosis of Islamic society as immoral as a precondition for Islamic resurgence.[451] Nursi does not present any detailed picture of the socio-moral system. He discusses in detail only those problems which seem important from his moral point of view and which relate to his time. That is to say, he does not deal with how to structure society bit by bit, or with how to build a state structure.

---

[449] See Jacques Waardenburg, 'Islam as a Vehicle of Protest,' in *Islamic Dilemmas: Reformers, Nationalists and Industrialization the Southern Shore of the Mediterranean*, ed. Ernest Gellner (New York: Mouton, 1985), 22–49.

[450] See Nursi, *The Damascus Sermon*, 76. In this context he also states, "Our way is also to adopt the morality of Muhammad [peace and blessings be upon him], and revive his practices." Nursi, *The Damascus Sermon*, 76.

[451] See Mikail Taşdemir, 'Political Thought of Bediüzzaman Said Nursi' (MA thesis, International Institute of Islamic Thought and Civilization (ISTAC), March 1999), 41–49.

While dealing with the issue of morality in society, Nursi stressed the sociological inheritance according to which, so he believed, the East responds more to religion than does the West. According to him, most of the Prophets appeared in the East and in Africa, while most philosophers emerged in the West and in Europe. He took this to be a sign of a Divine pre-ordaining that in Asia religion is dominant and philosophy takes second place. He points out the importance of dealing carefully with the socio-moral facts of Eastern or Western society on the basis of this analysis. He repeatedly said that the resurgence of the East would depend on upholding religious teachings and ethics.[452]

As Mardin argues, one of the significant points in Nursi's discourse was the idea of the rationality of Muslim ethics:

> The thesis that religion could not anymore be simply declarative (one of Said's oft-repeated statements) but had to rely on convincing arguments (which, incidentally does not mean the arguments of philosophy) was, no doubt, an aspect of his shrewd understanding of the process of modernization as it grew in Turkey after 1908.[453]

Nursi's main aim, especially in the second part of his life, was to demonstrate that via the Qur'an, with its reasoned proofs and certain evidences, not only Muslims but all humanity could find a way to happiness in this world and hereafter. It was for this reason, according to Vahide, that he was always optimistic about the future.[454] Mardin draws attention also to his softening of the orthodox Sunni stress on the torments of hell which are promised to sinners: "There is conversely, a new stress on the benevolence of God and on *şefkat* (affection) as the bond that links God and the believer."[455] Nursi's discourse places significant emphasis on the Divine Names *Rahim* and *Rahman* (merciful and compassionate) as well

---

[452] See Nursi, *Rays*, 399.

[453] Mardin, *Religion and Social Change in Modern Turkey*, 173.

[454] See Şükran Vahide, 'Toward an Intellectual Biography of Bediüzzaman Said Nursi,' in *Islam at the Crossroads: On the Life and Thought of Bediüzzaman Said Nursi*, ed. Ibrahim M Abu-Rabi (Albany, New York: SUNY Press, 2003), 27.

[455] Mardin, *Religion and Social Change in Modern Turkey*, 172. Also see for more on this in Bediüzzaman Said Nursi, *Kaynakli- Indeksli-Lugatli Risale-i Nur Külliyatı* (The Epistle of Light), II vols (İstanbul: Nesil Basim, 1996), 650.

as on God's forgiveness. He also maintains that his way, or the *Risale-i Nur*, has the attributes of the Divine Names *Hakim* and *Rahim*.

In a period when philosophy-based, materialistic ideologies, whether capitalist or communist, were becoming increasingly influential, the importance Nursi attached to preserving individual belief by making all Muslims aware of long-forgotten Islamic ethics furnished his basic solution. It is difficult to find considerations of institutional or structural renewal in Nursi's writings.[456] His concern was materialism's moral and spiritual destruction of both the individual and society. He thought that the implementation of Islamic ethics would repair the harm caused by negative, philosophy-based ideologies.[457] According to Mardin:

> Of all the themes he presented in the Risale-i Nur, Said Nursi was most adamant about the necessity to revitalize Islamic ethics. Sometimes this emphasis had pragmatic overtones, as when he described religion as a balm to the wound suffered by individuals. More often it was a theme which underlined the harmony that one would achieve by remaining in tune with the frame of the universe as thought by Islam.[458]

One further thing needs to be clarified here. From the above statement it could be inferred that religion, according to Nursi, is a kind of cure, an ointment for healing a sore. Religion in this view is reactive to the practical and sociological issues in society, so that it may give relief to people. Contrary to this, Nursi saw religion as pro-active and self-sufficient; by means of it, people can safeguard their mortal and eternal lives. Nursi thought that the solution for the Islamic world's backwardness was to reactivate pro-active Islamic ethics and injunctions. He elaborates on a number of issues relating to the reactivation of Islamic injunctions, and maintains that immorality gives rise to the following:

> Firstly: The rising to life of despair and hopelessness in social life.
> Secondly: The death of truthfulness in social and political life. Thirdly:

---

[456] See Davutoğlu, 'Bediüzzaman and the Politics of the 20th Century Islamic World,' 302.

[457] In this regard see Vahide, 'Toward an Intellectual Biography of Bediüzzaman Said Nursi,' 27.

[458] Mardin, *Religion and Social Change in Modern Turkey*, 168.

Love of enmity. Fourthly: Not knowing the luminous bonds that bind the believers to one another. Fifthly: Despotism, which spreads, becomes widespread as though it was various contagious diseases. Sixthly: Restricting endeavor to what is personally beneficial.[459]

According to Fromm, one of the most disturbing facts in moral life in the contemporary world is the startling contrast between private and collective interests in morality, and also the fact that man has lost his appetite for being a part of society and has become selfish and egotistic.[460] In opposition to this, Nursi endeavored to re-establish the moral injunctions of Islamic ethics in social life. He was of the opinion that a fearful egotism arising from heedlessness and from love of this world rules at this time, and he attempted to re-establish the good society by an emphasis on practical worldly issues balanced with a view of the hereafter. Nursi was particularly adamant about reviving Islamic ethics in order to build up a culture of belief. Among the first things he opposed as the consequence of modern morality was egotism. According to Nursi, egotism is man's most dangerous vein:[461]

> A fearful egotism arising from heedlessness and love of this world rules at this time. The people of reality, therefore, have to give up egotism and selfishness, even if it is in a licit form. Since the Risale-i Nur students dissolve their egotism, which is an ice-block, in the joint pool of their collective personality, they will not be shaken by this storm, God willing.[462]

From his youth Nursi emphasized the importance of prevailing moral and spiritual needs. He believed that humanity's greatest present need is for moral and spiritual strength, solace and fortitude.[463] Nevertheless, for Nursi the Qur'an is primarily a means of placing restraints on the dangerous appetites of man:

> The aims of the Quran are to provide a barrier against the appetites of man (*hevesat-i nefsaniye*), thus encouraging him to engage in higher

---

[459]  Nursi, *Damascus Sermon*, 26–27.

[460]  See Fromm, *The Sane Society*, 202–8.

[461]  See Nursi, *Letters*, 497.

[462]  Nursi, *Rays*, 343.

[463]  See Nursi, *Damascus Sermon*, 66.

pursuits, giving satisfaction to his higher aspirations and directing him towards the achievements of human perfection.[464]

In this regard, it is worth mentioning some of the moral values Nursi discusses, especially after the 1920s. Nursi's emphasis on the different moral values underwent change, but they mainly consisted of the following. Throughout the *Risale-i Nur*, among the issues mentioned most frequently in relation to the Islamic ethics are: sincerity (defined by Nursi as the most important principle in works pertaining to the hereafter); love (Nursi stated that the way of Islamic society is love for love and enmity toward enmity); and brotherhood. He speaks of strengthening love between Muslims and of "routing the soldiers of hostility."[465] Among the other oft-repeated issues Nursi dealt with are *taqwa* and respect. In response to the decline in moral standards, Nursi urged the adoption of the Qur'anic concept of *taqwa*, fear of God or piety, as the basis of actions in the face of corruption and destruction. Elsewhere, he defines *taqwa* as "the avoiding of sins and what is forbidden, and acting within the sphere of obligatory good works," and said that those who fulfilled their obligations and did not commit serious sins would be saved.[466] Nursi, in many places in his writings, emphasizes the significance of *taqwa* as the greatest strength appertaining in social life:

> And so, after sincerity (*ikhlas*), our greatest strength at such a time in the face of these fearsome events is, in accordance with the principle of 'sharing the works of the Hereafter', for each of us to write good deeds into 'the righteous-act books' of the others with our pens, and with our tongues, to send reinforcements and assistance to the 'forts' of the others' *taqwa*.[467]

In this regard, Nursi thought that will, mind, emotion, and the subtle inner faculties which he thought constitute the four elements of the conscience and the four faculties of the spirit, each has an ultimate aim. The

---

[464] As quoted in Mardin, *Religion and Social Change in Modern Turkey*, 168. Also see Nursi, *Kaynaklı- İndeksli-Lügatli Risale-i Nur Külliyatı* (The Epistle of Light), 185.

[465] See the twenty-second letter in Nursi, *Letters*.

[466] See as cited in Vahide, *The Author of the Risale-i Nur*, 262.

[467] See as quoted in ibid.

ultimate aim of the will is worship of God; that of the mind is knowledge of God; that of the emotions is love of God; and that of the inner faculties is the vision of God. He believed that perfect worship, known as *taqwa*, comprises all four elements: Islamic injunctions correct these and direct them toward their ultimate goals.[468]

Nursi deals with the question of man's perfecting of his abilities and, on the other hand, with the shortness of his life, which serves as a counterbalance to his countless desires and appetites. As regards sensual pleasures, according to Nursi man may sink to a level a hundred times lower than the animals. He therefore was of the opinion that those who wish to be eternally happy, in this world and the next, should take as their guide the instruction of the Prophet Muhammad, peace and blessings be upon him, within the bounds of belief.[469] Nursi here is appealing on a psychological level.

According to Özbek, "In many places in the *Risale-i Nur* attention is drawn to man's inborn disposition, and methodical information is given as to how it should be guided."[470] Nursi affirmed that he was seeking to save men from anarchy and establish social harmony through the *Risale-i Nur*, by helping to plant belief-focused individuals in society.[471] In his view, social tranquility can be assured only through the continuous production of religiously-minded young people.[472] According to Vahide, "The *Risale-i Nur* was a 'repairer' resisting the destruction."[473] Nursi writes:

> Our aim and program is to save first ourselves, then our nation, from eternal extinction and permanent solitary confinement in the Intermediate Realm; to guard our fellow citizens against anarchy and aimlessness; and to protect ourselves with the steel-like truths

---

468  See Nursi, *Damascus Sermon*, 117.

469  See Nursi, *Words*, 157–59.

470  Abdullah Özbek, 'The Importance of Knowing Man,' in *A Contemporary Approach Towards Understanding the Qur'an: The Example of Risale's Nur* (İstanbul: Sözler, 1998), 60.

471  See Beki, 'The Qur'an and Its Method of Guidance,' 96.

472  See Bediüzzaman Said Nursi, Treatise for 'youth', 'Genclik Rehberi,' in *Kaynakli-Indeksli-Lugatli Risale-i Nur Külliyatı* (The Epistle of Light).

473  Vahide, *The Author of the Risale-i Nur*, 262.

of the Risale-i Nur against atheism, which destroys our lives in this world and the next.[474]

Nursi first appeals to the psychological level of the individual and then to the psycho-social level. He was especially adamant that this interrelation operates on a psychological and not on a supernatural level. He employs the *Risale-i Nur* as a means of training and educating people by means of Islamic ethics and injunctions, with the ultimate aim of building a good society founded on belief.

## Conclusion

According to Nasr, there are a vast number of Muslims whose belonging to the Islamic tradition is still defined by others in terms of the traditional Islamic categories rather than contemporary Islamic revivalist manners.[475] A brief categorization of Muslim peoples' public lives today, as formulated by Nasr, may be of help in concluding the subject at hand. In general public life, there are Muslims who never miss their daily prayers and live to the best of their abilities considering the manner of the *sharia* as the only manner. Yet there are some Muslims today who do not practice their religion properly and take the *sharia* as the central point of their life; however, they consider themselves definitely Muslims. Also, there are even others who do not do anything specifically Islamic, but who when called anything else would protest. Another group of Muslims are those who normally perform religious rituals, yet break many of the moral injunctions.[476] Lastly adding to the above group, there are some others who follow their parents' traditionalist form of Islamic life blindly, as they had grown out of questioning what they really believe in (God) or examining what they really carry out in terms of religious ritual. In other words, there are some Muslims who believe in atavistic Islam without questioning anything, but just performing it: *taqleed* (blind following).

---

[474] As quoted in Ahmed Akgündüz, 'The Risale-i Nur Movement: Is It a Sufi Order, a Political Society, or a Community?,' in *Third International Symposium on Bediüzzaman Said Nursi: The Reconstruction of Islamic Thought in the Twentieth Century and Bediüzzaman Said Nursi* (İstanbul: Sözler, 1995), 167.

[475] See Nasr, 'Islam in the Islamic World Today, an Overview,' 18.

[476] See and compare with ibid.

The Muslim masses are waiting for a radical change in their lives. The failure of the so-called ideologies, economic crises, and Western domination of scientific and military developments, make the indifferent masses fertile soil for generating Islamic militancy more and more. This idea appeals to the imagination of the masses, and internalist tradition does not get the attention it deserves. Externalist Islam appears as the foundation of a new world order. These kinds of leaders and members of Islamic groups become more highly respected day by day. The downfall of the Shah of Iran at the hands of a religious leader has given all young leaders of Muslim groups more self-confidence in terms of social and political change.[477] But no one speaks about internal and individual change any more. Muslims do not question what they really believe in, what they really pray for, and what the real and ultimate aims of this life and the Hereafter are.

Nursi approaches externalism and internalism—namely esoteric and exoteric—as the two aspects of the same truth. While he sees the adherence to the former as exotericism, he sees the latter as pure esotericism. The goal of both attitudes should be to draw one's attention from the 'outer' dimension of religion, and direct it to the 'inner' dimension of the religious life.

Nursi's middle way determines the individual and social evolution of Muslims. This leads the individual from political Islam to apolitical Islam, from the outward indulgence of Islam to a faith-based Islam, from blind faith to a reason-based faith, from a stable faith to a gradualist, progressive-active faith. Nursi set in motion a process of rational inquiry into *islam*, clearing up misunderstandings in Islam and paving the way for dialogue with the multicultural world.

---

[477] See Hanafi, 'The Origin of Modern Conservatism and Islamic Fundamentalism,' 101–102.

# Chapter 10

## Agents of Human Spirituality: Dominical Subtle Faculties of Man According to Said Nursi

*Kerim Balcı*

### Introduction

I n one of his letters to Refet Bey[478] recorded in the Sixteenth Flash,[479] Nursi replies to his disciple's questions,[480] but refuses to elaborate on his question about the Ten Subtle Faculties [*Letâif-i Aşere* in Turkish] as he believes that his "duty at the present time is the discovery of mysteries, not the relating of existent matters." Instead, he enumerates the

---

[478] Refet Barutçu (1886–1975) was a retired army officer and an imam who joined Nursi's close circle of students. His questions to Nursi played a significant role in provoking Nursi to write on controversial issues. In a letter to him Nursi attests to Refet Barutçu's role in the writing of The Letters: "My Dear, Loyal Brother, Refet Bey! I cannot meet with indifference your learned questions since they are the keys to important truths contained in the part of the *Risale-i Nur* called *Mektubat* (Letters)" (*The Rays*, 323).

[479] References to the *Risale-i Nur* (Epistles of Light) are made from Şükran Vahide's translations as they are repaginated in erisale.com apart from *Al-Mathnawi Al-Nuri* (Clifton, NJ: Tughra Books, 2007) and *The Reasonings* (Clifton, NJ: Tughra Books, 2008), both translations of Hüseyin Akarsu. References to Turkish texts are made from the *Risale-i Nur Külliyatı* (İstanbul: Nesil Basım Yayın, 1996) and to Arabic Mesnevi from Abdulkadir Badıllı's edition.

[480] *The Flashes*, 155. This correspondence is also recorded in *Barla Lahikası*, 1553 (Turkish).

Ten Subtle Faculties,[481] with a reference to the scholars of the Naqshbandi way, Ahmad Sirhindi in particular.[482]

Despite the fact that he did not want to "relate to this existent matter" in a systematic way, Nursi appeals to the subtleties in countless places in the *Epistles of Light*. It may securely be claimed that one of Nursi's projects in the *Epistles* is "harmonization of spirit, heart and intellect" and joint use of the purification mechanisms of these superior subtleties. This project invites an in-depth study of the subtleties according to Nursi. His treatment of spirit and heart is particularly valuable as he regards the spirit as the unifying law of all other subtleties, and the heart as their commander.

## Subtleties in Sufi Tradition

The term *latifa* (plural *lata'if*) is derived from the Arabic word *latif*, meaning "gentle," "sensitive," or "subtle." In Sufi terminology the word *latifa* refers to a psycho-spiritual organ or a faculty of sensory and supersensory perception that can be influenced, purified or awakened through spiritual practices.[483] *Latifa* has been translated as "subtlety," "tenuous body," "subtle point" and "subtle essence." A majority of the models developed on the subtleties were developed within the Naqshbandi Sufi tradi-

---

[481] Nursi counts the Ten Subtle Faculties as conscience, nerve, sense, intellect, desire, faculty of concupiscence, faculty of anger, heart, spirit and mystery. But he does not limit the number to ten, and lists arcane, super-arcane, faculty of fervor, faculty of inclination and premonition as other subtleties. Even then he suggests that there are other faculties he observed as subtle faculties of "man's comprehensive disposition and vital potentialities."

[482] Better known among Turkish Muslims as Imam-ı Rabbani, Ahmad Sirhindi (1563–1624) was a major figure of the Naqshbandi way. Sirhindi turned the ten subtleties [five belonging to the world of creation and five to the world of higher order] into the core of his model for purification of the soul. The first five subtleties refer to the soul and subtleties corresponding to the four basic elements of existence (water, air, earth, and fire), and the second five, in the case of Sirhindi, to heart, spirit, mystery, arcane and super-arcane, which needed to be activated for the attainment of the status of Man of Perfection.

[483] Marcia K. Hermansen, "Shah Wali Allah>s Theory of the Subtle Spiritual Centers (Lataif): A Sufi Model of Personhood and Self-Transformation," *Journal of Near Eastern Studies*, Vol. 47, No. 1 (Jan. 1988), 1–25.

tion. Three names are particularly important in the development of the Sufi *lata'if* tradition: Abu Hamid Ghazali (d. 1111), Ahmad Sirhindi (d. 1624) and Shah Wali Allah (d. 1762).[484] All were known to be the renewers (*mujaddid*) of religion in their ages, hinting at an unstudied relation between openness to dealing with subtleties and openness to renewal (*tajdid*).

The *lata'if* tradition is in a continuous process of renewal. This has resulted in a literature that is hard to follow. The names of subtleties[485] have replaced one other over time, and new subtleties have been discovered throughout the history of the tradition. Despite the fact that the *lata'if* tradition was considerably influenced by the Greek medical and Hindu *chakra* disciplines, there is no canonical text listing Sufi subtleties and giving universally accepted definitions for them. In any case, *lata'if* were not thought of only in psychological or psychical terms; in line with the *chakra* tradition they were taken to be local manifestations of identically named parts of a higher realm of the cosmological structure, one above the realm of created things.[486] In that sense, the science of *lata'if* was accepted as a part of the Sufi cosmology, in which an analogy between the macrocosmic and microcosmic realms was drawn through *lata'if*.

Sirhindi, for example, divided the world into two realms: World of God's Creation (*'alam al-Khalq*) and World of God's Command (*'alam al-'amr*). In the first level there were five lower *lata'if*, fire, air, earth, water and lower soul (*nafs*), and in the second five higher *lata'if*, heart (*qalb*), spirit (*ruh*), mystery (*sirr*), arcane (*khafi*) and super-arcane (*akhfa*). Again as in the *chakra* tradition, Sirhindi appointed to the five second-level sub-

---

[484] Shah Wali Allah's book on the *lata'if*, *Altaf al-Quds* (Gujranwala, 1964), was translated into English by G. H. Jalbani and Donald Pendleberry as *The Sacred Knowledge of the Higher Functions of the Mind: The Altaf al-Quds of Shah Waliullah* (London: Octagon Press, 1982).

[485] The problem of nomenclature gets even worse in English translations. For the sake of continuity this chapter uses Jalbani and Pendleberry's translations as listed: *nefis* (soul), *ruh* (spirit), *vicdan* (conscience), *asab* (nerve), *his* (sense), *akıl* (intellect), *heva* (desire), *kuvve-i şehevaniyye* (faculty of concupiscence), *kuvve-i gadabiyye* (faculty of anger), *kalp* (heart), *sır* (mystery), *hafî* (arcane), *ahfâ* (super-arcane), *şâika* (faculty of fervor), *sâika* (faculty of inclination) and *hiss-i kable'l-vuku* (premonition).

[486] Hermansen, 1988.

tleties sites on the body and colors, and Islamized them by appointing a Prophet to each *latifa*: *Qalb* was the subtlety of Adam and was located just under the physical heart; *Ruh* was the subtlety of Abraham and was located under the right breast; *Sirr* was the subtlety of Moses and was located above the physical heart; *Khafi* was the subtlety of Jesus and was located on the right side of the chest above the right breast; and finally *Akhfa* was the subtlety of Muhammad and was located in the center of the chest.

Shah Wali Allah, on the other hand, had a more anthropocentric understanding of the *lata'if*. He synchronized Greek medicine with the *lata'if* by saying that *al-ruh al-nafsani*, which is traditionally positioned in the brain, corresponds to the intelligence (*'aql*); *al-ruh al-haywani*, which is in the heart, corresponds to *Qalb* (the heart as a subtlety); and finally *al-ruh al-tab'i*, which is in the liver, corresponds to *Nafs*, the lower soul. These are the three lower *lata'if* in Shah Wali Allah's understanding. *'Aql* has its higher latifa, *Sirr*, the Mystery, while *Qalb*'s higher *latifa* is *Ruh*, the spirit. Shah Wali Allah also detected faculties related to the *lata'if*: *quwwa shahawaniyya* (the faculty of desire or concupiscence, which expresses desire of acceptance) and *quwwa ghadabiyya* (the faculty of anger, which expresses aversion or anger). Shah Wali Allah mentioned the extremes of these faculties and suggested that religion was needed for a balanced temperament.

## Lata'if in Nursi's Writings

Despite the fact that he was deeply influenced by the Naqshbandi school, Nursi never gave a central position to the *lata'if* in his writings. The letter to Refet Bey informs us that he was well informed about Sirhindi's classification of *lata'if*.[487]

Nursi's own understanding of *lata'if* preserves the main lines of Sirhindi's classification, but cleanses the discipline of any trace of early Greek medicine or the Hindu *chakra*. Thus Nursi is not interested in the

---

[487] "I shall only say this much: Imam-i Rabbani defined the ten subtle faculties as the heart, spirit, inner heart (*sirr*), *khafi*, *akhfa*, and a faculty related to each of the four elements in man, and he discussed briefly the progress of one faculty in each stage of the spiritual journeying." *The Flashes*, 155.

positioning of *lata'if* within the body, or giving colors to those centers of *lata'if*. Sirhindi's association of the higher *lata'if* with the Prophets Adam, Abraham, Moses, Jesus and Muhammad is also absent in Nursi's definition of the *lata'if*. It cannot be claimed that Nursi's understanding of *lata'if* wholly lacks the cosmological dimension that illuminates Sirhindi's and Shah Wali Allah's understandings, but it is fair to say that the cosmological dimension is not dominant in the *Epistles of Light*.[488]

Nursi's understanding of the subtleties is a part of his understanding of the human being as a combination of the "senses and feelings, limbs and systems, members and faculties, and subtleties and immaterial aspects"[489] with which God equipped man. In numerous places in his *Epistles of Light*, Nursi compares and contrasts external senses to subtleties. In one particular passage he compares the white and red blood cells circulating the body to the *lata'if* that circumambulate the heart,[490] and in another rather interesting passage he claims that the human disposition is prone to mistake the provisions of the senses for those of the *lata'if* at times of inattention.[491]

Apart from these two passages, unparalleled in the works of Nursi, the overall treatment of the issue of *lata'if* in the *Epistles of Light* revolves around five major claims: (1) the number of *lata'if* is not limited to ten

---

[488] A rare passage that suggests a link between the subtleties and the higher realm: "... just as man's self is endowed with the manifestation of Divine mercy and his heart with the manifestation of Divine compassion, so too does his intellect take pleasure at the subtleties of Divine wisdom" (*The Rays*, 654). In another passage Nursi reverses Shah Wali Allah's allegory between the cosmos and man: "... just as in man there are immaterial faculties apart from his body, like the mind, heart, spirit, imagination, and memory, certainly in the world, which is the macroanthropos, and in the universe, which is the tree of which man is the fruit, there are other worlds apart from the corporeal world" (*The Words*, 595). In a similar manner, Nursi uses man's qualities as proofs of universal realities: "For example, extremely decisive evidence for the existence of the Preserved Tablet in the universe and an example of it is man's faculty of memory. And a decisive evidence of the existence of the World of Similitudes and an example of it is man's faculty of imagination. And evidence for the existence of spirit beings in the universe and an example of them are the powers and subtle faculties in man" (*The Flashes*, 453).

[489] *The Words*, 676.

[490] *Arabic Mesnevi*, 315.

[491] *Arabic Mesnevi*, 254.

and there are also undetected *lata'if*; (2) just like the external senses, all *lata'if* have their passions, desires, sources of sustenance and duties; (3) faith, the Qur'an, invocations, prayers and reading the *Epistles of Light* appeal to all the *lata'if* according to their level of purification; (4) man can attain perfection only through felicitous utilization of the *lata'if*; (5) the capacity of human *lata'if* is so under-utilized that it is obvious they are given for another world, where they will be made full use of; and finally (6), *lata'if* that are not used in accordance with their reasons for creation will testify against their owners in the Hereafter.

## Number of *lata'if*

Nursi does not make a distinction between *lata'if* and the faculties of those *lata'if*. Hence, Nursi counts the lower soul and the faculties of concupiscence and anger categorized by Shah Wali Allah as the faculties of the lower soul as separate subtleties.[492] It is clear that Nursi is ready to increase the number of the *lata'if* open-endedly. He concludes a list of the ten subtle by noting the numerous other faculties that exist, "like the sense of premonition, and faculties of inclination and fervor."[493]

In other passages memory and thought are also counted as subtleties.[494] Nursi speaks of a number of *lata'if* that are not accountable and should not be held responsible for deeds they may induce.[495] A comparison of these two passages reveals that these unaccountable *lata'if* can be at work in both the layman and the ecstatic when they are immersed in divine contemplation. These passages open in front of us a vast space of possibilities that were not investigated by the former theoreticians of subtleties. Nursi is aware of the huge range of "immaterial powers and subtle faculties" he is thus investigating, from those that even if they "devoured the world … would not be satisfied" to those that "cannot sustain even a minute particle within themselves."

---

[492] *The Words*, 595.

[493] *The Flashes*, 155–56 (with alterations in the translation). In *The Letters* Nursi claims that he himself "discovered two senses … that impel and stimulate" (*The Letters*, 401). These should correspond to *sâika* (faculty of inclination) and *şâika* (faculty of fervor) mentioned in this passage.

[494] *Barla Lahikası, RNK*, 1486.

[495] *The Letters*, 518.

## Sustenance, Desires and Duties of the *lata'if*

In the *32nd Word* Nursi suggests that just as each man's many members and faculties performs different functions, equally they have "completely different pleasures, pains, duties and rewards."[496] In line with the generally accepted analogy between the external senses and the subtleties, Nursi gives a complete list of the five external senses, their duties, pleasures and pains, and notes that these differ for all man's faculties, "including his important subtle aspects such as the heart, intellect and spirit."[497] These subtleties also require their specific sustenance: "In the same way that a stomach requires sustenance, so too the subtle capacities and senses of man, his heart, spirit, intelligence, eye, ear and mouth, also request their sustenance from the Compassionate Provider and gratefully receive it."[498]

One particular duty of man in this world, for Nursi, is to be a mirror to the Divine Names and the subtleties are no exception. The different Names are to be expressed by man "through all his members and faculties, all his organs and limbs, all his subtle senses and faculties, all his

---

[496] *The Words*, 676.

[497] *The Words*, 677.

[498] *The Rays*, 195–96, with minimal changes in translation. Compare with: "And just as he strives to meet the need of his stomach for food, so he is by nature compelled to strive to provide for the stomachs of his mind, heart, spirit, and humanity" (*The Rays*, 242) and "Then just as in truly wondrous fashion He causes the appropriate sustenance to hasten to all the trees, which need a sort of food, so He bestows an extensive table of foods on man's senses, which require sustenance physical and non-physical, and on his mind, heart, and spirit" (*The Rays*, 582) and "God Almighty, with His glorious Divinity, His beautiful mercy, His mighty dominicality, His generous benevolence, His immense power, and His subtle wisdom, has equipped and adorned tiny man with many senses and feelings, limbs and systems, members and faculties, and subtle and immaterial aspects so that through them He might cause man to perceive, know, taste and recognize the limitless varieties and levels of His bounty, munificence and mercy; and so that, through these tools, He might cause man to ponder over, know and love the endless kinds of manifestations of His thousand and one Names. Just as each of man's great many members and faculties performs a completely different service and worship, so too does each of them have completely different pleasures, pains, duties and rewards" (*The Words*, 676).

feelings and emotions."[499] He also notes that aside from the literal recital of the sacred Names, man "causes [these] to be recited by reason of his spirit, heart, mind, and through the pages of life and other subtle qualities."[500]

Nursi also expresses the idea that the subtle faculties like spirit, heart and mind can weep together with the eyes.[501] In another passage Nursi claims that although each and every faculty has its distinct pleasures and pains, the members, senses and subtleties of man take a share from the pleasure, pain and affection of each other.[502]

## Lata'if Enjoying the Sacred Texts and Prayers

Nursi has a holistic understanding of man. Normally man observes the universe not only with his eyes, but with all his external and spiritual senses. As such, faith disciplines not only the intellect of the believer, but also all of his/her subtleties, and all subtleties want and take their shares from what one sense or subtlety experiences:

> You cannot say, therefore, that "One window is enough for me," because if your reason is satisfied, your heart wants its share as well, and so will your spirit want its share. Your imagination will also want its share of the light. The other Windows are also necessary, therefore, for each contains different benefits.[503]

Nursi is particularly interested in showing that recitation of the Qur'an, invocation of the Beautiful Names of Allah and reading of the *Epistles of Light* appeal to all the subtleties—not only to the intellect. In one passage he explains how he felt during repetitive reading of a passage from the Qur'an, noting how different faculties received sustenance in different ways and at different times until "[g]radually with repetition only a few of the subtle faculties would remain, becoming wearied long after the others. They would persist, leaving no need for further study and meanings."[504] Nursi noted further that "the subtle faculties that per-

---

[499] *The Words*, 719.
[500] *The Words*, 659.
[501] *The Rays*, 203.
[502] *Al-Mathnawi Al-Nuri: Seedbed of the Light*, 133.
[503] *The Words*, 723.
[504] *The Letters*, 392, with minor changes in translation.

sist do not need to study and comprehend but to recollect, turn towards, and be prompted."[505] The reason repetition of the Qur'an does not cause boredom is that "it is food and sustenance for the heart, strength and wealth for the mind, water and light for the spirit, and the cure and remedy for the soul."[506]

In another passage Nursi claims that subtleties are nurtured by the gaining of faith, just as food is digested and distributed around the body, "after entering the stomach of the mind, the matters of faith that come through knowledge are absorbed by the spirit, heart, mystery, soul, and other subtle faculties; each receives its share according to its degree."[507]

In similar passages Nursi says that the *lata'if* are enlightened through Daily Prayer;[508] that during Ramadan the subtle faculties benefit from f    a    s    t    i    n    g    ;    [509] and that the heart, spirit, mind, and all other subtle faculties of man should invoke the Beautiful Names of Allah together with the tongue.[510]

Last, but not the least, Nursi explains the influence of his *Epistles* on their readers with the claim that they do not appeal only to the intellect, as the works of other scholars do, or only to the heart, as the works of some Sufis do, but that instead "they fly with the union and harmony of the intellect and the heart together with the mutual aid of subtleties like the soul."[511]

## Man of Perfection and the *lata'if*

Nursi's path to perfection and God's love is a four-step path comprising impotence, poverty, compassion, and reflection. He contrasts this path with the Naqshbandi and Qadiri paths, claiming that his path is shorter and safer.[512]

---

[505] *The Letters*, 392, with minor changes in translation.
[506] *The Words*, 389.
[507] *The Letters*, 382.
[508] *Arabic Mesnevi*, 262.
[509] *The Letters*, 463.
[510] *The Flashes*, 34.
[511] *Kastamonu Lahikasi, RNK*, 1574.
[512] *The Letters*, 524.

However, in other passages dispersed within the *Epistles of Light* we see that Nursi's path in fact incorporates both the purification of the ten subtleties and the climbing of the seven stages of the lower soul. A passage in the *Addendum* of the *27th Word* describes the perfect man as one who purifies not only his heart, but also all of his senses and subtleties:

> If man consisted of only a heart, it would be necessary to give up everything other than God, and to leave behind even the Divine Names and attributes and bind one's heart to the Divine Essence alone. But man possesses many senses and subtle faculties charged with duties, like the mind, spirit, soul, and others. The perfect man is he who, driving all those subtle senses towards reality on the different ways of worship particular to them, marches heroically like the Companions in a broad arena and rich fashion towards the goal, with the heart as commander and the subtle faculties as soldiers. For the heart to abandon its soldiers in order to save only itself and to proceed on its own is the cause not of pride, but of distress.[513]

Nursi warns that the subtle faculties that are given to man are immensely capable, also extremely sensitive, to the point that "[t]hey are sometimes extinguished and die even."[514] The immaterial members and subtle faculties in man have expanded to a degree a hundred times greater than the animals',[515] but occasionally the animal and vegetable powers in man come to dominate man's subtle faculties.[516] These powers are blind to consequences and obsessed by immediate pleasure, inducing subtle faculties such as the heart and reason to give up their humane and far-sighted duties.[517] Nursi cautions: "Since it is thus, be careful, tread

---

[513] *The Words*, 511. Compare with: "Yes, true progress is to turn the faces of the heart, spirit, intellect, and even the imagination and other subtle faculties given to man towards eternal life and for each to be occupied with the particular duty of worship worthy of it. Progress is not as the people of misguidance imagine, to plunge into the life of this world in all its minute details and in order to taste every sort of pleasure, even the basest, make subject to the evil-commanding soul all the subtle faculties and the heart and intellect, and make them assist it; to do this is not progress, it is decline" (*The Words*, 331).

[514] *The Flashes*, 185–86.

[515] *The Words*, 334.

[516] *The Flashes*, 114.

[517] *The Flashes*, 117.

with caution, be frightened of sinking! Do not drown in a mouthful, a word, a seed, a flash, a sign, a kiss! Do not plunge your extensive faculties, which can swallow the world, in such a thing."[518] On other occasions Nursi reminds his readers that even the *lata'if* of good people may occasionally tend toward abjectness.[519] These warnings are, of course, a reminder about the need for constant awareness and vigilance about the state of the *lata'if*, since man is capable of being infinitely perfected as much as he is ultimately corrupt:

> Consider this: together with being physically small, weak, and pow-erless, and being one of the animals, man bears within him an exalt-ed spirit, and has vast potentiality, unrestricted desires, infinite hopes, uncountable ideas, and unlimited powers, and he has a nature so strange he is as though an index of all the species and all the worlds. [...] Worship also removes the rust of nature from his members, physical and spiritual, each of which when transparent is like a window onto his private world and that of humankind. Also, when performed with both conscience and mind and heart and body, worship raises man to the dignity of which he is worthy and to his appointed perfection.[520]

Nursi is rather interested in infinite perfection. He gives the exam-ples of such students of the Qur'an as Shah Jilani, Rufa'i and Shazali. In reference to the latter, Nursi notes that his subtle faculties were expand-ed to such a degree that "the beings in the mighty world appear inade-quate as prayer-beads for his invocations. He considers Paradise to be insufficient as the aim of his invocations and recitations of the divine names, yet he does not see himself as superior to the lowest of Almighty God's creatures."[521] At such a level of spiritual perfection men can take in their hands "the strings of particles, the droplets of water, the breaths of all creatures, and recite their invocations with them."[522]

Muslims remember the Companions of the Prophet and the Prophet himself as the embodiments of perfection. Nursi underlines the fact that

---

[518] *The Flashes*, 185–86.
[519] *Arabic Mesnevi*, 193.
[520] *Signs of Miraculousness*, 162.
[521] *The Flashes*, 164–65.
[522] Ibid.

since all subtle inner faculties of the saints among the Companions and of the following two generations were able to receive their share from the Qur'an directly, for them the Qur'an was a true guide and it was sufficient for them.523 Nursi adds that, thanks to the mighty social revolution brought about by the lights of the Qur'an, "all the senses and subtle inner faculties of the Companions were awakened, to such an extent that even senses like those of fancy and imagination, in an awakened and aware state, received the numerous meanings of those recitations and glorifications [included in the Qur'an] in accordance with their own perceptions, and absorbed them."524 In this state of awakened senses and alert subtle faculties, when the Companions recited from the Qur'an, "they did so in all their meaning and they partook of them with all their senses."525

If the Companions showed such level of purification and awareness of their subtleties, the Prophet should have been in a superior position. Nursi underlines the fact that, as the Messenger's "hand, fingers, spittle, breath, and speech, that is, his prayer" were "the means of numerous miracles," so also "his other subtle faculties and emotions and senses were the means of many wonders."526 Among these wonders related to the Prophetic subtleties, Nursi mentions the miracle of Ascension:

> God's Most Noble Messenger [peace and blessings be upon him], the lord of all the saints, opened up a mighty highway with his Ascension, which lasting forty minutes rather than forty years, was the supreme wonder of sainthood, and which he made not only with his heart and spirit, but also with his body and his senses and his subtle faculties. He rose to the ultimate degrees of the truths of faith.527

Nursi reminds his readers that the Prophet set an example of spiritual journeying in his Ascension and that all the saints of Islam travelled under the shadow of this highway he disclosed through the door of the Ascension, with their spirits and hearts, in accordance with their degrees.528

523 *The Letters*, 410–11.
524 *The Words*, 506–7 (with minor alterations in translation).
525 *The Words*, 507.
526 *The Letters*, 185.
527 *The Letters*, 356.
528 Ibid.

## Lata'if as Evidence of Resurrection

Any issue Nursi touches upon eventually leads to speaking about faith in God and the Hereafter. Contemplating the human subtleties, Nursi finds a hint of the existence of Paradise. Since it is a well-established belief that Allah never creates anything, including a subtlety, without reason, the subtleties that cannot be satisfied in this world attest to the existence of another world, where man will use all of his subtle faculties in their full capacity.

Nursi observes that this transitory world and brief life, even if man was given the rule of all the world with its wealth and pleasures, do not satisfy the ambitions of man, despite the fact that the subtleties of man are not yet fully activated in this world. So it is obvious that this finite world is not sufficient for the infinite needs of these subtleties:[529]

> Just as we saw by looking at the identity papers of an officer in our comparison that his rank, duty, wage, instructions and equipment prove that he exists not for the sake of some temporary battlefield, but rather that he is proceeding to some permanent kingdom, for the sake of which he is exerting himself—so too those to whom truth and certainty have been unveiled are unanimously agreed that the subtleties inscribed in the book of man's heart, the senses written down in the notebook of his intellect, the equipment contained in his essential character, are all turned towards Eternal Bliss; they have been given to man and fashioned in accordance with this ultimate goal.[530]

Nursi concludes that God has prepared for man a Paradise of "everlasting favors that will satisfy all the longings of your spirit, heart, mind, and other subtle inner faculties."[531]

## Testifying to lata'if

A particular duty of the subtleties mentioned in the *Epistles of Light* is testifying against the man who misuses them. Nursi claims that by leaving himself to his ego and the worldly life of temporary pleasures, man

---

[529] *The Words*, 518.
[530] *The Words*, 101.
[531] *The Words*, 369.

limits himself to an "extremely constricted sphere." Upon his departure from this world, "All the members, systems, and faculties given him will testify against him at the resurrection and will bring a suit against him."[532] This is so, because making "the elevated subtle faculties subject to the soul and caprice and [making] them forget their fundamental duties is certainly decline and not progress"[533] and man is accountable for how he used the "capital of *lata'if* and human abilities given to him to buy eternal diamonds," if he gives them to "temporary bottles and pieces of cold ice."[534]

## Two Dominical Subtle Faculties: Heart and Spirit

On several occasions Nursi gives special place to heart and spirit among all the subtleties and calls them the dominical subtle faculties.[535] Although on occasion Nursi uses the term independently of heart and spirit, and some of his passages give the sense that there is a dominical subtle faculty other than these two, the dominant tone in the *Epistles of Light* is that both heart and spirit are dominical subtle faculties. Whether there are other dominical subtle faculties or not, or whether Nursi uses this combination simply to connote subtleties in general, is not clear. Since the spirit is defined by Nursi as the law harmonizing senses and subtleties of the body, and the heart is defined as the commander of all other subtleties, it is legitimate to give special place to these two subtleties.

## The Spirit (*Ruh*)

The meaning of *ruh* in Islamic terminology has been a topic of discussion since the time of the Prophet. The Qur'an notes that the Prophet's interlocutors asked him about the spirit, and suggests that he answers: "The spirit is from the command of my Lord, and you have been given little knowledge!"[536] Throughout the history of Islam, this verse has also set the benchmark, and the issue of the spirit was left the least studied among

---

532 *The Words*, 333.
533 *The Words*, 332.
534 *Barla Lahikası, RNK*, 1520.
535 *The Reasonings: A Key to Understanding the Qur'an's Eloquence*, 16; *Signs of Miraculousness*, 86.
536 *Holy Qur'an*, 17:85.

the major subtleties. Nursi is no exception in terms of the amount of information he gives about *ruh*, but an exceptional passage claims:

> Spirit is a law possessing external existence, a conscious law. Like the stable and enduring laws of creation, spirit comes from the World of the Divine Command and the attribute of will. Divine power clothes it an existence decked out with senses. He [God] makes a subtle, flowing being the shell to that jewel. Existent spirit is the brother of the conceivable law. They are both enduring and come from the World of the Divine Command. If pre-eternal power had clothed the laws governing in the species of beings in external existence, they would have been spirits. And if the spirit banishes consciousness, it still would be an undying law.[537]

There is no other direct definition of the spirit in the *Epistles of Light*. Passages scattered throughout the *Epistles* about the spirit are either about the properties of the spirit, or about its perfection, its pleasures and its instruments. The following passage is particularly important as it creates a hierarchy among the living beings on the basis of spirit:

> ... the choicest result of the universe is life, and the choicest essence of life is spirit, and the choicest of beings with spirits are intelligent beings, and of intelligent beings the one with the most comprehensive nature is man; and since all the universe is subjugated to life and works for life, and living beings are subjugated to beings with spirits and they are sent to this world for them, and beings with spirits are subjugated to man and they assist him [...] He [God] surely would not offend men, who love Him greatly and are loved, by causing them to die then not raising them again to life, and while He created them for an eternal love, to make them feel eternal hostility; to do that would not be possible.[538]

---

[537] *The Letters*, 530–31. For a similar, and similarly difficult passage see *The Words*, 735. With a reverse logic Nursi also claims that if the laws that govern in species were clothed in external existence, each of them would become the spirit of the species (*The Words*, 537). This definition of spirit is informed by Sa'd al-Taftazani's definition in *Maqasidu't-Talibin fi i'-lmi Usuli'd-Din* (completed in 784) and the exegesis he wrote for this book named *Al-Jazru'l-Asam*. Nursi attests to his indebtedness to al-Taftazani in *Barla Lahikası, RNK*, 1515.

[538] *The Rays*, 64–65. A similar hierarchy is given in *The Flashes*, this time in a reverse order: "... just as life is the distilled essence of the universe; and consciousness

## Immortality of the Spirit

A major issue Nursi deals with in relation to the spirit is its immortality. In line with the orthodox Islamic doctrine of the spirit, Nursi underlines the fact that "the body subsists though the spirit; in which case, the spirit does not subsist through the body. Rather, since the spirit subsists and is dominant of itself, the body may be dispersed and gathered together again as it wishes; it will not infringe the spirit's independence."[539] Nursi uses commonplace experiences of engagement with the spirits of deceased people as empirical and objective evidence of immortality of the spirit. His logic is simple, but convincing: "Indeed, when it is understood that a single spirit continues after death, this necessitates the continuation of all spirits as a category of being. For according to the science of logic it is certain that if an intrinsic quality is observed in a single individual, the existence of that quality may be assumed in all individuals."[540]As Nursi regards the spirit as the unifying force of the machine called a human being,[541] that unifying force should not be subject to dissolution or destruction. Nursi explains:

> As for spirit, it is not subject to destruction and dissolution. This is because it is simple and uncompounded; it has unity. As for destruction, dissolution and decomposition, they are the function of com-

---

and sense perception are distilled from life and are the essence of life; and intelligence too is distilled from consciousness and sense perception and is the essence of consciousness; and spirit is the pure, unsullied substance of life, its stable and autonomous essence ..." (*The Flashes*, 430).

[539] *The Words*, 535.

[540] *The Words*, 536. A similar logic is used in the *Signs of Miraculousness*, in a passage that deals with the nature of death: "... the innumerable signs and tokens human beings have witnessed up to the present have planted in their minds the conviction and surmise that after death man is immortal in one respect, and what has immortality is his spirit. Thus, the existence of this inherent property in an individual is evidence of its existence in the race as a whole, because it is essential. Consequently [in accordance with the rule of logic], the particular proposition necessitates the universal one. Hence, death is a miracle of [divine] power the same as life is; it is not non-existence caused by the absence of the conditions of life" (*Signs of Miraculousness*, 245).

[541] See, below, the section that deals with the relationship between the body and the spirit.

plex and compound substances. As we explained above, life ensures a form of unity within multiplicity; it causes a sort of permanence. That is to say, unity and permanence are fundamental to spirit, from which they spread to multiplicity.[542]

Nursi uses nature as a metaphor to the immortality of the spirit, which is preserved just as the "large flowering and fruit bearing plants are formed and the representations of their forms are preserved and perpetuated in most regular fashion in tiny seeds throughout tempestuous changes."[543] In a rather intriguing passage, Nursi also claims that if the fruits created every year in exact similitude of the previous year had spirits like human beings, "they would be the actual fruits that died last year."[544]

## Relationship of the Spirit to Time and Space

Nursi believes in the relative freedom of spirit (and heart) from constraints of time and space. According to him, the expansion of time and space for a person is a sign of elevation to the life-level of the spirit. "Time, which for others consists of the past and the future, is as though the present for such a person," he says.[545] The precondition of breaking the constraints of time and space is belief, since

> belief takes from the hands of the body the reins of the faculty of will, which cannot penetrate to the past and future, and hands them over to the heart and spirit. Since the sphere of their life is not restricted to present time like the body, and included within it are a great many years from the past and a great many years from the future, the will ceases being limited and acquires universality. Through the strength of belief it may enter the deepest valleys of the past and repel the darkness of its sorrows; so too with the light of belief it may rise as far as the farthest mountains of the future, and remove its fears.[546]

---

[542] *The Words*, 536.
[543] *The Words*, 87–88.
[544] *Al-Mathnawi Al-Nuri: Seedbed of the Light*, 155.
[545] *The Letters*, 69.
[546] *The Letters*, 294.

The spirit can also move in space with utmost speed, because "near and far are the same in relation to the spirit."[547] Just as the air does not prevent us from walking, or water from diving, nothing can stop or prevent the spirit and its servants from wandering around, Nursi says.[548] Nursi uses this relative omniscience of the spirit to explain how "the people of Paradise, whose bodies have the strength and lightness of the spirit and the swiftness of imagination" will be in "hundreds of thousands of places at the same time."[549]

The spirit's freedom from time and space restraints reaches, for elevated spirits, to such a level that they can communicate with Paradise "by means of the telephone of the heart, and receive gifts from Paradise."[550] This also explains the ability of certain soothsayers to give news from the Unseen using jinn and the spirits,[551] and of certain saints to form a relation with the spirits "by going to their place and drawing close to their world to an extent, to benefit from their spirituality."[552]

## Sicknesses of the Spirit

Nursi believes that corresponding to the outer wounds and sicknesses of the body, man has "inner sicknesses of the spirit and heart."[553] "Sins are the chronic illnesses of eternal life, and in this worldly life they are sicknesses of the heart, conscience, and spirit,"[554] as "each sin that we commit and each doubt that enters our mind inflicts wounds on our heart and our spirit."[555]

The two greatest sicknesses of the spirit are disbelief and misguidance.[556] Disbelief is not only a sickness in its own right, it also causes pain and suffering to the spirit:

---

[547] *The Words*, 720.
[548] *Arabic Mesnevi*, 275.
[549] *The Words*, 519.
[550] *The Flashes*, 377.
[551] *The Letters*, 211.
[552] *The Words*, 266.
[553] *The Flashes*, 22.
[554] *The Flashes*, 270.
[555] *The Flashes*, 22.
[556] *Signs of Miraculousness*, 68.

The person, therefore, who does not believe in the everlasting life of the hereafter casts himself into a sort of Hell in this world, arising from his unbelief, and suffers constant torment. As is described in *A Guide For Youth*, through their death and parting, all the past and the future and creatures and universes continuously rain down endless pains on his spirit and heart, making him suffer the torments of Hell before going there.[557]

Nursi counts "worship of the human form,"[558] "struggle for livelihood together with lack of reliance on God,"[559] "to flatter the ego and give high status to the evil-commanding soul by attracting attention to oneself and public acclaim, driven by the desire for fame, renown, and position,"[560] "excess (*al-ifrat*) or deficiency (*al-tafrit*) in the three powers of intellect, anger, and animal appetites,"[561] and, for nervous spirits, "politics in this time"[562] as other sicknesses of the spirit.

## Sustenance and Pleasures of the Spirit

We have already seen that Nursi ascribes different pleasures and duties to each of the *lata'if* and that subtleties like heart, spirit and intelligence have their specific means of sustenance. The subtleties also have different perceptions of beauty:

> ... beauty perceived by the eye is not the same as something beautiful heard with the ears, and an abstract beauty comprehended by the mind is not the same as the beauty of food relished by the tongue; so too, the beauties appreciated and perceived as beautiful by the external and inner senses and the spirit are all different. For example, the beauty of belief, the beauty of reality, the beauty of light, the beauty of a flower, the beauty of spirit, and the beauties of form, compassion, justice, kindness, and wisdom. Similarly, since the utter

---

[557] *The Rays*, 583.
[558] *The Words*, 423.
[559] *The Words*, 508.
[560] *The Flashes*, 220.
[561] *Signs of Miraculousness*, 232.
[562] *Kastamonu Lahikası, RNK*, 1620.

and infinite beauties of the Most Beautiful Names of the All-Beauteous One of Glory are all different, the beauties in beings also differ.[563]

As disbelief is the prime sickness of the spirit (and heart), belief in God and in the Hereafter is the prime sustenance of these subtleties: "O man! Your one and only point of support is belief in God. The only source of assistance for your spirit and conscience is belief in the hereafter. One who does not know of these two sources suffers constant fear in his heart and spirit, and his conscience is perpetually tormented."[564]

Naturally, guidance to belief has to be counted among the bounties of the spirit. "For of itself it is the greatest bounty, and rapture of the conscience; it is the paradise of the spirit. ... Later it will produce the fruits of happiness and salvation in the hereafter."[565] Recitation of the Qur'an and repetitive reading of some of its passages comes third in Nursi's list of sustenance of the spirit. It is "food and sustenance for the heart, strength and wealth for the mind, water and light for the spirit, and the cure and remedy for the soul,"[566] Nursi says. In Nursi's understanding, the words of the Qur'an are like basic sustenance, not like fruits, since "they strengthen the mind and feed the spirit. The more they are repeated, the better they seem and the more familiar they become, like sunlight,"[567] unlike fruits, which give rise to boredom when repeated and provide pleasure when replaced with something new. This is because "for fourteen centuries at every moment its six thousand, six hundred and sixty-six verses have been read by the tongues of more than a hundred million men, training them, refining their souls and purifying their hearts."[568] Thus the Qur'an offers to spirits "a means of development and advancement," to intellects "an orientation and light," and to life "life itself and felicity."[569]

Daily Prayer is also a great sustenance of the spirit, as "the spirit, the heart, and the mind find great ease in Prayer"[570] and as Daily Prayer

[563] *The Rays*, 86 (with minor alterations in translation).
[564] *The Rays*, 651.
[565] *Signs of Miraculousness*, 68.
[566] *The Words*, 389.
[567] *Signs of Miraculousness*, 36.
[568] *The Rays*, 157.
[569] *The Rays*, 157.
[570] *The Words*, 33.

allows one's spirit to relax and one's heart to take a breather,[571] and these Prayers "attract the needs of your (of the soul's) companions in the house of my body, the sustenance of my heart, the water of life of my spirit, and the air of my subtle faculties."[572]

Prayer is also a sustenance for the spirit as its observation turns regular daily work or terms of imprisonment into Prayer,[573] just as the light of belief turns the bounty of hearing into a bounty for the subtleties also, causing the ear to hear the "dominical speech in the sighing of the blowing wind, the peals of the rolling thunder-clouds, the refrains of the billowing sea, the clamor of the throbbing stones, the pattering of the falling rain, and the songs of the twittering birds," turning the universe into a vast orchestra arousing in his heart an elevated sorrow and exciting passion in his spirit.[574]

Apart from these, Nursi mentions the believer's reading of the *Epistles of Light*,[575] travelling and visiting old friends "both in reality or in dreams"[576] as a healing for the spirit and a nourishment for the heart.

## Relationship between the Body and the Spirit

We have already seen that Nursi regarded the spirit as a kind of centripetal force keeping the parts of the human body together, orchestrating their moves and using them for various ends. Nursi elaborates on this point in *The Words*:

> The relationship between man's spirit and his body is such that it causes all his members and parts to assist one another. ... Thus, in administering the parts of the body, and hearing their immaterial voices, and seeing their needs, they do not form obstacles to one another, nor do they confuse the spirit. Near and far are the same in relation to the spirit. They do not veil one another. If the spirit wishes, it can bring the majority to the assistance of one. If it wishes, it can know, perceive, and administer through each part of the

---

[571] *The Words*, 279.
[572] *The Words*, 277.
[573] *The Rays*, 214.
[574] *Signs of Miraculousness*, 77.
[575] *Emirdağ Lahikası, RNK*, 1703.
[576] *Emirdağ Lahikası, RNK*, 1764.

body. Even if it acquires great luminosity, it may see and hear through all the parts.[577]

This relationship is further clarified when Nursi claims that "the body is the spirit's house, it is its home; it is not its clothes." He goes on to elaborate that the spirit itself is clothed in "a subtle, fine sheath, something which may be likened to a body, which is to some extent constant, and is ethereal and appropriate for the spirit," and that thus at the time of death "the spirit is not completely naked, it leaves its home dressed in its body-like sheath."[578]

This description of the cloth of the spirit resembles the aura of the theosophists. This thesis cannot be proved or disproved, however. In any event, Nursi believed that the spirit was a law clothed in a body-like sheath and that this body-like sheath overlapped with the physical body as long as the body was alive, and the relation between the two is cut when the spirit, together with its clothing, leaves the body at death.

The detachment between the body and the spirit is not eternal, however. Nursi makes it clear that the spirit and the body are united once again in Paradise, "because it is the body that is the means by which the duties of worship are performed and the means of innumerable pleasures and pains."[579]

The body, together with the spirit, houses all the other senses and subtleties of man, and the spirit is a unifying force coordinating the moves of these senses and subtleties. Inescapably, the spirit has relations with the physical organs or senses of the body. Nursi mentions the eye as a window through which the spirit looks out on this world,[580] the tongue as being to the spirit as a key is to a lock,[581] and the sense of taste as inducing the heart, spirit, and mind to thank God by recognizing and perceiving the varieties of divine bounty.[582]

---

[577]  *The Words*, 720.
[578]  *The Words*, 535.
[579]  . *The Words*, 596.
[580]  *The Words*, 39.
[581]  *Signs of Miraculousness*, 22.
[582]  *The Flashes*, 191.

The spirit (and heart and mind) also has a unique relationship with the soul. This relationship remains antithetical as long as the soul is at the level of "evil-commanding soul,"[583] where the soul rejects obeying the heart and the spirit.[584] But the soul can discipline itself and learn to listen to commands[585]—particularly through fasting—and the relationship between the spirit and the soul may turn into one of obedience. At this level, the spirit rules the body, the heart rules the desires of the soul, and reason rules the stomach.[586]

## Instruments and Powers of the Spirit

The spirit in charge of unifying the body, its senses and subtleties is given certain instruments and powers with which to realize its duties. A passage directly related to the powers of the spirit (*ruh*) counts three of them: the power of animal appetites (faculty of concupiscence) to attract benefits; the power of savage passion (faculty of anger) to repulse harmful and destructive things; and the power of angelic intellect to distinguish between benefit and harm.[587] Nursi then goes on to detail how these should be utilized:

> However, since His wisdom necessitated that humanity should achieve perfection through the mystery of competition, Allah placed no innate limitation on these powers, as He did on those of other living beings. He did however limit them through the Shari'a, for it prohibits excess (*ifrat*) and deficiency (*tafrit*) and enjoins the middle way (*wasat*). ... In the absence of any innate limitation, three degrees arise in the three powers: the degree of deficiency, which is negligence; the degree of superabundance, which is excess; and the middle way, which is justice.[588]

In another passage Nursi defines will, intellect, sense, and dominical subtle faculty as the four elements of the conscience and four senses of

---

[583] *The Words*, 46.

[584] *Emirdağ Lahikası*, 1764.

[585] *The Letters*, 463.

[586] *The Flashes*, 191–92.

[587] *Signs of Miraculousness*, 29.

[588] *Signs of Miraculousness*, 29.

the spirit. He suggests that each one of these four senses has a particular "aim of aims." The aim of aims of the will is the worship of God, that of the intellect is the knowledge of God, that of the sense is the love of God, and finally the aim of aims of the dominical subtle faculty is the sight of God.[589] On other occasions Nursi counts premonition (foresight)[590] and imagination[591] as faculties used by the spirit.

## Perfection of the Spirit

Just like the soul, which has seven stages, the spirit has a vast range of qualifications. At the two extremes Nursi puts "a spirit like coal" and "a spirit like diamonds."[592] This allegorical naming does not say anything about the state of a spirit that is like coal, but makes it clear that this life of examination and competition is intended to purify the spirit, together with other subtleties, and elevate it from inferior levels to superior ones.

We have already seen Nursi's four-step path to perfection, which included impotence, poverty, compassion, and reflective thought. As a general rule Nursi regards religion, particularly Islam, as the path to perfection of the subtleties.[593]

Nursi claims that the Islamic religion and Shari'a make up the essence of "the science of refining the spirit, and of training the heart, and of educating the conscience," together with all other material sciences.[594] For Nursi, the path to perfection is the wide path of religion and Shari'a, and there is no need to run after psychic methods. Only once does he mention the inverse relation between the size of the body and the quality of the spirit,[595] hinting at a kind of training of the spirit through fasting and

---

[589]  *Hutbe-i Şamiye, RNK*, 1980.

[590]  *The Flashes*, 312. Nursi is consistent in relating the premonition to the spirit. See *Tarihçe-i Hayat*, 201 for a similar use of the term. Only in Letters, 402, Nursi suggests that the premonition is used by a dominical subtle faculty. Whether this dominical subtle faculty is the spirit, or heart, or any other intermediary faculty is not clear.

[591]  *The Rays*, 607.

[592]  *The Words*, 275.

[593]  *Signs of Miraculousness*, 231.

[594]  *Signs of Miraculousness*, 188.

[595]  "The spirit weakens on account of the body, and the body becomes finer on account of the spirit," *The Words*, 551.

avoiding bodily pleasures. He also believed that active service to belief and the cause of spreading the message of the Qur'an would provide his students with such eternal merits, virtues, and joys of the spirit and heart that it would reduce their sorrows and hardships in this world to nothing.[596]

## Heart (*Qalb*)

In Sufi terminology the "heart" plays a large part, for it is viewed both as the source of man's good and evil aspirations and as the seat of learning or religious apprehension and of divine visitations.[597] It is regarded as the battleground of intellect and lower soul. There in the heart lies the secret and hidden (*sirr*) home of the conscience, and also the place of Satan. It is with his heart that man "understands," and receives inspirations and intuitions. It is also the seat of all moral impulses, both evil desires and instincts and the struggle to be free of them.[598] And the heart is the seat of belief. "The first evidences of the Maker are manifested from the heart's consultation with itself and from the conscience referring to the innate disposition."[599]

Nursi's definition of *qalb* as a dominical subtle faculty is quite clear:

What is meant by the heart is the dominical subtle faculty—not the piece of flesh shaped like a pinecone—the emotions of which are manifested in the conscience and the thoughts of which are reflected in the mind. The term heart indicates that the dominical subtle faculty is to man's spiritual dimensions what the cone-shaped piece of flesh is to the body. For just as the physical heart is a life-machine that pumps the water of life to all the parts of the body, and if it is obstructed or ceases from activity, [life departs and] the body stiffens; so the subtle inner faculty dispenses the light of true life to all the parts of the corpus composed of man's spiritual aspects, and his [mental] states, and hopes. And if, God forbid, the light of belief

---

[596] *The Rays*, 321.
[597] Gardet, L. and Vadet, J. C. "Kalb," *Encyclopaedia of Islam*, ed. P. Bearman, T. Bianquis, C. E. Bosworth, E. van Donzel and W. P. Heinrichs (Leiden: Brill, 2008).
[598] Ibid.
[599] *Signs of Miraculousness*, 85.

fades away, his being, with which he contends with the universe, becomes like a motionless spectre, dark in its entirety.[600]

It has to be underlined that the heart, and not the brain, is also the seat of the intellect. Nursi makes a clear distinction between the working of the brain and that of the heart:

> ... since man is a comprehensive index of the universe, his heart resembles a map of thousands of worlds. For innumerable human sciences and fields of knowledge show that man's brain in his head is a sort of center of the universe, like a telephone and telegraph exchange for innumerable lines. Similarly, the millions of light-scattering books written by incalculable saints show man's heart in his essential being to be the place of manifestation of innumerable cosmic truths, and to be their pivot, and seed.[601]

On other occasions Nursi defines heart as the mainspring of the human machine,[602] the seat of belief,[603] the seat of the remembrance and knowledge of God,[604] a most brilliant and comprehensive mirror to the universe's Maker,[605] the faculty the receives inspirations,[606] the arising place of meanings,[607] and the battleground of "inspirations and Satanic whisperings."[608]

## Sustenance of the Heart

We have already seen that the subtle capacities and senses of man require sustenance "from the Compassionate Provider" in the same way that the

---

[600] *Signs of Miraculousness*, 86.

[601] *The Letters*, 507.

[602] *The Letters*, 522.

[603] *The Words*, 766. A few lines below Nursi says that both "the heart and conscience are the seat of belief." See also *Signs of Miraculousness*, 85.

[604] *The Flashes*, 21.

[605] *The Words*, 641.

[606] *The Letters*, 447.

[607] "...when meanings arise in the heart, they enter the imagination stripped of form; it is there that they are clothed in an image or form" (*The Words*, 282).

[608] *The Words*, 195. See also *The Words*, 283, where Nursi reminds his readers of the proximity of Satan and the angel of inspiration to one another around the heart. In *The Flashes* Nursi suggests that man can mix the whisperings of Satan as coming from his heart (*The Flashes*, 110).

stomach requires feeding.[609] Nursi observes that the senses and subtleties of man are created in such a way that they will be able to receive
their sustenance:

> [God] had placed in my head a brain, and in my breast a heart, and
> in my mouth a tongue containing hundreds of scales and measures
> with which I might weigh up and know all the gifts of that Most
> Merciful One stored up in the treasuries of mercy. He had inscribed
> on these, thousands of instruments for unlocking and understand-
> ing the treasures of the infinite manifestations of His Most Beautiful
> Names, and given numerous smells, tastes, and colours to the assis-
> tance of those instruments.[610]

The utmost pleasure and sustenance of the heart is belief in one God
and in the Hereafter. The core of the heart accepts only the One, the Single. It is "content with nothing other than eternity and the Eternal One.
It can address itself to none but He."[611] "It is as if the heart has world-
filling adversities and hostilities. It is satisfied only with the One who
can make it independent of, and protect it from, everything."[612]

Belief is such sustenance for the heart that it changes the perceptions of man. In the *23rd Word* Nursi mentions a man "that attains to
Divine guidance and belief enters his heart, and ... the tyranny of his soul
is smashed." Eventually that man realizes the real nature of events of
this world that he previously perceived as bad. "He will even see death
to be the introduction to eternal life, and the grave, the door to everlasting happiness,"[613] contends Nursi. One who does not have a belief in God
and in the Hereafter "suffers constant fear in his heart and spirit, and his
conscience is perpetually tormented."[614] Human spirit and the heart, suffering countless needs and the attacks of innumerable enemies, are
saved from utter desolation and from aching sorrow only through belief,
which ensures an eternal joy, a perpetual happiness.[615] A critical dimen-

---

[609] *The Rays*, 195. See also *The Rays*, 582.
[610] *The Rays*, 76 (with minor alterations in translation).
[611] *The Flashes*, 158.
[612] *Al-Mathnawi al-Nuri: Seedbed of the Light*, 170 (with alterations in translation).
[613] *The Words*, 322.
[614] *The Rays*, 651.
[615] *The Letters*, 262–63.

sion of the joy and happiness that fill the heart through belief is the promise that believers will "behold the vision of Divine beauty in eternal happiness" in Paradise.[616]

Not unrelated to belief, listening to the Qur'an is also sustenance for the heart. Man listening to the Qur'an with the ear of his heart "may rise through the ascension of worship to the throne of perfections. He may become an eternal man."[617] Tranquility of the heart is only in the light of the Qur'an.[618] With its inimitability, the text of the Qur'an, "flowing like water and shining like the stars," is also sustenance for the heart.[619] The Qur'an "fills the spirit with ardor, the heart with delight, the mind with interest, and the eyes with tears."[620]

Together with recitation of the Qur'an, invocation of the Beautiful Names of Allah and phrases glorifying God are also a source of sustenance and of joy for the heart. Nursi finds a most effective means of working the heart in turning it toward the truths of faith through remembrance of God.[621] Hence, "all the saints and purified ones have found their sweetest illuminations and most delectable spiritual sustenance in repeated recitation of 'There is no god but God,' the profession of Divine unity."[622] Apart from the invocation of this phrase, Nursi described the invocation of "He is One" as a refuge and protector that will deliver the spirit and the heart from all the confusion and bewilderment,[623] and the invocation of "O Eternal One, You alone are Eternal!" as a kind of surgical operation that severs the heart from everything other than God.[624]

---

[616] *The Words*, 610.

[617] *The Words*, 374. See also *The Letters*, 471 and this poetic passage: "Since everywhere is a guesthouse, if the mercy of the guesthouse's Owner befriends one, everyone is a friend and everywhere is familiar. Whereas if it does not befriend one, everywhere is a load on the heart and everyone is hostile" (*The Letters*, 93).

[618] *The Letters*, 227. The translator uses "peace of mind" for "tranquility of heart."

[619] "It gives both pleasure and delight to the heart like dates. And it is sustenance" (*The Words*, 393).

[620] *The Words*, 394.

[621] *The Letters*, 508.

[622] *The Rays*, 17.

[623] *The Letters*, 263.

[624] *The Flashes*, 30.

Itself a disciplined and organized invocation of the Beautiful Names and recitation of sections from the Qur'an, Daily Prayer should also be counted as sustenance for the heart:

> Yes, it is by knocking through supplication on the door of One All-Compassionate and Munificent that sustenance and strength may be obtained for a heart afflicted with infinite grief and sorrows and captivated by infinite pleasures and hopes. And it is by turning towards the spring of mercy of an Eternal Beloved through the five Daily Prayers that the water of life may be imbibed by a spirit connected with most beings, which swiftly depart from this transitory world crying out at separation. And being most needy for air in the sorrowful, crushing, distressing, transient, dark, and suffocating conditions of this world, it is only through the window of the Prayers that a conscious inner sense and luminous subtle faculty can breathe, which by its nature desires eternal life and was created for eternity and is a mirror of the Pre-Eternal and Post-Eternal One and is infinitely delicate and subtle.[625]

The Daily Prayer is such sustenance that it turns transient time into permanent time[626] and mundane worldly works into Prayers.[627] Five Daily Prayers should not "cause man boredom," for Daily Prayer is "the sustenance of my heart, the water of life of my spirit, and the air of my subtle faculties."[628] It is not tiring for the body, and the spirit, the heart and the mind find great ease in Prayer.[629]

As in the case of the spirit, the heart also takes its share from reading the *Epistles of Light*. Nursi believes that this quality of the *Epistles* is based on it being a contemporary exegesis of the Qur'an. He believed wholeheartedly that being occupied with the *Epistles*, through "studying it, or reading it out loud, or writing it out," "affords an expansiveness to the heart, an ease to the spirit, health to the body, and makes sustenance plentiful."[630] Nursi observed that certain parts of the *Epistles* had a heal-

---

[625] *The Words*, 277.
[626] *The Rays*, 214.
[627] *The Words*, 279.
[628] *The Words*, 277.
[629] *The Words*, 33.
[630] *The Rays*, 483.

ing effect on his "various deep ills"[631] and that "those whose spirits are needy and hearts wounded search out and find those Qur'anic remedies" of the *Epistles*.[632]

On other occasions, Nursi counts the principles and matters of the Shari'a and practices of the Prophet,[633] good health and well-being,[634] as sources of pleasure and means of sustenance for the heart.

## Sicknesses of the Heart

Unsurprisingly, disbelief is a common sickness of the spirit and the heart.[635] Nursi comments that not only is disbelief a sickness that will hurt the heart in the Hereafter, but that unbelievers are losers "by reason of their pangs of conscience, anxious hearts, and desolate spirits" in this world also.[636] In particular the failure to believe in resurrection "arouses in the heart the pathetic sorrow of the orphan; that is, the lack of friends; and the desolation of alienation; that is, being without owner or guardian."[637] That is so, because the human heart yearns for eternity, and disbelief makes man regard death as separation from life and friends once and for all.[638]

Another major sickness of the heart is to use for other purposes the love that is included in man's nature for the Creator, or to use the fear that is given for fear of God for other fears.[639] In another passage Nursi goes further and claims, "the inner heart is the mirror of the Eternally Besought One and pertains only to Him." Accordingly, he warns his readers not to give other loves the opportunity to enter into their inner hearts.[640]

We have already seen while discussing the sicknesses of the spirit that sins are a common sickness of the spirit and the heart. They may,

---

[631] *The Rays*, 70.
[632] *The Letters*, 90.
[633] *The Flashes*, 88.
[634] *The Rays*, 338.
[635] *Signs of Miraculousness*, 74.
[636] *Signs of Miraculousness*, 237.
[637] *Signs of Miraculousness*, 77.
[638] *The Flashes*, 33. See also *The Rays*, 24 and *The Words*, 156.
[639] *The Words*, 367; *The Flashes*, 30.
[640] *The Words*, 670.

however, have further implications for the heart: "... the temptations and doubts that arise from those wounds will—may God protect us! —penetrate our inner heart, the seat of belief, and thus wound belief. Penetrating too the spiritual joy of the tongue, the interpreter of belief, they cause it to shun in revulsion the remembrance of God, and reduce it to silence."[641]

Unless the sin is swiftly obliterated by seeking God's pardon, it will grow from a worm into a snake that gnaws on the heart,[642] and, eventually penetrating the heart, repeated sins will "blacken and darken it until it extinguishes the light of belief."[643]

One particular sickness of the heart Nursi deals with is the sickness that exists even in the most sound and illuminated hearts:[644]

> Many great saints and holy men have complained about their evil-commanding souls although their souls were tranquil. They have lamented over sicknesses of the heart although their hearts were completely sound and illumined. But what afflicted these persons was not their evil-commanding souls, but the soul's functions that had been handed over to their nerves. Their ailments were not of the heart, but of the imagination.[645]

Despite the fact that he deals with the sicknesses of the heart in passages scattered around the *Epistles of Light*, it should be noted that Nursi ranks striving to "eliminate the sicknesses of the heart by way of Sufism and ... journey with the feet of the heart" third in importance in the Naqshbandi way. The first and second places go to serving the truths of faith directly, and to advancing the cause of the religious obligations and serving the glorious practices of the Prophet.[646]

On other occasions Nursi counts doubt cast by Satan into the heart,[647] worry about physical illnesses,[648] feelings of materialism,[649] feelings of

---

[641] *The Flashes*, 22.
[642] *The Flashes*, 22.
[643] *The Flashes*, 22.
[644] *The Letters*, 380.
[645] *The Letters*, 380.
[646] *The Letters*, 38–39.
[647] *The Words*, 281.
[648] *The Flashes*, 272.
[649] *The Words*, 770–71.

enmity toward others,[650] disquiet in the heart,[651] and desire for position[652] as sicknesses of the heart.

## Relationship between the Heart and Other Subtleties

Nursi's main observation about the relationship between the heart and other subtleties is that ideally the heart is the commander of all other subtle faculties.[653] This is not always the case. "Sometimes the soul's emotions affect certain veins of character, and predominate to an extent in spite of the heart, mind, and spirit ... the soul, desires, emotions, and imagination sometimes deceive."[654]

Nursi observes a natural alliance between the heart and the spirit. "Just as one hand cannot compete with the other, so one eye cannot criticize the other, nor the tongue object to the ear, nor the heart sees the spirit's faults,"[655] he says. But he is also aware that occasionally the external senses may obstruct the heart and the spirit, since "if a finger is wounded, the eye, mind, and heart neglect their important duties and become preoccupied with it. Similarly, our lives, which reach this pitch of distress, busy our hearts and spirits with their wounds."[656]

Ideally, the relationship between heart and intellect[657] is a dialogic one. The heart predominates over the intellect, but intellect has its control over what comes out of the heart also. "The light of reason comes from the heart ... So long as the lights of the mind and of the heart are

---

[650] "If you wish to nourish enmity, then direct it against the enmity in your heart, and attempt to rid yourself of it. Be an enemy to your evil-commanding soul and its caprice and attempt to reform it, for it inflicts more harm on you than all else. Do not engage in enmity against other believers on account of that injurious soul" (*The Letters*, 309).

[651] *The Letters*, 411.

[652] *The Letters*, 476.

[653] *The Words*, 511; *The Flashes*, 185. Also: "It is the sovereign of your senses and faculties" (*The Flashes*, 158).

[654] *The Flashes*, 221.

[655] *The Flashes*, 215.

[656] *The Rays*, 326.

[657] The Turkish words for mind, intellect, and reason are interchangeable and there is no way to detect Nursi's intended choice between these three. It if most probable that he saw no distinction between these concepts.

not combined, there is darkness, producing oppression and ignorance."[658] Nursi is aware that at certain times and for certain people the heart predominates over reason.[659] But the dominant tone in the *Epistles of Light* is that Nursi would prefer "the light of the Qur'an," which has connotations of the heart, to "the genius of Rome," that is rationalism, since the guidance of the Qur'an "works in the heart, and works the mind," while "genius works in the mind and confuses the heart."[660]

As for the relationship between the heart and the external senses, Nursi is of the idea that for "those who approach reality with their hearts" external senses may work as servants of the subtleties, particularly those of the heart and spirit. The sense of taste can work as a "supervisor and inspector in the kitchens of divine mercy," helping the heart, spirit, and mind recognize and perceive the varieties of divine bounty and carry out their duty of thanks.[661]

Accordingly, if man's spirit rules his body, "and his heart rules the desires of his soul, and his reason rules his stomach, and he wants pleasure for the sake of offering thanks, then he may eat delicious things."[662] In a similar manner, the tongue functions, apart from being the organ of tasting, as "an accurate interpreter and telephone exchange for the heart, spirit, and mind in the function of speech," pointing to an all-encompassing knowledge.[663]

## Relationship of the Heart to Time and Space

We have already seen that the spirit is relatively free of time and space constraints. In almost all the passages that mention the spirit's level of life and the vastness of its universe, the heart is mentioned also. In only one passage does Nursi contend that the freedom of the heart from time and space constraints is not at the level of the spirit's freedom:

---

[658] *The Words*, 739; *The Letters*, 532.
[659] *The Letters*, 447. Compare with this passage: "This lesson looks to the heart more than the reason, and regards spiritual pleasure and perception rather than rational proofs" (*The Words*, 18).
[660] *The Words*, 747.
[661] *The Flashes*, 191.
[662] *The Flashes*, 192.
[663] *The Rays*, 616.

Just as the hands of a clock counting the seconds, and those count-ing the minutes, hours, and days superficially resemble each other but differ in respect of their speed, so too the spheres of the body, soul, heart, and spirit in man differ from one another. For example, the body possesses an immortality, a life, and an existence in the present day, and even in the present hour while its past and future are dead and non-existent, but the heart's sphere of existence and life extends from many days previous to the present day and to many days in the future. Then the sphere of the spirit is vast; its life and existence extends from years previous to the present day to years subsequent to it.[664]

The fact that the spirit has greater freedom from time and space does not suggest a superiority of the spirit over the heart. The imagina-tion is completely free of any limitations of time and space, yet it is still a servant of the heart and mind.[665] It will be useful to remember here that the freedom of heart and spirit from the constraints of time and space is not a given but a taken quality. Only through belief are man's narrow time and space "transformed into a broad and easy world. This extensive world becomes like man's house, and the past and the future like present time for his spirit and heart. The distance between them disappears."[666]

## Instruments and States of the Heart

Nursi speaks of the eye,[667] ear,[668] and telephone[669] of the heart on differ-ent occasions. All of these usages are allegorical. The eye of the heart is the window of the heart opened to the unseen, and "the telephone, it is a

---

[664] *The Flashes*, 32.

[665] *The Rays*, 604–5.

[666] *The Rays*, 651; *The Words*, 489; *The Flashes*, 294.

[667] "The eyes of my heart wept ..." (*The Words*, 228); "he will see with the eye of the heart ..." (*The Words*, 322).

[668] "if he listens with the ear of his heart" (*The Words*, 374); "Whichever of them you listen to with the ear of the heart" (*The Words*, 715). Also, *The Words*, 374; *The Words*, 715.

[669] "He left a telephone in every heart" (*The Words*, 684); "by means of the telephone of the heart, may communicate with elevated spirits" (*The Flashes*, 377). Also, *The Words*, 646; *The Flashes*, 375.

link and relation with God that goes forth from the heart and is the mirror of revelation and the receptacle of inspiration. The heart is like the earpiece of that telephone."[670] The eyes of the heart see better than the external eyes, and the ears hear better than the material ears.[671] Nursi believes the heart to have eyes, ears, and a kind of telephone line that reaches the dominical realm, since "it is a necessary and essential consequence of His Divine solicitousness and His dominical compassion that He should also communicate His presence and existence by speech, from behind the veil of veracious inspiration—a mode of dominical discourse— to individuals, in a manner peculiar to them and their capacities."[672]

Apart from the eye, ear, and telephone, the heart uses intuition as an instrument to rapidly attain new knowledge.[673] Nursi also mentions the faculty of memory as an instrument of the heart:

> Furthermore, tiny man's tiny heart may hold a love as great as the universe. Yes, the fact that writings equivalent to a library of thousands of books may be inscribed in the faculty of memory, which is a coffer of the heart's the size of a lentil, shows that the human heart may contain the universe and bear love that great.[674]

Both intuition and the faculty of memory may well be regarded as distinct subtleties under the command of the heart also. But nowhere in the *Epistles of Light* are these named among *lata'if*.

It is inescapable that according to its sicknesses, its level of attainment of sustenance and its capacity to use its various instruments, the heart should have different states, similar or corresponding to the seven states of the soul. There is no established list of states of the heart in the Sufi tradition. In different places in the *Epistles*, Nursi speaks of the hardness and unfeelingness of the heart,[675] of its tiredness,[676] of a sound

---

[670]  *The Words*, 65.

[671]  *The Rays*, 17.

[672]  *The Rays*, 149.

[673]  *The Words*, 534.

[674]  *The Flashes*, 90. See also *Al-Mathnawi al-Nuri: Seedbed of the Light*, 170–71.

[675]  *The Words*, 258.

[676]  "And sometimes the heart becomes tired, and the mind occupies itself with anything it encounters in order to entertain itself" *The Words*, 283.

heart,[677] of a corrupt heart,[678] of an aware and attentive heart,[679] of a sick heart,[680] of an unshakeable heart,[681] of a luminous hearts,[682] of stout hearts,[683] of hearts deficient in submission and obedience,[684] of vigilant hearts,[685] and of a righteous and a depraved heart.[686]

In its different states, the heart perceives the world, God and the Hereafter in different manners. "A black-hearted, cruel person sees the universe as weeping, ugly, dark, and tyrannical,"[687] says Nursi. This brings us to the necessity for the purification of the heart.

## Purification of the Heart

Purification and emancipation of the heart (and soul) from eternal perdition are regarded by Nursi as the main struggle of this life:[688]

> Since the human heart and brain ... comprise the members of a mighty tree in the form of a seed, and within them are encapsulated the parts and components of an eternal, majestic machine pertaining to the hereafter, certainly the heart's Creator willed that it should be worked and brought out from the potential to the actual, and developed, and put into action, for that is what He did. Since He willed it, the heart will certainly work like the mind. And the most effective means of working it is to be turned towards the truths of faith on the Sufi path through the remembrance of God in the degrees of sainthood.[689]

The remembrance of God can take several forms. It can be realized through invocations of the Beautiful Names, or through declarations of

---

[677] *The Words*, 316.
[678] *The Flashes*, 110, 168.
[679] *The Flashes*, 176; *The Words*, 711.
[680] *The Flashes*, 177.
[681] *The Flashes*, 92.
[682] *The Words*, 690.
[683] *The Letters*, 490.
[684] *The Words*, 177.
[685] *The Words*, 258.
[686] *The Words*, 49.
[687] *The Rays*, 583.
[688] *The Words*, 35.
[689] *The Letters*, 507–8.

faith like "There is no god but God," [690] or it can take the form of reflective thought.[691] The Qur'an comprises both invocations and reflective thought and hence provides for "the surrender of the heart and conscience," and "the subjugation of the reason and intellect."[692]

Nursi suggests that if the heart is purified, it will "stir the other subtle faculties into motion," and drive them to fulfill the purposes of their creation, making a person into a true human being.[693] It is obvious that Nursi regards the purification of the heart as a central project of the perfection of man. Thus, any attempt to use any subtlety or sense for the real reasons for which they were created is a way toward purification of the heart. Nursi suggests a kind of fasting for all the senses and organs, such as the eyes, ears, heart, and thoughts, together with the stomach, as a means of purification. This involves banning the tongue from lying, backbiting, and obscene language; making it fast; and busying it with such activities as reciting the Qur'an, praying, glorifying God's Names, asking for God's blessings for Prophet Muhammad, and seeking forgiveness for sins. All other human organs, senses, and subtleties have their special forms of fasting too.[694]

## Conclusion

Said Nursi's understanding of the subtleties of man is largely shaped by the Naqshbandi way, particularly by Ahmad Sirhindi. Sa'd al-Taftazani's understanding of spirit as a law clothed in an external body found a place in Nursi's theory of the spirit. What is unique to Nursi is his unified and collective understanding of man. Hence it is very difficult to study subtleties in the *Epistles of Light* on their own, without reference to other subtleties and senses. This is true for the two dominical subtle faculties: the spirit and the heart. Despite the fact that Nursi gives clear definitions of the spirit and heart as distinct subtleties of man, an in-depth study of the sicknesses, sustenances, instruments, relations, and purifications of

---

[690] *The Flashes*, 178.
[691] *The Letters*, 508.
[692] *The Words*, 378.
[693] *The Letters*, 522.
[694] *The Letters*, 462.

the spirit and the heart suggests that what holds for the spirit holds for the heart also. In line with Nursi's general tendency of prioritizing belief as a means of perfection, and the Qur'an as a means of attainment of belief, and Daily Prayer as an external representation of belief, these three find their places among the top three sustenances of the spirit and the heart, and strategies of purification of these *lata'if* also have to be built on this trio.

This chapter falls short of studying the intellect, the soul (*nafs*) and the self (*ana*, the I), for various reasons. Attainment of purification through elevating the seven states of the soul is not a part of Nursi's project. His understanding of the self has already been studied extensively. Nursi's project of harmonization of spirit, heart, and mind is also well studied. The intellect as a subtlety deserves a separate study.

# Index